Stock Market Scams, Swindles and Successes

Dr. Bryan Taylor
Chief Economist
Global Financial Data

GFD | GL⊕BAL
FINANCIAL DATA

Published by

Global Financial Data
29122 Rancho Viejo Rd. Suite 215
San Juan Capistrano, CA 92675

Contents

Illustrations

Tables

Acknowledgments

I would like to thank Michelle Kangas for her invaluable help in reviewing and editing the chapters in this book. She has provided useful insights into making each chapter more interesting and appealing to the average reader. Her focus on what part of each chapter to emphasize and expand, which portions to remove, how to make each chapter funny and interesting, and providing intriguing taglines for many of the sections helped to ensure the book is fun to read and not a soporific study in economics.

I would also like to thank my editors, Erica Orloff and Jon VanZile, for all of their suggestions for improving the book. I also received insights and valuable feedback from Maureen Burton, Mike Cerneant, Josh Silverman, and Pierre Gendreau and would like to thank them for their suggestions.

part I

Stock Successes

chapter one

The Famous Whiskey Dividend, or What a Way to End Prohibition

Successful companies pay dividends to their shareholders. Usually, they share their profits by issuing a cash dividend. Companies can also give extra shares of stock through a stock dividend or stock split, or in some cases, they provide dividends in kind, such as coupons for free bowling or sticks of gum. The first stock company, the Dutch East India Company, often unloaded the treasure brought back from the Far East onto its shareholders.

Whiskey Dividends

The most creative in-kind dividend of all time was given to shareholders of National Distillers Products Corp. (later Quantum Chemical Corp.) on October 15, 1933. What did each shareholder receive? Nothing less than a Warehouse Receipt for one case of 24 pints of 16-year-old whiskey for every 5 shares of stock they owned. So if you owned 100 shares of stock, you got 20 cases of 16-year-old whiskey. After 14 years of Prohibition, that was an answer to prayer.

Actually, given the company's history, shareholders were lucky to receive the whiskey. National Distillers Products Corp. had been founded as Distillers Securities Corp. on September 18, 1902, to acquire all the outstanding stock of the Distilling Co. of America. The company changed its name to U.S. Food Products Corp. on April 5, 1919, and went into bankruptcy in 1924 when it reorganized as National Distillers Products Corp. on April 18, 1924. With so many changes in corporate structure, you would think that the directors of the company were keeping a large portion of their output for their own use. Luckily, the company's most valuable asset, its pre-Prohibition whiskey passed on to the surviving company after the previous company went bankrupt.

The 18th Amendment to the Constitution was passed on January 16, 1919, and introduced Prohibition. The Volstead Act, passed on October 28, 1919, provided the legal framework to enforce Prohibition, though not very successfully. Prohibition was repealed by the 21st Amendment to the Constitution on December 5, 1933.

During Prohibition, a company such as National Distillers Products Corp. could not make any alcohol for consumption but had to concentrate on the production of industrial alcohol and other chemicals. This meant that any whiskey they had already produced when Prohibition was adopted could not be sold, so the company put its whiskey in a warehouse and waited for Prohibition to end.

Whiskey Profits

By 1933, the war was over. Prohibition was repealed, and National Distillers could produce alcohol once again. And what did shareholders think? They loved it. Not only did they get free whiskey, but the company's stock price shot up. With Prohibition repealed, National Distillers Products Corp. stock went from 19 at the beginning of 1933 to 111.25 by September 1933 (Figure 1.1). *The stock then split three-for-one and continued to rise.*

Although shareholders didn't receive any more in-kind dividends, the rise in the price of the stock paid for plenty of more booze. You wonder what the annual corporate meeting was like. After 1933, shareholders only had cash dividends to look forward to, but I'm sure there were many shareholders who loved to share the story at the local bar of the best dividend they had ever received.

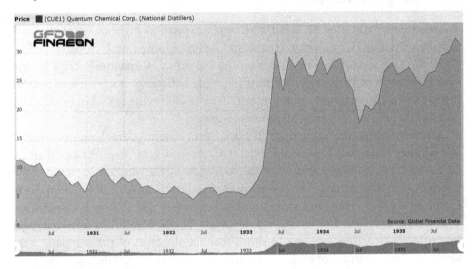

Figure 1.1 National Distillers Product Corp. Stock Price, 1930 to 1935.

chapter two

Why No One Asks, "Can You Make Me a Haloid?"

The company everyone knows as Xerox was originally called the Haloid Co. It introduced the first commercially-successful machine using xerography, which is why Haloid Co. changed its name to Xerox.

Of course, Xerox had competitors, like A. B. Dick & Co., who introduced mimeograph machines around 1900. Mimeograph machines forced ink through a stencil onto paper, allowing a small number of copies, often in purple, to be made. Minnesota Mining & Manufacturing introduced its Thermo-Fax in 1950, American Photocopy introduced its Dial-A-Matic Autostat in 1952, and Eastman Kodak introduced Verifax in 1953. However, all three required special paper. The Autostat and Verifax were hard to operate and turned out damp copies, and Thermo-Fax copies darkened when exposed to too much heat. Xerox overcame these problems and allowed regular paper to be used for copies.

The Haloid Co. was incorporated on April 17, 1906, in Rochester, New York, also home to Eastman Kodak. The xerography (Greek for "dry writing") technique was developed by Chester Carlson and Otto Komei. They put together a five-step process for copying a piece of paper that included sensitizing a photoconductive surface to light by giving it an electrostatic charge; exposing the surface to a written page to form an electrostatic image; developing the latent image by dusting the surface with a powder that adhered only to the charged areas; transferring the image to paper; and fixing the image by applying heat. All these steps had been used in other technologies, but no one had combined these five steps to make a copy as Carlson and Komei did.

Although they had discovered this process in 1938, it took Carlson and Komei 20 years to perfect xerography and produce a machine that did this efficiently. In the intervening 20 years, Haloid bet the company on developing the new process. Not only did they pour every penny of profit back into perfecting the xerography process, but they kept their salaries to a minimum, got the University of Rochester to invest in the company, got friends and relatives to buy shares, and even took out mortgages on their houses to raise money for further research and development.

The investment paid off handsomely not only to the developers at Xerox, but to the University of Rochester, which by one estimate had a capital gain of over $100 million on its investment.

One of the keys to the success of the xerography process, which Carlson and Komei discovered through trial and error, was replacing the sulfur in the drum with selenium, which succeeded where other elements had failed. There were other unexpected problems along the way which only experience could foresee (what do you do when a staple falls into the machine?), but through repeated innovation, their Yankee ingenuity succeeded in overcoming each little problem that appeared.

The first commercial xerographic copier, the Xerox A was introduced in 1949; however, it wasn't until the release of the Xerox 914 copier in 1959 that the company was able to invade the offices of the world. The Xerox 914 could copy originals up to 9 inches by 14 inches and could make a copy in only 26.4 seconds. The copier weighed *650 pounds* so it couldn't be placed on a desk top. The 914 usually had an operator who oversaw the machine, changed the toner, cleaned the selenium drum, and fixed the machine when it jammed, which curiously was referred to as a "mispuff."

The company had an interesting pricing structure for its premiere product. The Xerox 914 could be rented for $25 a month plus at least $49 worth of copies at four cents a copy. The more copies that were made, the higher the fees paid to Xerox. If you wanted to avoid the monthly fees, you could buy a Xerox 914 for $27,500, but few customers did. By 1965, the Xerox 914 represented two-thirds of Xerox's revenues. The 914 was followed by the 813, which was a smaller, desktop version of the 914, the 2400, which could copy 2,400 pages an hour, the Copyflo, which could enlarge microfilmed pages, and the LDX, which allowed copies to be transmitted by telephone or microwave.

Haloid Co. changed its name to Haloid Xerox Inc. on April 15, 1958, introduced the Xerox 914 in 1959, and changed its name to Xerox Corp. on June 1, 1961. Although Haloid stock began trading over-the-counter in 1938, Xerox Corp. didn't join the NYSE until July 11, 1961. As with many other companies, most of the stock appreciation occurred when the stock was traded over-the-counter, not after it was listed on the New York Stock Exchange.

Figure 2.1 shows Xerox's performance before listing on the NYSE in July 1961. The stock made a 15-fold move between mid-1961 and mid-1965. Unfortunately, for shareholders, that was the end of the stock's appreciation. In 2015, Xerox stock was at the same level it had traded at in 1965. During those 50 years, Xerox printed lots of copies, but didn't provided much of a return to shareholders.

The pre-NYSE history of Haloid Xerox is quite interesting. Xerox had 3:1 splits in March 1936 and April 1955, a 4:1 split in December 1959, before joining the NYSE, and a 5:1 split in January 1964 after joining the NYSE. These four splits sum to 180:1.

Haloid Co. was at its nadir at $15 a share in February 1949 when the company introduced its first commercial copier. With the success of its first xerography

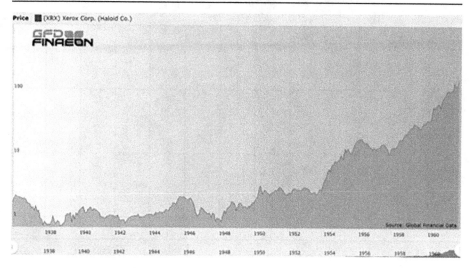

Figure 2.1 Xerox Corp. 1936 to 1961.

machine, the stock roared ahead. The stock doubled in price, reaching 32.5 by the end of 1953, and thence began its spectacular rise. By the time Xerox joined the NYSE in July 1961, the stock was trading at 104. Allowing for its two splits, this was the equivalent of 1,248 in the old stock, an 83-fold increase from its low point in February 1949 when the Xerox A was introduced.

By the end of 1965, Xerox was at 215, or 12,900 in the old stock, an 860-fold increase from 1949, and one of the most spectacular runs by any stock in history. Xerox's all-time high was reached on May 3, 1999 when it closed at 63.6875, quite an increase from the split-adjusted price of $0.014 the stock had been at

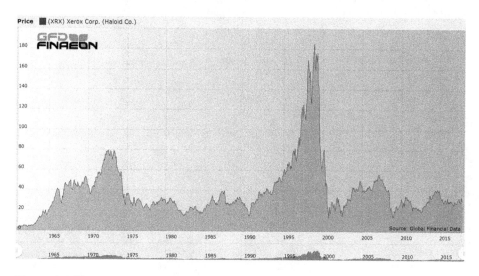

Figure 2.2 Xerox Corp. 1961 to 2018.

7

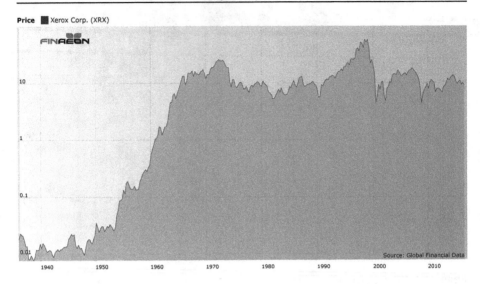

Price ■ Xerox Corp. (XRX)

FINAEON

10

1

0.1

0.01

Source: Global Financial Data

1940 1950 1960 1970 1980 1990 2000 2010

Figure 2.3 Xerox Stock Price, 1936 to 2018.

in February 1949, an increase of over 4,500-fold over a period of 50 years. By contrast, Xerox stock only rose 55-fold between July 1961, when Xerox joined the NYSE, and its peak on May 3, 1999 (Figure 2.2).

Before the advent of the NASDAQ in 1971, it was common for stocks to trade over-the-counter before they could list on an exchange. Unfortunately, the pre-exchange history of many companies is ignored because data was not available before the stock listed on a major exchange such as the NYSE, AMEX or NASDAQ. Now these pre-exchange histories are available through Global Financial Data. Without a complete history of a company's stock, the true returns to shareholders would never be known.

chapter three

Kentucky Fried Chicken— Finger-Lickin' Profits

Before the advent of NASDAQ in 1971, it was common for stocks to trade over-the-counter before they could list on an exchange. As a result, data on the stock price of many companies before they listed on an exchange is often ignored , and some of the greatest moves in stock market history lie undiscovered.

A good example of this is Kentucky Fried Chicken Corp (KFC). The company was founded by Colonel Harland Sanders in North Corbin, Kentucky, in 1930. Sanders opened a Shell Oil service station and paid a share of the sales to Shell Oil Corp. To supplement his income, he began serving fried chicken, steaks, and country ham in the adjacent living quarters before opening a restaurant. The restaurant provided 24-hour service, with lunch and dinner for $1 or less.

Chicken Shoot Out

The Colonel didn't run the only restaurant in town. Matt Stewart ran another restaurant in North Corbin, and the Colonel got involved in a shoot-out with his competitor over a traffic sign he had put up that directed traffic to Sanders's restaurant. Unfortunately, an official from Shell Oil was killed by Matt Stewart in the shoot-out. Matt Stewart was convicted of murder, effectively eliminating Sanders's competition.

Colonel Sanders franchised his first KFC restaurant in 1954 to Pete Harman in South Salt Lake, Utah. The Colonel received $0.04 per chicken sold, and a local sign painter, Don Anderson, coined the phrase Kentucky Fried Chicken. In the 1960s, Kentucky Fried Chicken grew to 600 restaurants, including franchises in Canada, England, Mexico, and Jamaica. The expansion proved too much for Colonel Sanders, and in 1964, at the age of 74, he sold the company to an investment group led by John Y. Brown, Jr. (a future governor of Kentucky) and Jack C. Massey for a mere $2 million.

The Chicken Exchange

Kentucky Fried Chicken Corp. was incorporated by its new owners on March 4, 1964, and became one of the fastest-growing restaurant chains of the 1960s. KFC was acquired by Heublein, Inc. on July 8, 1971, for $285 million, over 100 times the price paid to Col. Sanders in 1964. Heublin was later taken over by R.J. Reynolds in 1982. KFC was sold to Pepsi Corp. in July 1986 for $850 million and then was spun off as part of Tricon Global Restaurants, Inc. in 1997. The company changed its name to Yum! Brands, Inc. on May 17, 2002. KFC is now the second-largest restaurant chain in the world by sales after McDonald's.

Before being acquired by Heublin, Inc., KFC had one of the most spectacular stock runs of the 1960s, but most of this occurred before KFC joined the NYSE. The chart below shows the performance of KFC stock both over-the-counter between 1966 and 1969 and on the NYSE between 1969 and 1971. The company's performance while it was listed on the NYSE was quite poor with shareholders losing half of their money between the time KFC listed on the NYSE on January 16, 1969, and it was acquired by Heublein, Inc. on July 8, 1971, declining in price from 46.875 to 22.5 (Figure 3.1).

KFC's performance OTC was quite a different story. In March 1966, the stock was trading at 21.50. The stock had 5:4 splits in December 1965 and December 1966, a 3:1 split in December 1967, and a 2:1 split in October 1968, for a cumulative 9.375:1 split. Consequently, between March 1966 and January 1969, a period of less than 3 years, KFC enjoyed a 20-fold move in its stock!

Since 1971, shareholders have been unable to exclusively own stock in KFC since it has always been part of other companies: Heublin, Inc., R.J. Reynolds, Pepsi Corp. Tricon Global Restaurants, Inc. and Yum! Brands, Inc. Still, anyone who owned KFC stock before it listed on the NYSE was able to make enough money to feed themselves for years to come.

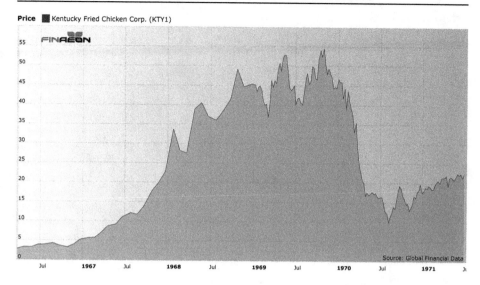

Figure 3.1 Kentucky Fried Chicken, 1966 to 1971.

chapter four

Dr. Pepper: The Portfolio Pepper Upper

Since I grew up in Dallas where the old Dr. Pepper plant was located on Mockingbird Avenue (now demolished), I have always been a Dr. Pepper fan, and though not everyone refers to this soft drink as the elixir of life as I do, it is still popular among those with discriminating taste like mine, especially if you grew up in Texas.

Dr. Pepper was first made in Waco by Wade B. Morrison in 1885, a year before Coca-Cola was introduced. The Artesian Manufacturing and Bottling Co. was founded in 1891 to manufacture Dr. Pepper. The Southwestern Soda Fountain Co. of Dallas acquired the right to purchase and sell Dr. Pepper on September 8, 1898, and changed its name to the Dr. Pepper Co. on September 25, 1902. The Circle "A" Corp. purchased Artesian Manufacturing and Bottling works in 1920 and was the only bottler of Dr. Pepper concentrate. Circle "A" Corp. went bankrupt on June 12, 1923, due to rising commodity prices and high taxes. Circle "A" Corp incorporated in Colorado on July 6, 1923, absorbing the remnants of the old Circle "A" Corp. and Dr. Pepper Co., and changed its name to Dr. Pepper Co. on September 7, 1924.

The company grew dramatically over the years until it was acquired by Forstmann and Little, a New York Investment firm, in February 1984. Dr. Pepper merged with Seven-Up in 1986 to form the Dr. Pepper/Seven-Up Companies, which went public in 1993 only to be acquired by Cadbury Schweppes plc in June 1995. Cadbury Schweppes merged Dr. Pepper/Seven-Up with the Snapple Group to form Dr. Pepper Snapple Group, Inc. in 2007, which went public in May 2008 and was traded on the NYSE until 2018 when Keurig Green Mountain acquired the company.

The first Dr. Pepper shares, which traded on the regional St. Louis Stock Exchange and OTC, had two spectacular moves before listing on the NYSE on March 18, 1946. The first move occurred between 1934 and 1937, when the stock made a 32-fold move as the company's expanded its reach beyond its roots in Texas. Dr. Pepper stock listed on the NYSE on March 18, 1946, and was one of

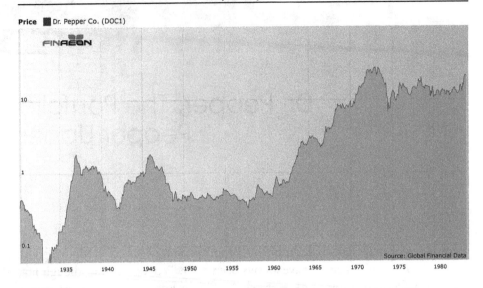

Figure 4.1 Dr. Pepper Stock Price, 1929 to 1984.

the original members of the S&P Composite when it expanded from 90 members to 500 companies in March 1957 (Figure 4.1).

The Uncola

The stock traded sideways during the 1940s and 1950s before making a 64-fold move between 1960 and 1972, when Dr. Pepper was able to extend its reach nationwide. Dr. Pepper's success was due in large part to a favorable court ruling. In 1963, the United States Fifth District Court of Dallas declared that Dr. Pepper was not a cola. Independent bottlers had contracts forbidding them from carrying other cola drinks that could compete with Coca-Cola or Pepsi Cola. Consequently, independent bottlers could carry Dr. Pepper without violating the exclusivity clauses they had signed with Coca-Cola or Pepsi Cola since Dr. Pepper was not legally a cola drink. Between 1968 and 1977, Dr. Pepper sales and profits increased five-fold. Even though Dr. Pepper wasn't one of the "Nifty 50" stocks from the 1960s, it should have been. Between these two moves in the 1930s and the 1960s, Dr. Pepper made a 480-fold move, making it one of the best-performing stocks of the 20th century.

However, without the data on Dr. Pepper stock before the company joined the NYSE in 1946, no one would know that Dr. Pepper had already made one spectacular move, had built a 25-year base, and was ready to join the Hall of Fame of Outstanding stocks after its spectacular rise in the 1960s. True stock analysts shouldn't only worry about the survivorship bias that comes from ignoring delisted stocks, but from the exchange bias that comes from ignoring the pre-exchange history of a stock, as Dr. Pepper clearly illustrates.

chapter five

The Bank of England—Safe for Widows and Orphans

The stock for which Global Financial Data has the longest history is the Bank of England, or as it was originally known, the Governor and Company of the Bank of England.

The origin of the Bank of England lies in naval warfare. In 1694, the French had the strongest navy in the world, and following the 1690 Battle of Beachy Head, England needed to rebuild its navy, but King William III lacked the resources and the credit to do so.

This problem was resolved by creating the Bank of England. In exchange for creating a limited liability corporation, which would act as a bank for the government and have the right to issue banknotes, shareholders loaned the bank £1,200,000 at 8 percent interest. The Royal Charter was granted on July 27, 1694, and the £1,200,000 of capital was subscribed in only 12 days.

A Central Bank Owned by Shareholders

Although today no central bank is owned by shareholders, until the 20th century, this was common. The Bank of the United States, Bank of England, Banque de France, Reichsbank, and others all issued shares to the public.

Over time, the Bank of England took on the responsibilities of managing the government's debt, becoming a banker's bank, controlling interest rates through discounting and establishing a base interest rate, having the exclusive right to issue banknotes within 20 miles of London, and then within the entire country, and other duties of a central bank.

The Bank of England maintained its independence for 250 years, but it was nationalized on October 29, 1945. Shareholders received £400 in bonds for each £100 in par value of bank stock. The bonds paid 3 percent interest (as opposed to the 12 percent yield on the stock), and the bonds were redeemable at par on April 5, 1966.

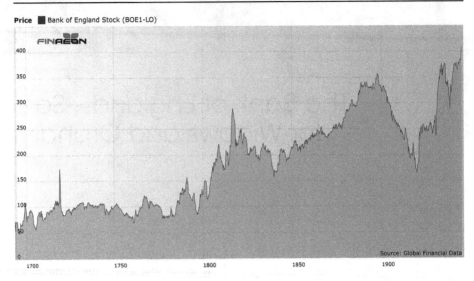

Price ■ Bank of England Stock (BOE1-LO)

Source: Global Financial Data

Figure 5.1 Bank of England Stock Price, 1694 to 1944.

Bank of England's stock traded for over 250 years before the bank was nationalized. The stock participated in the South Sea Bubble of 1720, though only doubling in price rather than showing the 10-fold increase South Sea stock enjoyed before collapsing. Bank of England stock, along with East Indies Co. stock and South Sea Co. stock, were the "three sisters" whose shares were safe enough, because of their government connection, to trade regularly on the London Stock Exchange during the 18th century. Until the rise of canals and the liquidity created by the Napoleonic Wars, stock trading in other shares remained almost non-existent between 1720 and 1800.

Only British government bonds were safer than Bank of England stock; however, Bank of England stock had the potential for dividend increases that the government bonds did not. Although the dividend fluctuated in its first dozen years, the dividend settled down to infrequent changes after the 1720 South Sea Bubble. From 1720 when the South Sea bubble burst until the 1860s, the Bank of England had the largest market capitalization of any company in the world.

As you can see by the 250-year chart of Bank of England stock in Figure 5.1, the shares showed no real trend during the 1700s, rose in price during the Napoleonic Wars as England left the gold standard and suffered inflation, declined in price from around 1818 to 1845 during the deflation that followed the war, rose in price for the rest of the 1800s as the Bank gradually increased its dividend, plunged until 1920 as inflation occurred without any compensating rise in the dividend, then gradually rose in price until the Bank was nationalized in 1945. The behavior of the Bank of England's stock encapsulates the general behavior of the British stock market over that 250-year period.

Bank of England stock was about as safe as they come. There was virtually no risk of bankruptcy since the Bank was backed by the British government. The Bank's stock could participate in price increases because the Bank could raise its dividend as profits rose. This provided investors some protection against inflation.

By contrast, British consols, which were originally issued in 1729 and traded until they were called in by the British government in 2015, could not raise their interest payments. In fact, as a result of two refundings, the consols paid 2.5 percent in the 1900s rather than than the original 3 percent coupon that was paid in 1729, while the dividend on Bank of England stock rose from 8 percent in 1694 to 12 percent in 1945 and the price of the stock quadrupled over time.

Nevertheless, most of the return to Bank of England shareholders came through dividends. £100 invested in Bank of England stock in 1694, assuming all dividends had been reinvested and there were no taxes, would have grown to £41,870,819 by 1945. By contrast, £100 invested in British government consols during the same period would have grown to only £2,637,476, a 20-fold difference. Bank of England stock clearly provided the superior return. Of course, in order to have received this, you would have had to live 250 years, but why worry about details?

chapter six

The South Sea Company—
The Forgotten ETF

Most people in the stock market have heard about the South Sea Bubble, the first stock market bubble in England, which took place in 1720, but few people realize that the South Sea Co. was also one of the first exchange traded funds (ETFs) in market history. Many people have seen a chart of the stock rising from 100 to 1,000 within a few months, then collapsing back to 100. But why did the stock price rise so suddenly and then collapse, and what happened in the hundred years that followed?

The South Sea Company Sails

The South Sea Company was a British joint-stock company founded in 1711 as a public-private partnership to consolidate and reduce the cost of British national debt. The company had a monopoly on British trade with South America, and the potential profits from this monopoly were used to justify the rise in price of South Sea Co. stock. When it was discovered the projected profits would not occur, which they did not, the price of the stock collapsed.

The South Sea Company was, in modern parlance, a debt-equity swap. The British government significantly increased its debt as a result of the War of the Spanish Succession, which occurred between 1701 and 1714. The government debt was over £50 million, or about 100 percent of GDP. Following in the footsteps of John Law, who had created the *Banque Royale* in France to reduce French debt, the British government decided to do the same.

In 1720, South Sea Company shares were backed by government bonds paying 5 percent interest, and unlike British government debt, South Sea Co. shares had the potential for increases in dividends, and thus in share price, as the South Sea Company profited from its monopoly. The British government benefited because it reduced its debt, and holders of British government debt could benefit from a higher rate of return and the potential for capital gains. The conversion of British government debt to South Sea Co. stock was perceived as a win/win.

The South Sea Scam Succeeds

When things are too good to be true, they usually are. If the Securities and Exchange Commission had existed in 1720, they would have arrested everyone associated with the South Sea Co. since they broke almost every rule in the SEC book. Rumors about profits were spread, members of Parliament were bribed, and shares could be bought with a small down payment or no down payment. Shares could be purchased at the par price of £100 and sold at the higher market price, allowing purchasers to arbitrage a profit.

Shares were sold to members of the government at the market price without them having to pay for the shares. When the price of the stock rose, the shares could be sold at a profit. This cost the "investors" nothing, made sure their interests lay with the South Sea Co., and insured profits to the supporters of the company. Even George I's mistress was allowed to benefit from the South Sea stock scheme.

The rise in the price of South Sea Co. stock led to numerous additional companies emerging to take advantage of the stock market bubble. Almost all of these companies became worthless, which led to the passage of the Bubble Act in June 1720. The whole South Sea Bubble was pilloried by William Hogarth and others after it was over with (Figure 6.1). The Bubble Act required that a joint stock company could only be incorporated by Act of Parliament or by Royal Charter. The prohibition on unauthorized joint stock ventures was not repealed until 1825. The Bubble Act limited potential competition and drove the South Sea Co. stock price to £890 in early June.

The price of South Sea stock finally reached £1,000 in early August, and sellers began to outnumber buyers. Liquidity started to dry up, in part because the first installments for shares purchased by investors on credit came due. By the end of September, South Sea stock had fallen to £150.

The Bubble Bursts

Despite forays into the slave trade and Arctic whaling (an oxymoron for the South Sea Co.), the company never made a profit, but consistently lost money, and as is always true of large companies that lose money, it sought subsidies from the government for their Arctic whaling, which it got, and it sought a bailout from the British government, which it did not get.

After 1732, the company's slave trading and Arctic whaling were shut down. Thence until 1855 when the company was liquidated, the South Sea Co. simply managed the government debt it owned. After the Bank of England stock and East Indies Co. stock, the South Sea Co. stock was the third most traded stock on the London Stock Exchange for the rest of the 1700s, not for its monopoly profits, but for the steady income from government bond interest payments that shareholders

Figure 6.1 William Hogarth: Emblematical Print on the South Sea Scheme (1721).

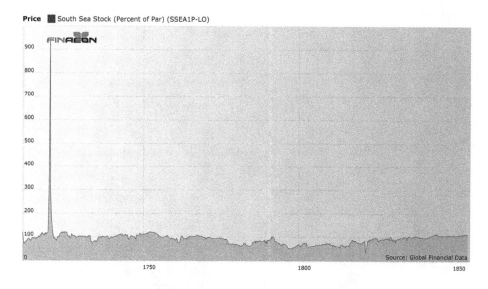

Figure 6.2 South Sea Company Stock Price, 1700 to 1854.

received. In effect, the South Sea Company became an ETF for government debt, 250 years before ETFs became a mainstay of the United States stock market.

By 1855, the South Sea Co. had outlived its purpose and was closed down. Figure 6.2 shows the history of the South Sea Co. from its inception in 1711 until its liquidation in 1855. Except for the blip in 1720, the share price rarely moved away from its 100-par value. Although the South Sea Co. will always be remembered for the bubble of the 1720s, it should not be forgotten that it also laid the foundations for the ETF mania of the 21st century.

chapter seven

Alexander Hamilton and the First Bank of the United States

The President, Directors, and Company of the Bank of the United States, or the First Bank of the United States as it is more commonly known, was chartered for a term of 20 years, by the United States Congress on February 25, 1791. The bank was part of Alexander Hamilton's plan for stabilizing and improving the nation's credit by establishing a central bank, a mint, and introducing excise taxes.

Andrew Hamilton Creates the Bank of the United States

The Bank of the United States was established with $10 million in capital, of which $2 million would be subscribed by the government. The $8 million in shares sold to the public (20,000 shares at $400) were quickly purchased and the price of the stock initially rose to $600. Of the first $8 million in shares that were sold, one quarter had to be paid in gold or silver. The rest could be paid in bonds, scrip, or similar financial instruments.

Shares were priced at $400, and to understand how much money this was by today's standard, the per capita income in the United States in 1791 was only $50 (vs. over $50,000 today), so one share of stock cost the equivalent of $400,000 in today's purchasing power, making Berkshire Hathaway Class A stock seem cheap by comparison.

Hamilton modeled the Bank of the United States on the Bank of England. The bank could be a depository for collected taxes, make short-term loans to the government, and could serve as a holding site for incoming and outgoing money. Nevertheless, Hamilton saw the main goal of the bank as a way of promoting commercial and private interests by making sound loans to the private sector. Most of the bank's activities were commercial, not public.

The Bank of the United States was a privately owned bank and was the only Federal Bank that Congress allowed, though states could also charter banks. The

Figure 7.1 The First Bank of the United States in Philadelphia.

bank had a 20-year charter; foreigners could be stockholders (and owned about three-fourths of the stock) but could not vote; and the Secretary of the Treasury had the right to inspect the bank's books as often as once a week.

There were a couple ways, however, in which the First Bank of the United States differed significantly from the Federal Reserve Bank today. The Bank of the United States could not buy government bonds, and the bank could neither issue notes nor incur debts beyond its actual capitalization. Alexander Hamilton would have been a strong opponent of Bernanke's quantitative easing, and if Bernanke had studied the First Bank of the United States rather than the Great Depression, he might not have been Fed Chairman.

Bank Battles

The same battles that exist today between tight-money and easy-money factions existed when the Bank of the United States was established in 1791. The "moneyed interests" of the northern, commercial businessmen generally favored the bank while the southern, agricultural groups opposed it. The reason for this is quite simple. Since farmers had to borrow money to fund their crops and people in the southern and western United States needed capital to buy land and establish new communities, they wanted interest rates to be as low as possible. Lenders of money wanted to keep interest rates high and provide sound money. Since the wealthy had suffered from the depreciation of the Continental Dollar, which lost 99.9 percent of its value during the Revolutionary War, lenders wanted to avoid another debasing of the currency. Moreover, the Bank of the United States was the largest bank in the country, so state banks were naturally opposed to its competition.

When the Bank's charter came up for renewal in 1811, the Democrats, who opposed the bank, were in control of Congress, while the Federalists, who had set up the bank, were not. The vote to renew the charter failed by one vote in both the House (65-64) and in the Senate, where the vote was deadlocked at 17, and Vice President Clinton cast the deciding vote against the renewal of the charter. The Bank of the United States was born of politics and died of politics. Votes along party lines are nothing new in Congress.

This battle between lenders and borrowers over the nation's financial sector continued for the rest of the 18th century. It occurred again when the second Bank of the United States was established in 1816, and when William Jennings Bryan ran for President three times at the end of the nineteenth century and made his "Cross of Gold" speech. Today, in the twenty-first century, the same battle lines are drawn between easy-money advocates in favor of quantitative easing, and tight-money opponents who believe these policies will lead to another bubble and financial crash. No doubt, 200 years from now, the same battle lines will be drawn between other opponents.

An Investment to Bank On

For shareholders, the Bank of the United States was a good investment (Figure 7.2). While US government bonds paid 6 percent interest, Bank of the United States stock paid an 8 percent dividend. When the bank's charter was not renewed, the bank liquidated and paid off investors in full. Global Financial Data not only has price data for the First Bank of the United States, but a complete record of dividend payments for the bank as well. The price of the stock fluctuated between $400 and $600, and the bank paid $634 in dividends on the original $400 investment.

Stephen Girard purchased most of the bank's stock as well as the building in Philadelphia (Figure 7.1) where the Bank had its headquarters. Philadelphia and not New York was the financial capital of the United States at that time, and Philadelphia was also the capital of the United States from 1790 to 1800 before the capital was moved to Washington, D.C.

The Bank of the United States was succeeded by Girard's Bank in 1811. Girard's Bank was chartered by Pennsylvania on September 1, 1832, was chartered under the National Bank Act on November 30, 1864, as the Girard National Bank, and was closed on March 31, 1926. Girard's Bank spun off the Girard Life Insurance Annuity and Trust Co. which incorporated on March 17, 1836, and merged into Mellon National Corp. on April 6, 1983. Thus, the legacy of the First Bank of the United States ended.

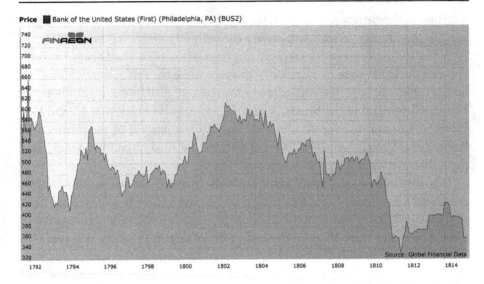

Figure 7.2 First Bank of the United States Stock Price, 1791 to 1815.

chapter eight

The Bank War

The previous chapter discussed the founding and dissolution of the First Bank of the United States, which existed from 1791 to 1811. After the First Bank of the United States recharter was defeated, the United States suffered defeat in the War of 1812, and faced financial problems due to a lack of fiscal order and an unregulated currency. As industrial and commercial interests expanded after the War of 1812, politicians advocated the creation of a second Bank of the United States to promote the economy.

The Second Bank of the United States is Founded

After the War of 1812, there was sufficient support to overcome the opposition to the second Bank of the United States. Opponents of a second Bank of the United States saw its charter not only as a threat to Jeffersonian agrarianism and state sovereignty, but to slavery since, as John Taylor of South Carolina put it, "If Congress could incorporate a bank, it might emancipate a slave." The bank's constitutionality was established in 1819 in *McCulloch v. Maryland*, a landmark decision in constitutional history, but many still felt the establishment of a bank by the Federal government was unconstitutional.

The Bank of the United States was created to be a depository for collected taxes, make short-term loans to the government, issue currency (Figure 8.1), and serve as a holding site for incoming and outgoing money. The main goal of the bank was to promote commercial and private interests by making sound loans to the private sector.

The second Bank of the United States charter was signed into law on April 10, 1816, by President Madison. The second Bank of the United States was modeled on the first with the government owning 20 percent of the $35 million in equity, and its capital divided into 350,000 shares of $100 each. The bank had 4,000

Figure 8.1 Bank of the United States $1,000 Bill.

investors, of which 1,000 were Europeans, though the bulk of the shares were owned by a few hundred wealthy Americans.

Bank, Bubble and Bust

The second Bank of the United States had 25 branch offices in addition to its main office in Philadelphia. After the Bank of the United States was established, southern and western branches issued credit to fund expansion. This led to a financial bubble that burst in the Panic of 1819, leading to sharp declines in property prices, similar to what happened in 2008 when the most recent bank-induced bubble led to a financial crash.

The public was unhappy about the prolonged recession that resulted from the Bank of the United States–induced Panic of 1819. Nicholas Biddle took over the Bank of the United States in 1823, and switched to a sound money policy. At that point in time, state-chartered banks could issue their own banknotes, but when their currency was deposited at the Bank of the United States, the bank demanded gold or silver from the issuing bank, limiting the issuance of currency by state banks. Because the number of banks in the United States grew from 31 in 1801 to 788 in 1837, state-chartered banks began to oppose the Bank of the United States because it limited their ability to issue currency and make profits.

Shares in the Second Bank of the United States were the most liquid and most secure of all shares listed on US exchanges. The bank paid steady dividends to its shareholders, increasing the dividend from $5 in 1819 to $7 by 1834. Since the US government succeeded in paying off all of its outstanding bonds by 1835, the stock of the Bank of the United States was not only the largest issue on the stock exchange, but it was also the safest since it was backed by the United States government, or so it seemed.

Andrew Jackson Begins the Bank War

In the election of 1824, Andrew Jackson received the largest number of votes, the largest number of electoral votes, and carried the most states, but failed to gain a majority. The House of Representatives elected John Quincy Adams as president instead.

When Jackson was elected in 1828, he felt rancor toward his opponents for keeping him from being chosen president in 1824. Jackson was a populist, and even though the Bank was popular because the economy was growing as a result of its sound-money policies, Jackson opposed the Bank of the United States as unconstitutional, corrupt, and a danger to American liberties. In Jackson's mind, the Bank of the United States was at the center of the class warfare of the 1830s, which pitted "farmers, mechanics, and laborers" against the "rich and powerful," in words that seem reminiscent of Occupy Wall Street's opposition to the 1 percent.

Jackson's opposition to the Bank of the United States led to the "Bank War" between Jackson and Biddle over the re-chartering of the Second Bank of the United States, which became the focal point of the 1832 election. Pro-bank forces tried to get a vote on the charter before the 1832 election to discourage a presidential veto, but anti-bank forces delayed the vote until after the election, when Jackson vetoed the re-charter which Congress failed to override.

One of Jackson's first actions after re-election was to remove all government deposits from the Bank of the United States and spread them out among state-chartered banks, crippling the Second Bank of the United States. Biddle counterattacked by contracting bank credit, but this led to a financial downturn that only added to opposition against the Bank of the United States. Business leaders in American financial centers became convinced that Biddle's war on Jackson was more destructive than Jackson's war on the Bank.

When the Second Bank of the United States's charter expired in 1836, the bank re-chartered as a Pennsylvania private corporation. In 1839, the bank suspended payments, and it went into liquidation in 1841. The performance of its stock is shown in Figure 8.2.

As was true of the First Bank of the United States, the bank was born of politics and died of politics. Andrew Jackson won the bank war, and the Bank of the United States charter lapsed in 1836. The United States was without a central bank for the next 77 years.

At one point during the Bank War, Jackson had offered to charter a new bank if it were publicly owned, and if it did not compete with state-chartered banks by issuing commercial loans. Although Jackson's version of a Central Bank never came

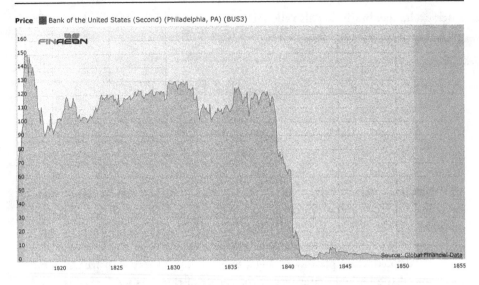

Figure 8.2 Second Bank of the United States Stock, 1816 to 1855.

into existence, when the Federal Reserve was chartered in 1913, Jackson had his way at last because the Federal Reserve is 100 percent owned by the government, does not compete with commercial banks; and to avoid the political battles over re-chartering, the charter for the Federal Reserve is perpetual.

Today, the battles are over who is appointed Federal Reserve chairperson, not over whether the Federal Reserve should be re-chartered. The advocates of hard money and soft money continue to battle over interest rates, quantitative easing, the federal deficit, funding the government, and the other subjects related to the availability of credit. The Bank War was not just part of the 1832 presidential election, but it is part of every election and almost every battle involving the economy today, and in the future.

chapter nine

The Mississippi Bubble, or How the French Eliminated All Their Government Debt

The government is running a large deficit, and it can't cover its expenses. The government debt exceeds GDP. The Central Bank's balance sheet is exploding as the government buys its own debt. Sound familiar? That was France in 1719.

Everyone has heard of the South Sea Bubble, but few have heard of the French version, the Mississippi Bubble, which happened one year before. Not only was the Mississippi Bubble bigger than the South Sea Bubble, it was more successful. It completely wiped out the French government's debt obligations at the expense of those who fell under the sway of John Law's economic innovations.

The *Compagnie du Mississippi* was chartered in 1684 at the behest of Rene-Robert Cavelier, who had been appointed governor of Fort Frontenac, located at the mouth of the Mississippi. After getting his charter, Cavelier went to Mississippi with four vessels full of inhabitants, but the venture floundered, and Rene-Robert Cavelier died there, killed by a party that mutinied against him.

John Law Takes over the *Compagnie d'Occident*

In August 1717, Scottish businessman John Law (shown in Figure 9.1) acquired a controlling interest in the then-derelict *Compagnie du Mississippi* and renamed it the *Compagnie d'Occident*. The company's initial goal was to trade and do business with the French colonies in North America, which included much of the Mississippi River drainage basin and the French colony of Louisiana.

As John Law bought control of the company, he was granted a 25-year monopoly by the French government on trade with the West Indies and North America. In 1719, the company acquired the *Compagnie des Indes Orientales*, the *Compagnie de Chine*, and other French trading companies and combined these

Figure 9.1 John Law, Creator of the French Stock Market Bubble.

into the *Compagnie Perpetuelle des Indes*. In 1720, it acquired the *Banque Royale*, which had been founded by John Law as the *Banque Generale* in 1716, and which was the source for the quantitative easing which enabled the government to eliminate its debts.

How Debt Begat a Bubble

Once he took control of the company, John Law schemed to create speculative interest in the *Compagnie des Indes*. Reports were skillfully spread about gold and silver mines discovered in America. Law exaggerated the wealth of Louisiana with an effective marketing scheme, which led to wild speculation on the shares of the company in 1719. This was the way Gregor McGregor was to generate interest in Poyais 100 years later (see Chapter 19).

Law had promised the French regent that he would extinguish the public debt. To achieve this goal, Law required that shares in the *Compagnie des Indes* should be paid for one-fourth in coin and three-fourths in *billets d'Etat* (public securities), which rapidly rose in value on account of the foolish demand that was created for them. The speculation was further fed by the huge increase in the money supply introduced by John Law in order to stimulate the economy. The South Sea Company and the British government learned from John Law and imitated these techniques in 1720.

Compagnie des Indes shares traded around 300 at the end of 1718, but rose rapidly in 1719, increasing to 1,000 by July 1719, 5000 by August 1719 and broke 10,000 in November 1719, an increase of over 3,000 percent in less than one year (Figure 9.2). By contrast, South Sea Company shares rose by 900 percent in 1720. It was downhill from there. The fall in the price of the stock increased, and at the end of 1720, John Law was dismissed by Regent Philippe II of Orleans.

The number of outstanding shares of the company was probably around 500,000 in 1720. A stock price of 10,000 livres would have given the company

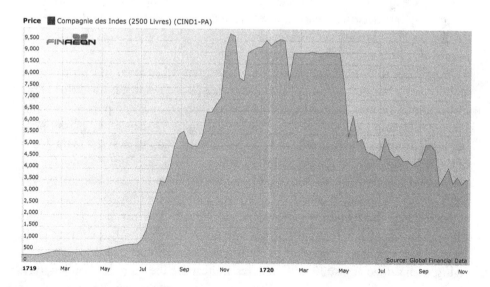

Figure 9.2 *Compagnie des Indes* stock, 1718 to 1721.

a market capitalization of 5 billion livres. By comparison, the French government expenses in 1719 were around 150 million livres, and the French government debt in 1719 was 1.6 billion livres.

At its height, the capitalization of the *Compagnie des Indes* was greater than either the GDP of France or all French government debt. With the demand for company shares being so high, the government and John Law set out to buy back the whole 1.6 billion livres government debt for shares in the company. The plan was successful, and in 1720 the whole government debt was acquired by the company.

As the creditors bought shares in the company with their bonds and debt papers, the whole government debt became property of the company. The company then became property of the former creditors, now the shareholders, and the effective control fell into the hands of the government that paid an annual 3 percent interest to the company, which amounted to 48 million livres. Through these transactions the French government successfully unloaded their gigantic debt (perhaps 200 to 400 percent of GDP) and became basically debt free.

Life after the Bubble and Bankruptcy

The company sought bankruptcy protection in 1721. It was reorganized and opened for business in 1722. In 1723 it was granted fresh privileges by Louis XV. Among these were the monopoly of the sale of tobacco and coffee, as well as the right to organize national lotteries.

Compare this outcome with that of the South Sea Company, which was unable to find any business that enabled it to make a profit for its shareholders after its collapse in 1720, but relied on the government bonds the South Sea Company held to provide income to its shareholders.

From 1726 to 1746, the *Compagnie des Indes* flourished from its overseas trade and domestic business. It brought wealth to the port cities it was operating from: in Bordeaux, Nantes, Marseille, and, in particular, in its home port of Lorient . During this period, the company lost its trading rights for the western hemisphere, but it kept trading with the east and prospered from that business. Its main goods of trade during the period were porcelain, wallpapers, lacquer and tea from China, cotton and silk cloth from China and India, coffee from Mocha (Yemen), pepper from Mahe (South India), as well as gold, ivory, and slaves from West Africa.

After 1746, the spendthrift policies of the French government began to hurt the company, and the Seven Years' War brought severe losses. In February 1770, an edict required the company to transfer to the state all its properties, assets, and rights, then valued at just 30 million livres, quite a decline from the 5 billion livres the company had been valued at in 1719. The king agreed to pay all the company's debts and annuity (*rente*) obligations. The company was officially dissolved in 1770, although its liquidation dragged on into the 1790s (Figure 9.3).

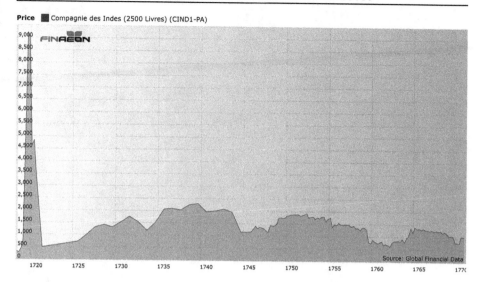

Price Compagnie des Indes (2500 Livres) (CIND1-PA)

Source: Global Financial Data

Figure 9.3 *Compagnie des Indes* Stock Price, 1717 to 1770.

The debt-laden governments of today probably wish they could create a scheme similar to the Mississippi Bubble to unburden themselves of the debts they have accumulated over time. With many western government debts equal to or greater than GDP, it would provide them a great relief. Unfortunately for governments, investors are unlikely to fall for a similar scheme a second time. Or would they?

chapter ten

Amazon and Alphabet at $1000? Small Change, Buddy

With Amazon and Alphabet surpassing $1,000 (much less Berkshire Hathaway's Class A shares trading at $300,000), people are amazed that stocks can trade at such high levels without being overvalued or losing liquidity, but in reality, compared with the past, most stocks are cheap nowadays. In fact, the further you go back in time, the higher was the price of most stocks relative to incomes. In terms of purchasing power, stocks are as cheap and as liquid as they have ever been.

Not only was the average price of stocks 200 years ago higher than average stock prices today, they were also higher in terms of personal income. Shares of the First Bank of the United States were issued at $400 in 1791, and shares of the Massachusetts Bank of Boston were issued at $500 in 1792. One share was equivalent to the average annual income of most people back then. The majority of shares sold for $100, and some for $50 or $25. In London, most stocks were issued at a par value of £100, equal to about $486.

So how could investors afford stocks that make Amazon and Alphabet look cheap? Even if a stock was at $100, this was equivalent to $10,000 today in terms of earning power. Were there really that many rich people back then? The answer is no, but the difference is in the way shares were issued and traded.

Making Expensive Shares More Affordable

First, shares were rarely bought in round lots of 100 shares as they are today. Instead, shares were traded individually. Investors bought 1 share at $100, not 100 shares at $20. This means that even though the prices of individual shares have decreased, the average transaction size has not changed significantly.

Second, and most importantly, shares were often bought on the installment plan, at a discount, or in fractions in order to reduce the total cost of investing. I will focus on this second point.

To see how this worked, let's go back to the South Sea Bubble of 1720. It should be remembered that South Sea shares traded around £100 before the bubble began, which was equivalent to about $500 in 1720. One factor that allowed the Bubble to occur was that "investors" were allowed to pay for their shares in installments. The initial purchase required only 10 percent down with the rest of the payments spread over the remaining months of 1720. This was the 18th century version of buying on margin. It encouraged buying because speculators, as always, thought they could make a profit before the next payment was due. It was the 18th century equivalent of flipping houses. Many investors, no doubt, knew they didn't have the full amount of money for a share, but they did have enough to get in the game. Unfortunately, the game got them.

Without the speculative allure of buying on down payment, as occurred in the 1720s, trading remained quiet in London for the next 100 years. Speculation only returned during the Canal Bubble of the 1810s, the South America and Mining boom of the 1820s, and the railroad boom of the 1840s. The difference between how stocks traded in the 1840s and today is particularly striking. Again, the difference is what I call buying on the installment plan.

The par value of most stocks was £100 or about $486 using the fixed, gold exchange rate. This was almost a year's income for the average person. Of course, the average person wasn't investing, and most investors were people who had an endowment they relied upon for their income. The problem was, if you want to build a railroad and raise large amounts of money, how do you get people to part with their money? As in 1720, the answer was to pay on the installment plan.

Show Me the Money

A railroad stock would be issued at £100 par. This was the amount investors were expected to put into the company; however, the company would only ask for the money as it was needed. The amount actually paid in was the paid amount, and this could differ significantly from the par value. The agreement was that as the building of the railroad progressed, the corporation could assess shareholders for additional money, which they would then be required to pay in, or lose their shares. This allowed shareholders to get in on the cheap and spread out their £100 in payments over a period of years, starting off at £10 and working their way up. As always, the hope was that if the railroad were successful, investors could use the profits the railroad produced to pay for the shares, and if the railroad were not successful, this process would minimize their losses. In theory, after several years, the £100 would be paid in full, and the shareholder would have made a successful investment.

In reality, this process created a number of complications. First, there was always the problem that someone might not have the cash ready when an assessment was due. For this reason, shareholders began to resent the fact that at any point in time, the corporation could ask them for more money with the threat of the loss of shares if the shareholder did not pay. The goal was to receive money from the corporation, not pay money into it. Shareholders especially resented this when the railroad ran into unexpected problems creating a need for the investors to share the burden.

Shareholders were obligated to pay these assessments, even if the shares were worthless. As shareholders in Overend, Gurney and Co. (see Chapter 28) found out, it is one thing to lose all your money on a stock; it is another to have to pay money into the company in addition to losing your capital if it goes bankrupt. This is why all shares today are non-assessable, meaning companies cannot ask shareholders for more money.

Show Me the Losses

The oddest result of this system was that some shares might actually trade at a negative value! In other words, someone would pay you to take their shares in the company, and we have recorded negative values for shares from the London Stock Exchange. Let's say that a share is trading at £5 and a £10 assessment is due, but you don't have the £10, then you might pay someone £5 to take the shares off your hands and avoid the £10 assessment. Having to pay someone to take shares of a company you invested and lost money in would certainly add insult to injury.

Another problem this system created was that several shares could trade simultaneously. You might have shares with paid-in values of £30, £40, and £50 trading at the same time, reflecting the amount paid in and creating confusion. For this reason, prices were often quoted in the *London Times* at a premium or discount to the par value, so the same quotation could be provided regardless of which shares you were buying. If shares were trading at a £5 discount, you would pay £25 for the £30 shares or £35 for the £40 shares. Up until the mid-19th century, most shares on the London Stock Exchange that were not fully paid were listed at a premium or discount, not their nominal price.

There was another problem this created. When the railroad boom got going in the 1840s, stocks increased in value dramatically. If a railroad needed to raise more capital, and the shares were already fully paid in at 100 and had risen in price since then because the railroad was profitable, it became difficult to raise additional capital because the price of the shares was so high. So how do you raise additional capital? The answer was simple: you issue fractional shares.

Shares were issued in halves, thirds, fourths, fifths, eighths, tenths, sixteenths, and most fractions in between. At any given point, a company might have a half-dozen fractional shares issued and trading. This allowed smaller investors to jump on the bandwagon and make money along with their richer friends. In addition to this, the railroad might issue shares for different railroad routes, which would be separate from the main line. This allowed the railroad to issue new shares at lower prices on the installment plan, and since money is fungible, use the money as they best saw fit.

Of course, most shareholders wanted to receive income on their shares in the form of dividends. After the railroad mania of the 1840s was over, profits were lower and shares declined in value. It became more difficult to raise money from the investing public, so some of the railroads began issuing "preferred" shares, which were paid ahead of the common stocks. The London and Greenwich Railway was the first to do this, issuing a 5 percent preferred in April 1842.

By the time the railway mania of the 1840s was over, the outstanding securities of some railroads were a mess. Most railroads never made it to the full £100 par, so the paid-in value was only a portion of the shares' par value. In addition to that, various fractional shares were outstanding, there were the shares from extension lines of the railroad, and shares in railroads taken over during the boom, which often traded separately from the parent shares.

To eliminate the confusion, railroads consolidated shares once the building boom was over. If a £100 par share was at £20 paid, the company would do a 1:5 reverse split, turning the stock into a £100 par share. If there were half shares or quarter shares outstanding, they would do a 1:10 or 1:20 reverse so all the fractional shares were eliminated. If an extension rail line was at £10 par, it would have a 1:10 reverse. This way, all the shares would be consolidated into a single security.

By the late 1800s, capital was flowing freely enough that all the measures that had been used to make shares "affordable" were no longer needed. New shares were issued at £100 and the whole system of down payments, fractional shares, and other half-measures weren't necessary anymore.

Stock Splits Slide into the Great Depression

Nevertheless, there was a final interesting phenomenon that occurred in London to make shares more accessible to the public. When the bull market of the 1920s occurred, the high price of stocks kept most shareholders out of the market, even though punters wanted in. Companies found a quick solution to making their shares more liquid and bringing in more capital.

In the U.S., companies split their stocks 4:1 or 5:1 as prices rose during the bull market of the 1920s to make the shares more affordable, and speculators could go to bucket shops to trade on 10 percent margin, but in London, shares were sometimes split 100:1 to get the par value down from £100 to £1. There are even cases of stocks splitting 400:1 to get the par value down to 5 shillings (or about $1). This helped to feed the bull market in stocks in London, but as we all know, the 1920s bull market ended in the crash of the Great Depression. By making stocks cheaper, markets made sure it wasn't only the rich who lost money in the stock market crash. The London stock index fell around 50 percent between 1929 and 1933, but The Dow Jones Industrial Average fell by 89 percent.

The bottom line is, companies will always find a way to make their shares available to the public to raise money and maintain liquidity in their stocks. Some may criticize high-frequency trading, but it has made markets more liquid. It is easier and cheaper to trade odd lots than ever, so if you only want to buy ten shares of Google, then do so. Markets have always accommodated investors, and always will.

chapter eleven

The Grand Junction Canal:
Three Bubbles for the Price of One

The Company of Proprietors of the Grand Junction Canal was incorporated by Special Act of Parliament on April 30, 1793, to build a canal from Braunston to the River Thames. The stock for the canal went through three bubbles, in the 1790s, the 1810s, and the 1820s, before settling down once the railroads were built, providing competition to the canal.

The Speculative Bubble of the 1790s

Unfortunately, there is almost no price data for the Canal Mania of the 1790s. Only one canal was authorized by Act of Parliament in 1790, but by 1793 twenty were authorized. The capital authorized for canal companies in 1790 was £90,000, but rose to £2,824,700 by 1793. Most of the canals raised their money locally, mainly in the Midlands. Shares were not actively traded since most canals were small, and there were few transactions recorded in the stocks as a result. Though a stock exchange was established in Liverpool in the 1790s to trade shares, actual values are hard to come by and must be tracked down through local newspapers. Nevertheless, some of the stock increases were impressive. The Birmingham and Fazeley Canal showed one of the greatest increases in its shares, trading at a premium of £1170 in 1793.

The first canal bubble occurred in 1792 and 1793 and we only have two prices for Grand Junction Canal Shares (Figure 11.1), one at £472.75 in October 1792, a premium of 355 guineas. Amazingly, this trade occurred even before the company had started to dig the canal or gotten approval from Parliament! Talk about a speculative bubble. Shares had fallen to £441 by the time the approval for the canal was provided by Parliament, and the prices collapsed after 1795 when shares returned to their par level of around 100.

The London Stock Exchange wasn't formally established until 1801, which limited both the opportunity to trade canal stocks and to keep track of price

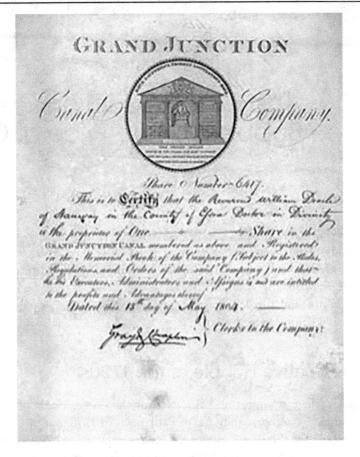

Figure 11.1 Grand Junction Canal Company Stock Certificate.

fluctuations. Even once the London Stock Exchange was established in 1801, most of the prices Global Financial Data has are bid-and-ask quotes from the *Gentlemen's Magazine* and other sources, not actual trades. Canal stock prices weren't provided in the *Course of the Exchange* until 1811. Nevertheless, these data are sufficient to outline the three bubbles in shares of the Grand Junction Canal.

Two More Bubbles

The next price we have for Grand Junction Canal shares after 1793 is at £94 in April 1806. The canal bubble began again in May 1808 when shares still traded at £96, but the price steadily rose to £313.5 by June 1808, whence they declined to £179 by August 1811, stabilized around £200 until 1815 when the Napoleonic War ended, then fell to £103 by September 1816. The second Canal Mania of the 1810s was not as wild as the one of the 1790s, since share prices tripled rather than quadrupled, but the difference was that the Canal Mania of the 1810s was not

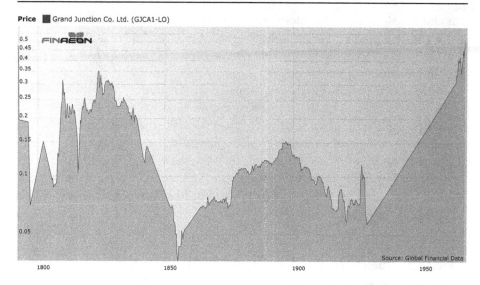

Figure 11.2 Grand Junction Canal Co. Stock Price, 1792 to 1967.

limited to the Midlands. Shareholders in London also participated as a result of the formal establishment of the London Stock Exchange.

The next move up in the shares began soon after the post-war plummet. Shares moved up steadily from September 1816 to hit £200 by the end of 1817, stabilized around £200 through the end of 1820, then hit £383 by April 1824. The canal stocks shared in the bubble of the 1820s even though that bubble mainly revolved around South American stocks and the mining companies that were established following the independence of the South American countries.

Unfortunately, Grand Junction Canal shares did not benefit from the railway mania of the 1840s since the railways were in direct competition with the canals and shareholders who sold their canal shares to invest in railways. Shares traded steadily between £200 and £300 between 1825 and 1845, but fell along with the Railway Mania crash in the 1840s, with shares declining to £51 by 1853 (Figure 11.2).

Shares of the Grand Junction Canal Co. generally rose for the rest of the 19th century, hitting £150 in 1897 before declining until the 1920s bull market began. The Regent's Canal bought the Grand Junction Canal and the three Warwick canals, and from January 1, 1929 they became part of the (new) Grand Union Canal. The Grand Junction Canal took the proceeds and became a REIT, which was renamed the Grand Junction Co., Ltd. The company was acquired by the Amalgamated Investment & Property Co. Ltd. in 1971.

Bubbles require a source for the speculation, a new technology that excites investors and causes cash to quickly flow into the new discovery, and excess credit being made available to invest in the shares. The initial canal mania of the 1790s was driven by strong profits, with one canal paying a £75 dividend. Many of the stocks were profitable and did quite well, but others were poorly thought out and failed. The two bubbles that drove Grand Junction Canal shares in the 1810s and 1820s were driven not only by the investment opportunities the canals provided, but by the liquidity created by the impact of the Napoleonic Wars on Britain's finances.

Between 1793 and 1818, UK government debt rose from £243 million to £843 million. The brief hiatus in the increase in government debt between 1808 and 1812 could help explain the canal mania of 1810–1812 since the Continental Blockade forced investors to put their money to work internally, but once Napoleon invaded Russia, this source of funding dried up. 1819 was when the UK government debt peaked at £844 million, declining from there in absolute terms, much less as a share of GDP, until 1914. The decline in the debt freed up capital for investing in individual companies.

London Becomes the Financial Capital of the World

It should be remembered that, more than anything else, Napoleon made London the financial center of the world. The French Revolution both destroyed the rich in France by driving wealthy financiers out of Paris and to London, and through inflation, which destroyed the value of the assets the rich had held. The other financial center in the 18th century in Europe was Amsterdam, but it never really recovered from the occupation of the country by French troops in 1795. Both financial expertise and capital flowed to London as a result of the French Revolution and the wars that followed. The laissez-faire approach England took to markets ensured that London would be the financial center of the world until World War I. The capital controls the British government introduced during World War I and maintained after the war kept London from continuing its role as the global financial center in the 20th century.

As capital flowed into London during and after the Napoleonic Wars, and investors were allowed to trade freely, stocks benefited. Anyone who questions the impact of the government on the price of financial assets, both positively and negatively, need only look at the Grand Junction Canal's history as well as that of the London stock exchange to see the impact the government can have.

chapter twelve

The First and the Greatest: The Rise and Fall of the United East India Company

The *Vereenigde Oost-Indische Compagnie* (VOC), or the United East India Company, was not only the first multinational corporation to exist, but also probably the largest corporation in size in history. The company existed for almost 200 years, from its founding in 1602, when the States-General of the Netherlands granted it a 21-year monopoly over Dutch operations in Asia, until its demise in 1796. During those two centuries, the VOC sent almost a million people to Asia, more than the rest of Europe combined. It commanded almost 5,000 ships and enjoyed huge profits from its spice trade. The VOC was larger than some countries. In part, because of the VOC, Amsterdam remained the financial center of capitalism for two centuries. Not only did the VOC transform the world, but it transformed financial markets as well.

The United East India Company Takes Over Asian Trade

The foundations of the VOC were laid when the Dutch began to challenge the Portuguese monopoly in East Asia in the 1590s. These ventures were quite successful. Some ships returned a 400 percent profit, and investors wanted more. Before the establishment of the VOC in 1602, individual ships were funded by merchants as limited partnerships that ceased to exist when the ships returned. Merchants would invest in several ships at a time so that if one failed to return, they weren't wiped out. The establishment of the VOC allowed hundreds of ships to be funded simultaneously by hundreds of investors to minimize risk.

The English founded the East India Company in 1600, and the Dutch followed in 1602 by founding the *Vereenigde Oost-Indische Compagnie*. The charter of the new company empowered it to build forts, maintain armies, and conclude treaties with Asian rulers. The VOC was the original military-industrial complex.

The VOC quickly spread throughout Asia. Not only did the VOC establish itself in Jakarta and the rest of the Dutch East Indies (now Indonesia), but it established itself in Japan, being the only foreign company allowed to trade in Japan. The company traded along the Malabar Coast in India, removing the Portuguese, traded in Sri Lanka, at the Cape of Good Hope in South Africa, and throughout Asia. The company was highly successful until the 1670s when the VOC lost its post in Taiwan and faced more competition from the English and other colonial powers. Profits continued, but the VOC had to switch to traded goods with lower margins. They were able to do this because interest rates had fallen during the 1600s.

Lower interest rates enabled the VOC to finance more trade through debt. The company paid high dividends, sometimes funded through borrowing, which reduced the amount of capital that was reinvested. Given the high level of overhead it took to maintain the VOC outposts throughout Asia, the borrowing and lack of capital ultimately undermined the VOC and led to its demise. Nevertheless, until the 1780s, the VOC remained a huge multinational corporation that stretched throughout Asia.

The Fourth Anglo-Dutch War of 1780–1784 left the company a financial wreck. The French Revolution began in 1789, leading to the occupation of Amsterdam in 1795. The VOC was nationalized on March 1, 1796, by the new Batavian Republic, and its charter was allowed to expire on December 31, 1799. Most of the VOC's Asian possessions were ceded to the British after the Napoleonic Wars, and the English East India Company took over the VOC's infrastructure.

The VOC Provides Innovations in Finance

The VOC transformed financial capitalism forever in ways few people understand. Although shares had been issued in corporations before the VOC was founded, the VOC introduced limited liability for its shareholders, which enabled the firm to fund large-scale operations. Limited liability was needed since the collapse of the company would have destroyed even the largest investor in the company, much less small investors.

Although this innovation changed capitalism forever, there were ways in which the VOC failed to transform itself, which led to its downfall. The company's capital remained virtually the same during its 200-year existence, staying around 6.4 million florins (about $2.3 million). Instead of issuing new shares to raise additional capital, the company relied on reinvested capital. The VOC's dividend policy left little capital for reinvestment, so the company turned to debt. The company first issued debt in the 1630s, increasing its debt/equity ratio to two. The ratio stayed at two until the 1730s, rising to around four in the 1760s, then

Price ■ Netherlands 10-year Government Bond Yield (IGNLD10D)

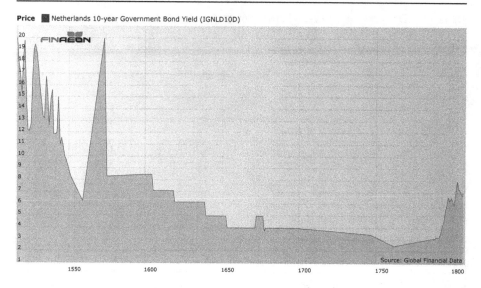

Figure 12.1 Netherlands Bond Yields 1517 to 1800.

increased dramatically in the 1780s to around eighteen, ultimately bankrupting the company, and leading to its nationalization and demise.

In the 1600s and 1700s, the Dutch had the lowest cost of capital in the world. This was because of an innovative idea: if you pay back your loans, your creditors will reward you with a lower interest rate in the future. This wasn't the way Spain, France, and other kings looked at borrowing money. They often defaulted, and their interest rates remained high.

As a result of Dutch fiscal rectitude, the yield on Dutch government bonds fell from 20 percent in 1517 to 8.5 percent by 1600 and to 4 percent by 1700 (Figure 12.1). The Dutch had the lowest interest rates in the world at that time. This pushed the Dutch to invest not only in joint-stock companies, such as the VOC, but in foreign government debt, helping to fund the American Revolution.

Another interesting aspect of the VOC was its dividend policy. Some of the dividends were paid in kind, rather than in money, and the dividends varied widely as Table 12.1 below indicates.

The dividend averaged around 18 percent of capital over the course of the company's 200-year existence, but no dividends were paid after 1782.

The VOC provided a high return to investors, but not always in the way shareholders wanted. The VOC basically unloaded its surplus inventories on shareholders in some years, providing them with produce, cloves, spices, or bonds. Some shareholders refused to accept them. Obviously, shareholders want money, not goods, and the three British companies, Bank of England, East India Company, and South Sea Company, learned from this and only paid cash dividends during the 1700s. The average dividends of 20–30 percent of capital were high, but since the price of shares traded around 400 during most of the company's existence,

Table 12.1 Dividends Paid to West India Company Shareholders, 1610 to 1644

Date	Action	Amount
1610-04-30	Dividend in Mace	75
1610-11-15	Dividend in Cash	7.5
1610-11-30	Dividend in Pepper	50
1612-03-31	Dividend in Nutmeg	20
1612-12-31	Dividend in Cash for those not accepting payment in kind	57.5
1613-08-31	Dividend in Cash for those not accepting payment in kind	42.5
1618-02-28	Dividend in Cash for those not accepting payment in kind	62.5
1620-04-01	Dividend in Cash	37.5
1623-04-30	Dividend in Cash	25
1623-11-15	Dividend in Cloves	25
1624-03-01	Dividend in Cash	12.5
1625-08-31	Dividend in Cash	20
1629-01-01	Dividend in Cash	25
1631-01-01	Dividend in Cash	17.5
1633-01-01	Dividend in Cash	12.5
1633-12-01	Dividend in Cash	20
1635-03-01	Dividend in Cash	20
1635-05-15	Dividend in Cloves	12.5
1635-08-20	Dividend in Cloves	12.5
1636-03-01	Dividend in Cloves	25
1636-11-01	Dividend in Cloves	12.5
1637-03-01	Dividend in Cloves	15
1637-11-01	Dividend in Cloves	25
1638-10-01	Dividend in Cloves	10
1638-12-01	Dividend in Cash	25
1640-01-01	Dividend in Cloves	15
1640-11-01	Dividend in Cash	25
1641-02-01	Dividend in Cloves	15
1641-11-01	Dividend in Cloves	25
1642-12-15	Dividend in Cash	50
1643-02-01	Dividend in Cloves	15
1644-11-01	Dividend in Cloves	25

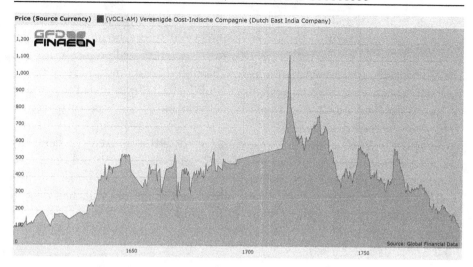

Figure 12.2 Dutch East India Company Stock Price, 1602 to 1795.

as Figure 12.2 shows the actual dividend yield was around 5–7 percent, better than Dutch bonds, but less than bonds from "emerging market" countries, such as Russia or Sweden.

As the chart shows, shares started at 100 in 1602, moved up to 200 by 1607, suffered a bear raid in 1609, moved up to the 400 range in the 1630s, fluctuated as the fortune of the company changed from year to year, participated in the bubble of the 1720s when shares exceeded 1,000, fell back to 600, rallied to 800 in the 1730s, then slowly declined from there (Figure 12.2). Perhaps no better indicator of the Dutch economy, or the global economy, prior to 1800 exists.

The Impact on the Amsterdam Stock Exchange

The VOC also transformed the Amsterdam Stock Exchange, causing a number of innovations to be introduced, such as futures contracts, options, short selling, and even the first bear raid. Isaac le Maire was the largest shareholder of the VOC in its early years, and he initiated the first bear raid in stock history, selling shares of VOC short in order to buy them back at a profit. These actions also led to the first government regulation of stock markets, attempting to ban short selling in 1621, 1623, 1624, 1630, and 1632, as well as banning options and other forms of financial wizardry. The fact that these laws had to be passed so many times shows that these regulations were not that effective.

One problem for the long-term success of the Amsterdam Stock Exchange was that the VOC and the West Indies Company (WIC) were the only shares of importance that traded on the Amsterdam Stock Exchange. Between 1600 and 1800, no new large companies listed in Amsterdam. Although Dutch fiscal rectitude kept debt and interest rates low, it also helped stifle the growth of the Amsterdam Stock Exchange because government bonds never became a prominent part of the trading on the exchange. Due to the decentralized political nature of the Netherlands, government debt was held locally. There was no large centralized national debt as in France and England, and ultimately, this inhibited the growth of the Amsterdam Stock Exchange. The Netherlands was as decentralized as France was centralized.

Because the VOC and WIC so dominated the share market, the company didn't issue new shares to raise capital. Dutch debt was so small and diversified among its cities that the Dutch invested in foreign debt to find an outlet for their capital. Dutch newspapers of the 1700s often listed the prices of French debt in Paris as well as British Consols, Bank of England stock, the British East India Company and South Sea Company stock in London, but no other debt or equity from Amsterdam was listed.

With the exception of colonial trade, until the 1800s no capitalist enterprise required the levels of capital of the VOC and WIC (Figure 12.3). So the Dutch capital that was available went into debt, not equity. America went to Amsterdam to raise capital, as did Sweden, France, England, Russia, Saxony, Denmark, Austria,

Figure 12.3 The Shipyard of the Dutch East India Company in Amsterdam, 1726, engraving by Joseph Mulder.

and other countries. This provided Dutch investors with higher returns, but didn't develop the Dutch economy in the way it could have.

Another factor that may have held the Amsterdam Exchange from expanding was the fact that shares could only be registered on a monthly or quarterly basis. The situation was different in London. Not only could British shares and debt be registered daily, but all of the shares were available for transfer. On the other hand, many VOC shares weren't traded at all. The amount of British and French debt grew throughout the 1600s and 1700s, requiring new investors on a regular basis. Not only did the VOC's capital remain constant, but centralized Dutch government debt didn't exist until the late 1700s. Amsterdam failed to provide its investors with new opportunities.

The Financial Capital of the World Shifts to London

Before the Industrial Revolution, companies were simply too small to require sufficient capital to be traded on exchanges. Shipping had long been a high-risk venture, providing high returns and high losses, and investors diversified their risk by putting their money in a number of different ships. The colonial trading companies of the 1600s and 1700s took financial capital to a different level, allowing thousands of people to invest in hundreds of shipping ventures, diversifying their risk.

After the Napoleonic Wars, the center of global finance shifted from Amsterdam to London. Although this process was spread out over several decades, it is amazing that the center of global finance could move from Amsterdam to London so quickly and so easily. There were some things, mostly political, which Amsterdam had little control over, such as the Napoleonic Wars, their occupation by the French, and the loss of its colonies after the war.

In retrospect, there were things the Dutch could have done to keep Amsterdam at the center of global finance after 1815, but the trend was inevitable. The Dutch failed to diversify away from VOC and WIC shares and allow other companies to take advantage of local capital markets; they failed to sufficiently develop the bond side of the market because there was no centralized government debt until the late 1700s; they failed to expand the capital of the VOC, but instead chose to borrow, adding to the debt load, which led to the bankruptcy of the VOC and WIC; the VOC and WIC did not sufficiently reinvest dividends for growth; and they failed to offer a large number of securities that encouraged trading as in London.

The company failed to raise additional capital when necessary, to limit borrowing, or to fund capital expenditures by cutting its dividend. Since the Netherlands lacked a centralized debt issuer, as the French, British, and Russians did, the Amsterdam Stock Exchange faded in importance after the VOC and WIC collapsed. Foreign government bonds became more prominent in Amsterdam, but even the foreign government bond trading moved to London in the 1820s, where capital was more readily available.

It is doubtful whether Amsterdam could have foreseen all the changes that happened, and perhaps they couldn't have prevented the move of the world's financial capital from Amsterdam to London that occurred after 1815, but it was a lesson London should have learned. London became the engine of global capitalism for the 19th century, only to lose its place to New York after World War I. The US should understand this lesson as well. The global center of finance must grow, innovate, and be as open as possible. Otherwise, the center will move to someplace that is.

chapter thirteen

The Happiest Shareholders on Earth—Disney Shareholders!

Invest $1 in 1948 and have $48,000 today! With the recent IPOs of Twitter and Facebook, two of the largest social/entertainment media giants, one would imagine that investing in those companies would pay big compared to the Walt Disney Co. However, the Walt Disney Co. outperformed them both by comparison in its day…and did it with an interesting story to tell.

Today, employees and venture capitalists reap most of the benefits before a company's IPO on the New York Stock Exchange (NYSE) or NASDAQ, but it wasn't always that way. In the past, most companies traded over-the counter for years before listing on the NYSE. Companies had to pay their dues before they moved to the NYSE, and for this reason, a majority of their outperformance occurred while they traded over-the-counter.

In the past, anyone could invest in fledgling companies before they listed on the NYSE. Today, this opportunity is rarely available to the average investor. By the time companies such as Xerox, Dr Pepper, and Kentucky Fried Chicken moved onto the NYSE, a good portion of the advance in their stock had already occurred. If you ignore the performance of the stock when it traded over-the-counter, you miss a substantial portion of the stock's historic move, and without this information, you will never fully understand the returns that were available to investors in the past.

Disney Trades OTC in 1946

Walt Disney Productions incorporated in 1938. The company issued its 6 percent cumulative convertible preferred to the public in 1940; its common began trading OTC in 1946; and the company listed on the NYSE on November 12, 1957. If you study the changes Walt Disney made to his eponymous company before it listed on the NYSE, you can see how he primed the company to increase in price and made sure the listing on the NYSE was successful. Walt Disney, his brother Raymond,

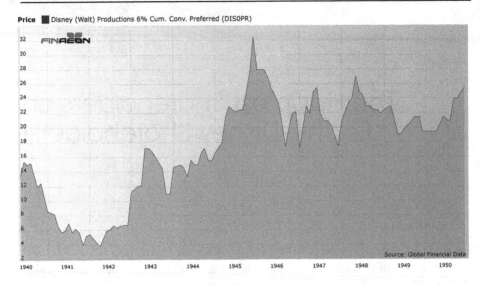

Price ■ Disney (Walt) Productions 6% Cum. Conv. Preferred (DISOPR)

Figure 13.1 Walt Disney 6 Percent Preferred Price, 1940 to 1950.

and their wives owned over 25 percent of the stock. Owning such a large ownership of the shares, Walt Disney had every incentive to drive the price up.

The preferred stock was issued at $25, but the company suffered large losses in 1941, caused by the disappointing returns from *Pinocchio* and *Fantasia*, which were not as successful as *Snow White* had been. The company fell in arrears on the dividend, starting in July 1941, but since the preferred was cumulative, there was always the chance the company would make up the lost dividends, and they did. Disney restarted the regular dividend in July 1947 and caught up on the $7.50 in arrears in 1948 and in 1949. You can see the impact this had on the preferred stock, which had fallen in price to $3.50 by April 1942, rising to $32.50 by the beginning of 1946, reflecting the expectation of the missed dividends being paid (Figure 13.1). This is also when the company's common began trading OTC. The preferred stock, whose chart is provided above in Figure 13.1, was redeemed on January 1, 1951, at $25 with all dividends paid.

Transforming Tomorrowland before Neverland

In the twelve years between 1946, when Disney common started trading OTC, and when it listed on the NYSE on November 12, 1957, Walt Disney introduced numerous innovations that transformed the company and increased its profits. Disney made animated films that had been delayed by the war, such as *Alice in Wonderland, Peter Pan*, and *Cinderella*. The company began making live-action movies with *Treasure Island* in 1950 and *20,000 Leagues under the Sea* in Cinemascope in 1954. For TV, Disney introduced the Disneyland TV show (later

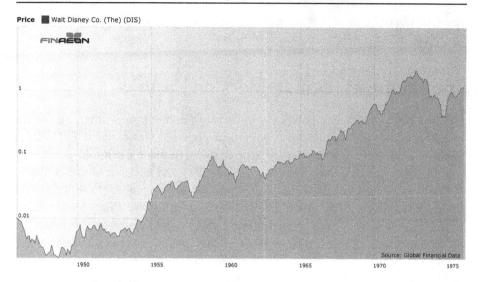

Figure 13.2 Walt Disney Stock Price, 1946 to 1975.

Walt Disney's Wonderful World of Color) in 1954, and the Mickey Mouse Club began production in 1955. Of course, Walt's greatest innovation was Disneyland, which opened on July 17, 1955, and for which Walt Disney hosted a live TV preview with Ronald Reagan and others.

Note that all of these events occurred *before* Walt Disney Productions, as it was known then, listed on the NYSE. In the year before the stock first traded on the NYSE, the company did a 2-for-1 stock split and paid its first dividend on the common stock.

One difference between Disney in the 1950s and Facebook or Twitter in the 2010s is that anyone could have bought Disney stock OTC before it listed on the NYSE. The stock wasn't restricted to employees and venture capitalists. Anyone who went to Disneyland in 1955, watched the Mickey Mouse Club or the Disneyland TV show, or saw the movies Disney was releasing could have taken advantage of the company's growth.

Figure 13.2 shows how Disney stock performed between 1946 and 1975. The stock traded at 3 in 1949, moved up to 52 by July 1956 before splitting 2-for-1. The stock closed at $13.75 on November 12, 1957, when it debuted on the NYSE, and moved up to $59.50 by April 1959. The stock traded sideways until 1966 when it began another significant move as one of the Nifty Fifty stocks of the 1960s, hitting 244 by the beginning of 1973.

The similarities between Walt Disney stock and Facebook or Twitter are striking in many ways. All of the companies had a CEO, Disney, Zuckerberg, or Costello, who was the driving force behind the company and benefitted immensely from the success of the stock. Each CEO provided innovations that appealed to young people at first, but which could eventually reach a wider audience. Their companies developed brand names that were easily recognizable, and they were able to take advantage of the publicity that came their way.

The Happiest Shareholders on Earth

One important difference between Disney and Facebook or Twitter was in the accessibility of the stock. Disney's 6 percent preferred was available OTC from 1940 to 1950, during which an investor could have made a ten-fold profit. The common stock made a ten-fold move between 1949 and its debut on the NYSE in 1957, then another ten-fold move by 1973 while it was a member of the Nifty Fifty in the 1960s. Since 1973, Disney stock has moved up another thirty-fold.

On a total return basis, even ignoring the ten-fold move in the Disney 6 percent preferred, $1 invested in Walt Disney Productions common in 1948 would be worth over $75,000 today, assuming all dividends had been reinvested in Disney stock. Even $1 invested in Disney on November 12, 1957, would be worth $5,000 today.

Disney certainly has been one of the top performing stocks on the NYSE since it debuted there in 1957; however, once you take into consideration the profits an investor could have made if they had bought Disney Preferred OTC in 1941, and switched to the common stock when the preferred was called, the returns increase 100-fold. Based upon Disney's returns OTC and on the NYSE, Disney probably has the "happiest" shareholders on Earth.

chapter fourteen

Six Ounces that Saved a Hundred Billion-Dollar Company

Today, Pepsi is one of the strongest brands in the world, with a capitalization of nearly $125 billion. But this wasn't always the case. It may be hard to believe, but Pepsi was on the verge of perpetual bankruptcy during its first forty years of business. Pepsi-Cola's financial situation was so bad that three times between 1922 and 1934, Pepsi-Cola approached Coca-Cola and offered to sell out to its competitor. All three times Coca-Cola rejected their offer.

Coca-Cola's rejections could be among three of the biggest marketing mistakes in history, while Pepsi's "12 ounce" jingle campaign turned out to be one of the most successful marketing efforts of all time. Not only did the campaign prove a success for Pepsi, but it revolutionized the soda industry as a whole. This case study is an interesting one that shows how perseverance in the marketplace and promotional advertising can be worth billions.

A Secret Recipe: Pepsin and Kola Nuts

First introduced in North Carolina as "Brad's Drink" in 1893 by Caleb Bradham, the drink's name was changed to Pepsi-Cola in 1898, mainly because of Pepsi's secret ingredients. Digestive enzymes named pepsin and kola nuts were used in the creation of this special drink. However, when Bradham unsuccessfully speculated on wildly fluctuating sugar prices after World War I (Figure 14.1), the company faced bankruptcy.

A series of buyouts and structural reorganizations occurred between 1922 and 1934. In 1931, the National Pepsi-Cola Co. reorganized as Pepsi-Cola Co., selling its assets to Roy C. Megargel. After Megargel also failed to make Pepsi-Cola Co. profitable, he sold the company to Charles Guth, president of Loft, Inc. Loft, a candy manufacturer and retailer that owned Happiness Candy Stores, had been around for twenty years prior to acquiring Pepsi. The Loft-operated Happiness

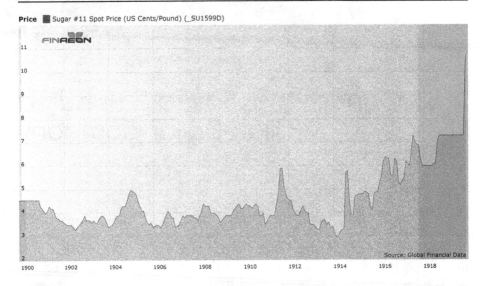

Price ■ Sugar #11 Spot Price (US Cents/Pound) (_SU1599D)

Figure 14.1 Sugar Spot Price, 1900 to 1919.

Candy Stores had soda fountains that could sell Pepsi and saw the marriage of the firms as a good fit.

Pepsi—Rejected by Coke, Acquired by Loft

Charles Guth wanted to cut costs at his soda fountains, so he tried to get Coca-Cola to lower the cost of its syrup. Coke refused, so Charles Guth turned to Pepsi-Cola. Guth bought an 80 percent controlling stake in Pepsi-Co. in September 1938 and had Loft's chemists reformulate the Pepsi-Cola syrup. Guth then quit Loft, Inc. as president to run Pepsi-Cola Co. and sold the syrup to Loft, Inc., his former employer, at a profit.

At the same time, Loft, Inc. was sliding into bankruptcy. Figure 14.2 shows how the price of Loft, Inc. sank to new lows in the 1930s.

The company's Happiness Candy Stores were consistent money losers and Loft, Inc. lost money on its candy for five years in a row. The Depression was so bad that not even candy could cheer people up! Figure 14.3. shows the desperate situation the company's shareholders were facing in the late 1930s.

Losses and Loft Suits

Where there are losses, there are lawsuits. Claiming that the companies had been mismanaged, shareholders sued Happiness Candy Stores, Inc. as well as Loft, Inc. Loft, Inc. sued Guth since he had used the finances and facilities of Loft, Inc. to help Pepsi-Cola, Co. succeed.

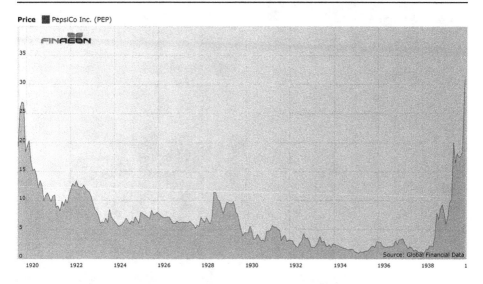

Figure 14.2 Loft, Inc. Stock Price, 1919 to 1939.

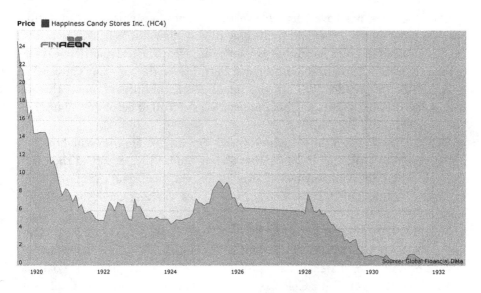

Figure 14.3 Happiness Candy Stores, Inc. Stock Price, 1919 to 1932.

Guth not only increased Pepsi's profits by selling the syrup to his former employer, but he made one of the most brilliant marketing decisions in history. He had the excellent idea of packaging Pepsi-Cola in twelve-ounce bottles rather than the 6.5-ounce bottles Coca-Cola used while keeping the price the same at five cents. Guth introduced the clever jingle "Pepsi-drink for you." As a result, Pepsi's sales increased and profits doubled between 1936 and 1938. Pepsi stock soared, rising 100-fold within two years, as shown in Figure 14.4.

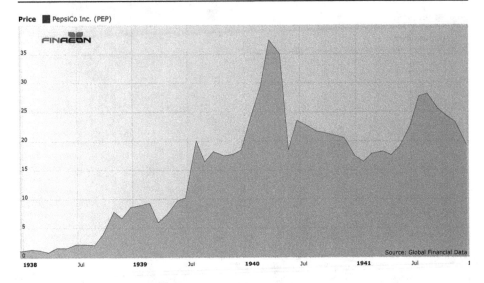

Figure 14.4 Pepsi Cola Co. (Old) Stock Price, 1938 to 1941.

Loft, Inc. may not have been able to run a candy business or a candy store business profitably, but they did know how to win a lawsuit. When *Guth v. Loft, Inc.* was decided in Loft's favor, the company was saved. The real question was how to turn all of these lawsuits for and against Loft, Inc. to the company's advantage. E. A. Le Roy Jr., president of Loft, Inc., made a series of brilliant moves that not only resolved all of the lawsuits, but put Pepsi on the road to becoming a hundred-billion-dollar company.

First, Le Roy spun off the Happiness Candy Stores, Inc. He eliminated the $1.5 million owed to Loft, Inc. by Happiness Candy Stores, Inc., absorbed the candy stores, of which the company owned over 70 percent, then spun the company off to shareholders as Loft Candy Stores, Inc. The loss-making candy business was eliminated from the company.

Next, Le Roy proposed that Loft, Inc. and Pepsi-Cola, Co. (Figure 14.4) merge into a single company. With 95 percent of Pepsi-Cola Co. shareholders and 75 percent of Loft, Inc. shareholders approving, the merger was given the go-ahead and on June 30, 1941, Pepsi-Cola Co. shareholders received 8.43 shares Loft, Inc. common stock for their old stock. Loft, Inc. changed its name to Pepsi-Cola Co. in a reverse acquisition.

You have to admire how Le Roy Jr. handled the situation, getting rid of the loss-making candy business, the loss-making candy stores, settling several lawsuits with shareholders over mismanagement in a favorable manner, winning the lawsuit against the company's former president for failing in his fiduciary responsibility, and organizing a reverse acquisition that turned a company that suffered losses year-after-year into a profitable company that has become a global brand recognized throughout the world.

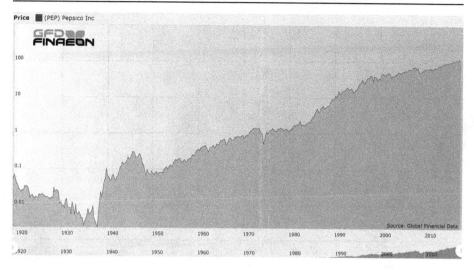

Figure 14.5 PepsiCo Inc. Stock Price, 1938 to 2018.

From a marketing point of view, giving away an extra six ounces for free was a stroke of genius on Guff's part. Pepsi's little jingle produced a 100-fold increase in its stock price, rising from $3.25 in June 1937 to $350 in April 1940. Since Loft, Inc. changed its name to Pepsi-Cola Co. in June 1941, on a nominal basis, the stock has increased in price 130-fold. On a total return basis, $1 invested in Pepsi-Cola, Co. on June 30, 1941, would be worth $10,000 today. Figure 14.5, on a log scale, shows how PepsiCo stock rose after the acquisition of a controlling stake in Pepsi in 1938.

Compare this performance with that of Loft, Inc. whose stock had fallen from $25 in 1919 to $2 when the company established its 80 percent ownership of Pepsi-Cola, Co. The stock rose to $22 by the time the reverse acquisition of Pepsi-Cola occurred on June 30, 1941 (Figure 14.2). The story of the Happiness Candy Stores was similar, with its stock falling from $25 in 1919 to $0.125 in 1941 when the company ceased to exist (Figure 14.3).

As for Loft Candy Stores, Inc. where all of the assets of the Loft Candy and retail stores were placed and spun off, its stock traded at $0.50 on June 30, 1941, rising to $8 by 1946, subsequently falling to $3 by 1951, rising again to $14 in 1968, and settling at $0.25 in 1972 after the company changed its name to Briarcliff Candy Corp. The company was dissolved in 1981. Figure 14.6 provides a chart of Loft Candy Stores stock after the company was spun off.

Today, Pepsi is one of the strongest brands in the world. Had it not been for the decisions of Charles Guff and E. A. Le Roy Jr., Pepsi might have met the same fate as Loft Candy, to become something you only read about on the Internet. Of course, PepsiCo had to make many good corporate decisions over the past seventy-five years to bring the company to the point it is at today, but you have to admire the way Guth and Le Roy turned around a loss-making company to

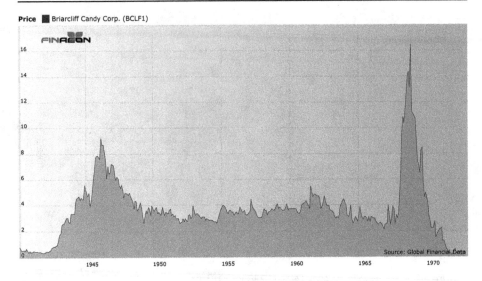

Figure 14.6 Briarcliff Candy Store Stock Price, 1940 to 1972.

become a global giant. Along with Coca-Cola, Pepsi dominates the soft drink business worldwide and shows no signs of slowing down.

chapter fifteen

American Tobacco and the Legacy of the Antitrust Laws

One of the twelve stocks that made up the original Dow Jones Industrial Average (DJIA) in 1896 ceased to exist in 2014, though few people noticed. General Electric Co. was the only one of the original twelve members that remained in the DJIA in 2014. Two other stocks, the National Lead Co. (now NL Industries Inc.) and Laclede Gas Co. (now Laclede Group Holding Co.) still exist, but were removed in 1916 and 1899 respectively. Other companies among the original twelve, such as the United States Leather Co., American Spirits Manufacturing Co., and United States Cordage Co., disappeared long ago.

Beam, Inc. was acquired by Suntory Holdings on April 30, 2014. Although you may not immediately recognize Beam, Inc., originally known as the American Tobacco Co., as an original member of the DJIA, the company played a significant role in American corporate history.

Automated Cut and Roll

The American Tobacco Co. was originally incorporated in New Jersey by James Buchanan Duke on January 21, 1890, as a merger of five tobacco companies: W. Duke & Sons (begun in 1879), Allen & Gintner, W.S. Kimball & Co., Kinney Tobacco, and Goodwin & Co. Duke gained a competitive advantage by using machines manufactured by the Bonsack Machine Co. to roll and cut cigarettes. Until then, cigarettes had been rolled and cut manually. A skilled worker could roll 200 cigarettes in an hour. Bonsack's machines could roll 200 cigarettes in a minute.

Duke got a secret contract with the Bonsack Machine Co. and used this competitive advantage to cut his prices and slowly take over the American tobacco industry. The five companies that formed the original American Tobacco Co. in 1890 produced 90 percent of the cigarettes in America. Duke increased his control over the tobacco industry on October 9, 1904, when he reincorporated the American Tobacco Co. after acquiring both the Consolidated Tobacco Co.

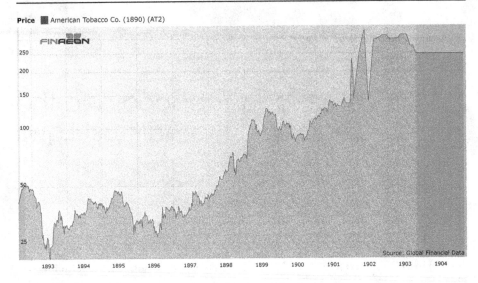

Figure 15.1 American Tobacco Co. (Old) Stock Price, 1892 to 1905.

and the Continental Tobacco Co. As Figure 15.1 shows, the stock for the original American Tobacco Co. rose from 100 to 250 between 1890 and 1904, rewarding shareholders handsomely.

In 1890, the American Tobacco Co. had a capitalization of only $25 million. After that, the company dominated the tobacco industry, absorbing another 250 companies in all areas relating to tobacco over the next two decades. By the first decade of the twentieth century, the American Tobacco Co. produced 80 percent of the cigarettes, plug tobacco, smoking tobacco, and snuff products produced in the United States. Having taken over the American market, the company expanded into Great Britain, China, Japan, and other countries.

In 1907, the American Tobacco Co. was indicted for violation of the Sherman Anti-Trust Act of 1890. Though the American Tobacco Co. neither grew tobacco itself, nor sold cigarettes at the retail level, its vertical integration gave it complete control of every other aspect of the tobacco industry. Nevertheless, the company continued to expand. The equity of the American Tobacco Co. grew to over $300 million by 1911. Though the American Tobacco Co. was half the size of the Standard Oil Co. and U.S. Steel, it was still one of the largest companies in the United States.

The Monopoly Becomes an Oligopoly

On May 29, 1911, the Supreme Court ordered both the Standard Oil Co. and the American Tobacco Co. to dissolve because of their violation of anti-trust laws.

The problem with dissolving the American Tobacco Co. was that Duke had integrated production in such a way that it was difficult to break up the American

Tobacco Co. cleanly. The solution that was reached was to break the American Tobacco Co. into several competing firms. The government would allow shareholders to buy shares at par in two new companies, Liggett & Myers and Lorillard, while distributing shares directly to shareholders in fourteen subsidiaries including:

- American Snuff Co.
- George W. Helme Co.
- Weyman-Bruton Co.
- McAndrews & Forbes Co.
- R.J. Reynolds & Co.
- United Cigar Stores
- British-American Tobacco Co.

Shareholders received odd fractions in each subsidiary, for example, 75,908/401,824 of a share of American Snuff Co. common. The monopoly became an oligopoly.

The two most famous brands of the American Tobacco Co. were Lucky Strikes and Pall Mall, which were sold to British American Tobacco in 1994. As Figure 15.2 shows, though American Tobacco Co. stock did well between World War I and 1929, rising eight-fold in price after the 1920s, the stock stagnated until the 1970s. At the market bottom in 1974, the stock still traded where it had been in 1929, forty-five years before.

Tobacco Sells Off

Since the Surgeon General declared cigarettes to be dangerous to consumers' health in the 1960s, the American Tobacco Co. decided to diversify away from cigarettes. Symbolically, on July 1, 1969, the company removed the word tobacco from its name and was rechristened American Brands, Inc. The company diversified into office supplies through its ACCO subsidiary, golf through its Acushnet division, home and hardware through names such as Moen and Master Lock, and alcohol through spirits such as Jim Beam. In 1994, the company sold off its tobacco division to Brown & Williamson. The American Tobacco Co. was no more.

On May 30, 1997, American Brands, Inc. changed its name to Fortune Brands, Inc. and on October 3, 2011, the company spun off its Fortune Brands Home & Security Division, and changed its name to Beam, Inc., keeping its spirits business (after acquiring twenty-five additional spirits from Allied Domecq and selling its wines to Constellation Brands). The tobacco company was now named after a brand of alcohol. On January 13, 2014, Suntory Holdings of Osaka, Japan, entered into a deal to acquire Beam, Inc. for about $13.6 billion, and on April 30, 2014, the deal was completed.

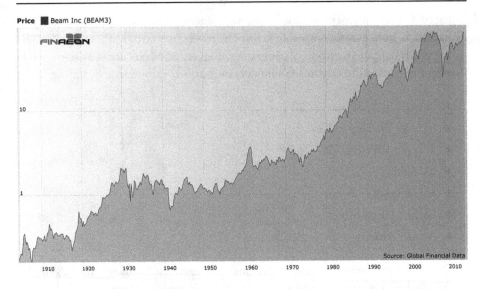

Figure 15.2 Beam Inc. (American Tobacco Co.) Stock Price, 1904 to 2014.

Allowing for splits and stock distributions, the company's strategy of diversification worked well. By the time the company was bought out, its stock had risen over 40-fold from around $2 a share in 1974 to the acquisition price of $83.50 in 2014 (Figure 15.2).

The Legacy of the Antitrust Laws

It was a simple innovation, the application of machinery to rolling and cutting cigarettes, which allowed the American Tobacco Co. to dominate the tobacco industry. By the time the company was finally acquired in 2014, it was a shadow of its former self. While the Standard Oil Co. (now ExxonMobil) grew from $600 million in 1911 to over $400 billion, Beam, Inc. grew from a $300 million capitalization to only $13 billion when it was taken over in 2014.

A century has passed since the American Tobacco Co. was broken up by the Supreme Court. Standard Oil, broken up in 1911, and AT&T, broken up in 1982, have gradually reformed themselves through mergers and acquisitions until they are now two of the largest companies on the NYSE. On the other hand, the American Tobacco Co. was never able to reorganize itself and dominate its industry after its breakup in the way Standard Oil still does.

chapter sixteen

Why Wilt the Stilt Got the Jilt

Global Financial Data has stock histories for over 50,000 securities. Some of these stocks cover centuries of data; others are quite short, lasting only a few months or even a few days. One of the most interesting of these is Wilt Chamberlain's Restaurants, Inc. for which there are only two days of data.

Wilt the Stilt

Wilt Chamberlain was one of the greatest, some would argue **the** greatest, basketball players in history. He holds seventy-one NBA records, and he is the only person to score 100 points in a single game. He averaged more than forty to fifty points per game in some seasons, and in one season he played every minute of every game. Chamberlain was 7-foot, 1-inch and played for the University of Kansas, Harlem Globetrotters, the Philadelphia/San Francisco Warriors, Philadelphia 76ers, and the Los Angeles Lakers. He dominated the NBA between 1959 and 1973 and left a legacy that few can match.

After Chamberlain left the NBA, he promoted the short-lived International Volleyball Association, wrote a book, appeared in the movie *Conan the Destroyer* alongside Arnold Schwarzenegger, and tried several business ventures. One of these was Wilt Chamberlain's Restaurants, Inc.

Wilt Chamberlain's restaurant (Figure 16.1) opened on December 20, 1990, in Boca Raton, Florida. The restaurant was a sports-themed, casual-dining family restaurant. The goal of the restaurant was fine food and service for families, a sports bar for drinkers, and an entertainment complex for kids of all ages. The restaurant had over fifty televisions broadcasting sports events for its patrons as well as a basketball court and hoops where customers could shoot a few shots while enjoying their drinks or waiting for a table. The restaurant had a live arcade with over forty games, and a redemption center where customers could either cash in their tickets or purchase sports-related goods.

The menu offered a full range of food including some of Wilt Chamberlain's favorites. Recommended starters included Wild Mushroom Christini and his

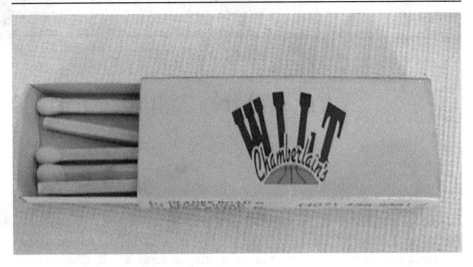

Figure 16.1 Matches from Wilt Chamberlain's Restaurant.

Downtown Dip, salads included the Bangkok Chicken, Noodle Salad and Cashew Shrimp Salad, sandwiches included Wilt's Clubhouse Sandwich and a Barbecued Beef Brisket Sandwich, specialties included the Ribs and Broasted Chicken Combo as well as Shrimp Enchiladas, pasta included Chicken and Penne and Penne Classico, and pizzas included the French Quarter, Grilled Vegetarian and Goat Cheese. Almost all dishes were under $10.

The IPO that went PU

The restaurant was successful, so in 1992, Wilt Chamberlain decided to go public. The Hard Rock Café had begun its expansion in 1982, and in 1991 Planet Hollywood was founded by Sylvester Stallone, Bruce Willis, Demi Moore, and Arnold Schwarzenegger. There was no reason why a sports-themed restaurant shouldn't succeed as well, but to do so Wilt Chamberlain would need more capital.

Chamberlin contracted with New York–based brokerage Meyers, Pollock, Robbins Inc. to go public. The goal was to raise $8 million through the initial public offering (IPO) in order to fund the restaurant's expansion. The company filed an SB-2 registration in which the brokerage firm said they would offer 1.4 million shares, priced at $6 to $8. The company had reported a profit of $222,706 for the nine months ended Sept. 30, 1992, so the restaurant was a profitable IPO.

Wilt Chamberlain signed an agreement to allow his name, likeness, and persona to be used in connection with marketing the company. Although there was only one Wilt Chamberlain restaurant at the time, the company had plans to open additional restaurants across the United States and possibly worldwide. The company would trade under the symbol WILT.

Price ◼ Wilt Chamberlain`s Restaurants Inc (WILT1)

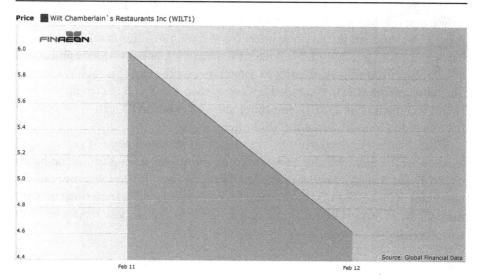

Figure 16.2 Wilt Chamberlain Restaurants, Inc. Stock Price, 1993.

Unfortunately, the IPO was a disaster. Although Meyers, Pollock, Robbins, Inc. had been in business for fifty years, they had never underwritten an IPO. Their inexperience contributed to the fiasco, and they botched the placement completely. Most investment bankers will guarantee the IPO price for thirty days after the debut, but shares in Wilt Chamberlain Restaurants, Inc. stayed above the offering price for only a few minutes.

Wilt Chamberlain Restaurants, Inc. went public at $7 a share on Thursday, February 11, 1993. The first trade in the stock was at $7.50, but the price fell to $6.75 a few minutes later. Over one million shares traded on its opening day, and the stock price closed at $6, $1 below the IPO price. This brought on short-sellers when it was apparent the firm could not or would not support the stock. By the next day, the stock closed at $4.625 a share (Figure 16.2). Everyone who owned stock in the company was losing money, many of whom were clients of Meyers, Pollock, Robbins, Inc.

IPO Money on the Rebound

Meyers, Pollock, Robbins, Inc. had gauged the price of the stock inaccurately and were unable to support the stock when it fell below its offer price. Over the weekend, the company and the underwriter huddled to figure out a strategy for their failed IPO. Before trading began on Tuesday, Meyers, Pollock, Robbins, Inc. announced that they would cancel the public offering. The underwriter had the legal right to do this because an IPO can be cancelled if the shares have not been distributed and no trades have settled. The stock became a two-day wonder.

What made the cancellation unusual was that the only reason given for pulling the IPO was the fall in the stock price. Cancellation of IPOs is rare, but it does happen. An IPO in July 1992 was cancelled when the Central Garden and Pet Co. of Lafayette, California, suffered a warehouse fire on the day of its public offering. The most infamous case of a failed IPO was when the BATS electronic platform IPO'd their own stock in 2012 and computer crashes on BATS caused the stock to fall to pennies from its initial $15 IPO price.

Wilt Chamberlain died in 1999. The restaurant remained popular and changed hands several times over the next few years, ultimately ending up in the hands of Joel Kron. A dispute between the landlord and Kron led to the closure of the restaurant in 2007. Though the restaurant is gone, memorabilia from the restaurant can still be found on Ebay. That and a failed IPO are all that remain of Wilt Chamberlain Restaurants, Inc.

chapter seventeen

Mickey Mantle Strikes Out,
Then Hits a Homer

Wilt Chamberlain wasn't the only sports star to go into the restaurant business. Few people realize it, but Mickey Mantle set up restaurants twice, once in Texas in the 1950s when he struck out, and a second time in the 1980s in New York City when he hit a home run.

Mickey Mantle played for the New York Yankees between 1951 and 1968 and is one of the few baseball players to hit over 500 home runs during his career, and believe it or not, without the aid of any steroids. Many consider Mantle to be the greatest switch hitter of all time, a skill that enabled him to hit for both average and for power. His lifetime batting average was 0.298, and he hit some of the longest home runs in history, including one measuring 643 feet at Tiger Stadium in 1960.

Mickey Mantle replaced Joe DiMaggio in centerfield in 1952, appeared in twelve World Series, helped the Yankees win seven of them, and played in sixteen All-Star games. Mantle was Most Valuable Player three times, and by 1961, he was the highest paid player in baseball.

Country Cooking Without the Sizzle

Mickey Mantle incorporated Mickey Mantle's Country Cookin', Inc. in Texas on April 22, 1968, during the last year of his baseball career. The company authorized 2,000,000 shares, and 1,000,000 shares were outstanding on July 11, 1969. Mickey Mantle's Country Cookin', Inc. offered 200,000 shares at $15 per share on July 11, 1969, through Pierce, Wulbern, Murphy, Inc. of Jacksonville, Florida, and through D.A. Campbell Co., Inc. in New York.

The restaurant's menu focused on country vittles, including Chicken & Dumplins, Ham and Lima Beans, Country Beef Stew, Country Fried Chicken, Texas Chili, Catfish Filets, Chili & Beans, Chicken Fried Steak, a Country Smoked Ham Sandwich, and a Country Pork Sausage Sandwich. Meals were $1.25, and

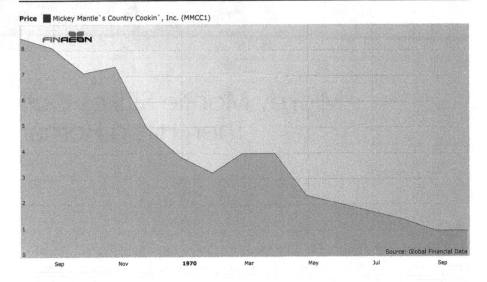

Price ■ Mickey Mantle`s Country Cookin`, Inc. (MMCC1)

Figure 17.1 Mickey Mantle's Country Cookin' Inc. Stock Price, 1969 to 1970.

the sandwiches were $1.00. If you wanted to go all-out, you could get an eight-piece Chicken Bucket for $3.25.

The first Country Cookin' restaurant opened up at 3651 Martin D. Love Freeway in Dallas, Texas. Company-owned restaurants were also located in San Antonio and in Irving, Texas. Mickey Mantle franchised the restaurant, and soon ones popped up in Florida, Louisiana, and Texas. In 1970, the company tried to acquire thirty-five Best Steak Home restaurants, but the deal fell through. Largely because of lawsuits, overextension, and poor management, the restaurants did not do well.

Shares in Mickey Mantle's Country Cookin', Inc. traded over-the-counter, and as you can see in Figure 17.1, the shares steadily declined in value. Offered at $15, shares fell below $10 by the end of the month and were down to $1 a year later. The company received more income from franchise fees than from sales, and this could only spell long-run trouble for the restaurant. As a sign of its problems, the company changed its name to Invesco International, Inc. on June 30, 1969, and reincorporated in Nevada, where it became a coal mining company.

Want a souvenir? The 1952 Topps Mickey Mantle #311 rookie baseball card can sell for over $10,000, but if that is beyond your budget, hundreds of souvenirs remain from the Mickey Mantle's Country Cookin' restaurant and can be purchased on Ebay. Souvenirs include postcards, china, coffee mugs, carrying trays, menus, chairs, pot holders, ordering pads, stock certificates, and prospectuses. Souvenirs are also available from Mickey Mantle's Holiday Inn located in Joplin, Missouri, including bars of soap, postcards, matches, and even room keys, though they probably don't work anymore.

Mantle's Business Career Booms

The Country Cookin' restaurants weren't Mickey Mantle's only business venture. As mentioned above, he ran a Holiday Inn in Joplin, Missouri. Mantle also created real estate and land developments (WIllowwood and Arbolado), the Mickey Mantle Billiard Center in Milwaukee, Wisconsin, and the Mickey Mantle Bowling Center at 200 Exchange Park North in Dallas, from which some cigarette lighters survive.

In 1988, Mickey Mantle's Restaurant and Sports Bar was opened in New York at 42 Central Park South at 59th Street. Although Mantle made frequent appearances at the restaurant, he let others run the business. The sports bar continued to operate successfully for over twenty years, perhaps because it focused on a single theme, avoided expansion, and let Mantle act as promoter rather than manager.

For the record, Mantle's favorite food at his restaurant was the chicken-fried steak, usually topped off with some drinks from the bar. Mantle died in 1995 and the sports bar closed on June 2, 2012, after failing to pay rent for several months. Though the sports bar remains closed, it has a Facebook page for the curious.

Mickey Mantle was an entrepreneur throughout his life, and the success of the sports bar shows that he learned from his first time at bat in the restaurant business.

chapter eighteen

Berkshire Before Buffett

Everyone is aware of the incredible returns that Berkshire Hathaway has provided shareholders over the past fifty years that Warren Buffet has run the company. In the late 1960s, when Warren Buffett became CEO of Berkshire Hathaway, shares in the company were trading at under $20. Today, shares trade around $300,000. During the same period, the S&P 500 Total Return Index went from around 38 to 5,300. While the S&P 500 increased 140-fold, Berkshire Hathaway increased 15,000-fold. That is what I call value added.

But how well did Berkshire Hathaway perform before Buffett took over the company? Had the company performed well even before Buffett took over, or did Buffett change the company's performance dramatically?

Berkshire Hathaway is Born

Berkshire Fine Spinning Associates, Inc. incorporated under Massachusetts laws in 1929 as a consolidation of Berkshire Cotton Manufacturing Co., Valley Falls Co., Coventry Co., the Greylock Mills, and Fort Dummer Mills. The company changed its name to Berkshire Hathaway in 1955 when it acquired Hathaway Manufacturing Co.

Berkshire Fine Spinning Associates, Inc. manufactured fine grades of cotton textiles and specialized in fine lawns, batistes, nainsooks, organdies, dimities, handkerchief cloths, broadcloths, oxfords, sateens, rayon, and silk mixtures. Plants were located in New Bedford, Massachusetts.

Berkshire offered 33,000 shares of common stock in 1929 at $40 per share, as well as 4,860 shares of 7 percent preferred stock, also at $40 per share. Unfortunately, the shares were offered in the middle of the 1929 bull market, and the share price collapsed soon after. In November 1929, the ask price for Berkshire stock was still at $40, but by November 1931, shares sank to $0.50. Sales for the company declined, and Berkshire ran losses until 1936.

As late as 1940, shares traded as low as $3, but profits and the share price picked up with the war. The company did well enough that it was able to reinitiate a

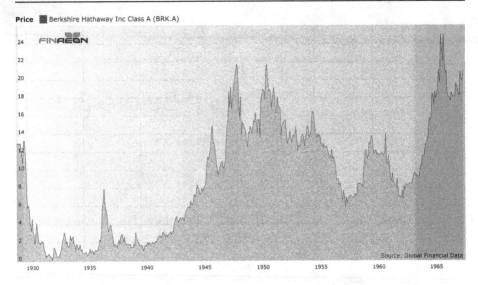

Price ■ Berkshire Hathaway Inc Class A (BRK.A)

Figure 18.1 Berkshire Hathaway Inc. Stock Price, 1929 to 1967.

regular dividend in 1942 (the dividend had been suspended in March 1930), and in September 1947, the company had a 3-for-1 split. Of course, the split marked the high mark for Berkshire and the stock began a downward trend that lasted until 1962.

Figure 18.1 shows the performance of Berkshire Hathaway, Inc. stock from 1929 until 1967, when Warren Buffett took over the company. As you can see, there was little change in the stock price in the forty years before then. Berkshire lost money between 1930 and 1936, and it lost money in 1957, 1958, and 1961 to 1963. Despite the fact that sales had tripled between the 1930s and the 1960s, there was no comparable increase in profits. In 1963, Berkshire stock was still trading below the price it had been offered at in 1929!

Buffet Buys Berkshire

Buffett began buying shares in Berkshire Hathaway at less than $8 in 1962, and by 1966, Buffett and his partners had taken over the company.

As soon as Buffett took over Berkshire, he began focusing on insurance and other businesses rather than textiles. Buffett invested in American Express when Anthony de Angelis's fraud (see Chapter 23) caused the price of American Express to drop dramatically in 1964. In the 1970s, Buffett expanded his investments to include media companies (the *Washington Post* and ABC) as well as other companies that fit his investment criteria. The final Berkshire mill was closed down in 1985.

Berkshire Hathaway paid a regular dividend between 1942 and 1960, when the dividend was suspended due to losses. Buffett paid a $0.10 dividend in November

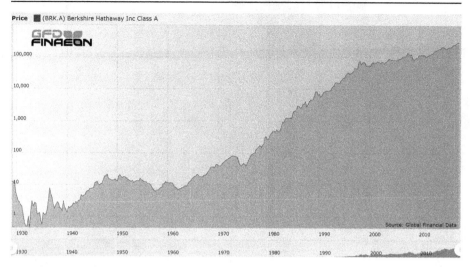

Figure 18.2 Berkshire Hathaway, Class A, 1929 to 2018.

1967, but that was the only dividend the company ever paid under Buffett. Thenceforward, profits were reinvested in the company to allow the share price to grow. Buffett lived off his $50,000 salary and outside investment income.

Berkshire Hathaway stock continued to trade OTC until October 1976, when it listed on NASDAQ. The shares moved to the New York Stock Exchange in November 1988, and in May 1996, Berkshire issued lower-priced Class B shares to investors who could no longer afford to buy a share of Berkshire Hathaway, Class A shares, which by that time had risen in price to $35,000.

Berkshire Booms

The impact of Buffett on Berkshire was incredible. Shares in Berkshire, which had gone nowhere for forty years, began increasing at a rapid pace. The stock closed at $18.625 in 1966. Shares first broke the $100 mark in 1977, the $1,000 mark in 1983, the $10,000 mark in 1992, and the $100,000 mark in 2006. Shares now trade around $300,000 each (Figure 18.2).

Buffett could have bought any company and the results would have been the same. As soon as Buffett took over Berkshire Hathaway, he began to focus on other businesses and ignore the company's core manufacturing subsidiaries. In fact, at one point, Buffett said that buying the textile business had been the worst trade of his life. I guess everyone is allowed one mistake.

part II

Stock Scams

chapter nineteen

The Fraud of the Prince of Poyais

Charles Ponzi built the original pyramid scheme; Michael Milken sold junk bonds; Nick Leeson was the rogue trader who broke Barings Bank; and Bernie Madoff bilked investors with trading that did not exist. All of these men were unambitious amateurs when compared to Gregor McGregor, the financial fraudster to top all fraudsters.

Gregor McGregor was a selfish swindler who returned nothing to any of his investors. At least Madoff and Ponzi returned some of the money they took from investors to perpetuate their Ponzi schemes, but McGregor kept all the money for himself. He also granted himself the title of Sir Gregor McGregor, as well as Grand Cacique (Prince) of Poyais, indicative of his vanity and narcissism.

It is one thing to convince people to invest money in a company that doesn't produce anything yet, as has often happened, but it takes real skill to convince investors to invest in a country that doesn't exist. How did he do it?

During the Napoleonic Wars, Spanish control over its South American colonies weakened and the colonists in those countries fought for their independence. Between 1809 (Ecuador) and 1825 (Uruguay), all of the South American countries gained their independence from Portugal and Spain. However, these newly independent countries needed money, and the local tax base was limited.

Most of the South American countries had mines that produced gold and silver, epitomized by the riches of Potosí in Bolivia. In the early 1820s, Argentina, Brazil, Chile, Colombia, Peru, and other countries issued bonds that were backed by their new governments. Local mines issued stocks, making promises of large profits to investors. The promises of riches exceeded the feeble finances of the issuers, and the collapse in the bonds and shares that followed imposed huge losses on investors.

The result was one of three bubbles on the London Stock Exchange in the early half of the 1800s: the Canal Bubble of the 1810s, the South American Bubble of the 1820s, and the Railroad Bubble of the 1840s. In the midst of this investment mania came McGregor, who sold bonds and anything else he could muster in his mythical country of Poyais.

McGregor had joined the Royal Navy in 1803 and was a colonel in the Venezuelan War of Independence, fighting under Simon Bólívar. In 1820, McGregor returned to London. Not content to merely talk about what he had done in the war of independence, McGregor announced that he had been named the Cacique (Prince) of the Principality of Poyais. The country, he assured everyone, was located on the Bay of Honduras and the land had been bestowed upon him by the native chief King Frederic Augustus I of the Mosquito Shore and Nation. This beautiful and fruitful country, he promised, included over 12,500 square miles of untapped, rich lands that only lacked settlers to develop.

To help promote his cause, McGregor published a book, *Sketch of the Mosquito Shore, including the Territory of Poyais*, supposedly written by Captain Thomas Strangeways, to describe in detail the wonders of this fantastic, fraudulent country. The book said English settlers had founded the capital of St. Joseph in the 1730s. They allegedly discovered untapped gold and silver mines, fertile soil, and ample resources that settlers could profit from. In his book, Strangeways described the country's resources: a civil service, a bank, an army, a democratic government, and natives who, of course, were eager to work for their British masters. In case you would like to review this tall tale of tantalizing hyperboles, the book can be downloaded for free from Google Books, where you can read for yourself the wonders of this nonexistent country. Unfortunately, the most fertile thing about Poyais was McGregor's imagination.

In reality, King Frederic Augustus had signed the document granting the land to Gregor McGregor in April 1820 after being plied with whiskey and rum. The land only had four run-down buildings in it, and was surrounded by uninhabitable jungle with no fertile lands, no gold or silver mines, and no compliant natives as described by McGregor in his book. But to a fraudster, facts are irrelevant.

McGregor took up residence in London, where he offered to bestow the benefits of Poyais on gullible investors. Many of the people who read about the Territory of Poyais and all of its riches had the misfortune to meet the Cacique of Poyais in London's inner circles of the rich and famous. Here his swagger and self-confidence impressed and reassured them that investors were facing a once-in-a-lifetime opportunity.

McGregor sold 2,000 bonds at £100 each on October 23, 1822, to the rich, which resulted in £200,000 in sales. The bonds were offered at 80 and paid a mere 3 percent interest. For the poor, he offered land for sale in Poyais at the rate of 3 shillings, 3 pence per acre (later 4 shillings, or about $1), an amount which was about a day's wages in 1822. Not to leave any stone unturned, McGregor sold places in his military, the right to be shoemaker to the Princess of Poyais, and opportunities to be a jeweler, teacher, clerk, or other craftsmen in his nonexistent government and country. McGregor even issued his own currency (see Figure 19.1), which settlers could use once they arrived in McGregor's El Dorado.

The Poyaisian Legation to Britain opened offices in London, and land offices were opened in Glasgow, Stirling, and Edinburgh to sell land to his fellow Scots. McGregor employed a group of people who promoted and sold land, sinecures, and

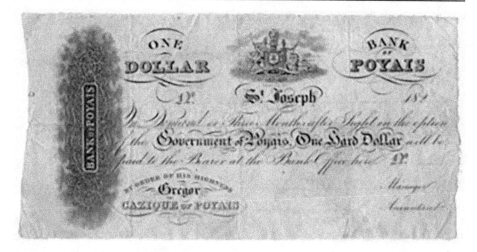

Figure 19.1 Poyais Hard Dollar.

other Poyaisian goods, sharing the profits with McGregor. By 1823, McGregor was a multi-millionaire in today's terms.

As amazing as it may seem, the Legation of Poyais even chartered two boats to take settlers to Poyais. Why they would take this risk, knowing that the settlers would soon discover that Poyais was little more than a swamp once they arrived, staggers the imagination, but perhaps the fraudsters had started to believe their own falsehoods. On September 10, 1822, the *Honduras Packet* departed from London with seventy settlers including doctors, lawyers, and a banker, and on January 22, 1823, the *Kennersley Castle* left Leith Harbour in Scotland with almost 200 settlers.

When they arrived in Poyais, the settlers, some of whom had risked their life savings, found an uninhabitable jungle that had more tropical diseases than silver and gold. In reality, they not only risked their life savings, but their lives as well. Of the original 240 settlers who reached Poyais, only sixty survived. The rest died.

The *Mexican Eagle*, an official ship from British Honduras, happened upon the Poyaisian settlers in April 1823 and brought King George Frederic to the settlers to tell them he had revoked the land grant because McGregor had assumed sovereignty. Fifty settlers sailed back to London on August 1, 1823, and arrived in London on October 12, 1823. The next day, the story of the ill-fated investors and settlers hit the newspapers of London.

The result can be seen in Figure 19.2. Until then, the price of Poyais bonds had held their own on the London Stock Exchange, but when news that Poyais was a fraud became clear, the price of the bonds collapsed overnight.

Amazingly, many of the settlers defended McGregor, believing the Cacique had been duped. Unwilling to admit that they were the ones who had been deceived, they protected the perpetrator of the Poyais fraud. One of the settlers, James Hastie, who lost two children to tropical diseases, published a book, *Narrative of a Voyage*

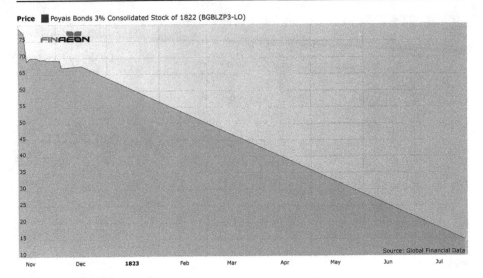

Price ■ Poyais Bonds 3% Consolidated Stock of 1822 (BGBLZP3-LO)

Figure 19.2 Poyais 3 Percent Consolidated Stock of 1822.

in the Ship Kennersley Castle from Leith Roads to Poyais, in which he blamed his advisors and publicists for the false information about Poyais, but not McGregor.

Realizing that eventually the truth would catch up with him, McGregor fled to France. Once in France, McGregor continued his fraud. He wrote a constitution for the Republic (no longer a Principality) of Poyais and tried to sell land to French settlers. In 1825, he tried to issue new bonds and shares in a new Poyaisian company.

When potential settlers began applying to the French authorities to sail to a country that didn't exist, the French began investigating. McGregor was arrested on December 7, 1825, and spent two months in prison on remand. There were two trials, one in April 1826 and another in July 1826, in which McGregor was acquitted, but one of his co-conspirators, Lehuby, was sentenced to thirteen months in prison. Despite all the evidence against him, McGregor managed to avoid incarceration.

McGregor returned to London, and still claiming to be the Cacique of the Republic of Poyais, opened an office at 23 Threadneedle Street (near the Bank of England). McGregor tried to issue new Poyais bonds in 1827 through Thomas Jenkins and Company as brokers, but with little success. In 1828, he tried to sell land in Poyais at 5 shillings an acre (about $1.20), which was more than the nonexistent land had sold for in 1822. In 1831, McGregor, now president of the Poyaisian Republic, issued Poyaisian New Three per cent Consolidated Stock bonds. He tried to sell land certificates in Poyais in 1834 and in 1837 and wrote a new constitution for Poyais in 1836.

Despite all these efforts, few believed McGregor's stories anymore. In 1839, McGregor moved to Venezuela, where he received a pension as a general who had fought in the Venezuelan War of Independence. That he would move from London to Venezuela to receive a pension shows that his attempts to perpetuate and profit from Poyais were failing. McGregor died on December 4, 1845.

The history of Poyais and McGregor should forever remain a cautionary tale to investors. Though not everyone will get the opportunity to invest in a country that does not exist, the hot air of Poyais has spread and will continue to spread to new schemes designed to deprive investors of their hard-earned money. Investors should beware lest they fall prey to the next Cacique.

chapter twenty

The Greatest Stock Market Loser of All Time

The stock for Hutech21 Co., Ltd. (CLGZF on the OTCQB) can lay claim to being the greatest destroyer of equity of all time as a result of the multiple reverse splits its stock has suffered and the decline in the value of the stock that followed these splits. The stock for Hutech21 Co., Ltd. itself has never had a reverse split, but the companies that preceded it had multiple reverse splits which, if compounded, would produce a cumulative one-to-twenty quintillion split (in numbers, that is 1:20,000,000,000,000,000,000)!

In the OTC markets where penny stocks (a term that gives the company the benefit of the doubt) like this reside, as the stock plunges in price, the company will do a reverse split to raise the price of the stock back to a level that allows them to sucker more investors into losing their money. When the company is close to bankruptcy, rather than declaring bankruptcy and putting investors out of their misery, the stock gets turned over to new owners who begin the process of equity destruction all over again.

Hutech21 Co., Ltd. was originally known as Vector Aeromotive Corp. back in 1990. Vector Aeromotive Corp. recapitalized as Vector Holding Corp. on August 15, 2000, changed its name to NCI Holdings on June 17, 2003, to Dark Dynamite, Inc. on May 7, 2004, to China International Tourism Holdings Ltd. on October 26, 2007, to China Logistics Group, Inc. on August 10, 2009, and reorganized under the laws of the British Virgin Islands as Hutech21 Co., Ltd. On March 21, 2011. The different companies had little if anything to do with their predecessors.

Since 1990, the following reverse splits have occurred:

July 9, 1990:	1:50
December 26, 1998:	1:5
July 10, 2000:	1:100
January 18, 2002:	1:25
May 7, 2003:	1:200
November 17, 2004:	1:2000

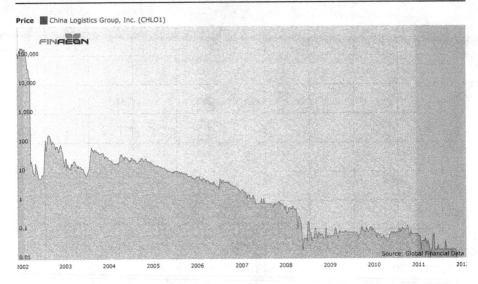

Figure 20.1 Hutech21 co., Ltd., 2002 to 2012.

March 28, 2005	1:1000
November 3, 2005:	1:4
April 3, 2009:	1:200
March 21, 2011:	1:100

Multiply this out and you get a cumulative 1:20 quintillion reverse split. The last trade we could find in Hutech21 Co. was on August 17, 2016, at $0.0001, which means that if you had invested $2 sextillion in Vector Aeromotive Corp. back in 1990, your wealth would have shrunk to $1. Since the money was invested over time and investors were subjected to a slow, torturous death rather than a sudden collapse, the company succeeded in luring in more investors. The long, sad decline in the stock is illustrated in Figure 20.1

So next time someone encourages you to invest in a penny stock, just remember, there is a reason they have that name.

chapter twenty-one

The Great Stock Exchange Forgery: Who Committed the Perfect Crime?

Most British stamp collectors are aware of the Great Stock Exchange Forgery that occurred in London in 1872 and 1873, though most philatelists and most Americans are not.

In 1870, the telegraph system of the United Kingdom was nationalized and run by the Post Office. The telegraph was useful to people on the stock exchange because without a ticker tape, traders used the telegraph to send stock quotes to customers throughout the United Kingdom.

If someone wanted to send a stock quote, they would go to the telegraph office at the Stock Exchange, write down the information, purchase a stamp generally costing one shilling, depending upon the number of words, then send the message off to the customer. The broker would purchase the stamp, put it on the telegraph message, and then have the message sent off, only seeing the actual stamp for a few seconds. The clerk would then cancel the stamp and send off the message.

The Great Stock Exchange Forgery occurred because a fraudulent clerk supplied forged stamps and pocketed the one-shilling fee. He used both fraudulent and real stamps so when the actual stamps were audited, none showed up missing. The stamps were only used on certain days, were convincing forgeries, and the stamps were not retained by the customers who might have noticed the fraud.

Although the telegraph messages were filed in a bag for disposal, the stock exchange kept the forms and they were later disposed of as waste paper. By obtaining some of these stamps after they were disposed of, some of the stamps were saved from oblivion. It wasn't until twenty-five years later, in 1898, that a philatelist, Charles Nissen, noticed differences between the forged stamps and the real stamps.

Three factors distinguished the fraudulent stamps from the genuine stamps. First, the stamps used letters that indicated the position of the stamps on the sheets of stamps, but some of the letters were incorrect. These letters were also slightly larger than on the genuine stamps and the corners of the stamps were blunter. Second, the stamps were not watermarked, while genuine stamps did have

Figure 21.1 Forged Stock Exchange Stamp.

a watermark. Third, the forged stamps were lithographed while the real stamps were typographed, producing a lower-quality stamp (see Figure 21.1).

By the time the forgeries were discovered in 1898, the clerk who had committed the forgery had disappeared, and to this day, no one knows who committed this perfect crime, perfect because no one knows who committed the crime and the criminal kept all the proceeds. In 1873, one shilling was equivalent to twenty-five cents or about $6 in today's money, and over a year, the forgeries could have added up significantly for the perpetrator. Perhaps after 1873, the fraudster simply retired.

Stock exchange forgery stamps are available to collectors but sell for more than the originals since they are scarcer. You can buy one on eBay for about $800 if you want a piece of stock market history, but if you try to imitate this perfect crime, the government will provide you with a change of address.

chapter twenty-two

The Land Co. of Florida and the Florida Real Estate Bubble

The Florida land bubble of the 1920s has been hailed as a precursor both to the stock market bubble of the late 1920s and the real estate bubble of the 2000s. Unlike the stock market crash of 1929 or the real estate bubble of the 2000s, there is insufficient evidence for the price fluctuations, so most of the data are anecdotal.

One of the stories, possibly apocryphal, that illustrates the impact of the Florida land boom was this story. An elderly man in Pinellas County was committed to a sanitarium by his sons for spending his life savings of $1,700 on a piece of Pinellas property. When the value of the land reached $300,000 in 1925, the man's lawyer got him released to sue his children and profit from his "unwise" investment.

Global Financial Data has data on a company that can provide some evidence of the crash in prices that followed the bursting of the Florida real estate bubble: The Land Company of Florida. Although it doesn't track the rise in Florida real estate prices, the company was formed in 1924 and does illustrate the fall in real estate prices that occurred.

The Florida real estate bubble was the most egregious example of a trend that had started during World War I. The post-war commodity inflation encouraged many farmers to borrow against their farms and buy additional property, anticipating further increases in both food and real estate prices. This led to a general increase in real estate prices during the 1920s throughout the United States before foreclosures started becoming more common in the late 1920s, culminating in the massive foreclosures of the 1930s caused by the Dust Bowl and the Great Depression.

In the middle of this real estate boom was the Florida bubble. In the 1920s, Americans had more money, more leisure time, were more willing to speculate, and were able to use their automobiles to travel to Florida and other places, creating markets that hadn't existed before. All of these factors enabled Florida to take advantage of these trends to promote the Florida land boom.

The Florida legislature passed laws in 1924 prohibiting state income and inheritance taxes to convince wealthy visitors to make Florida their permanent residence. Land developers then promoted real estate by building cities where none existed before. The most spectacular developments were in southeast Florida, where Henry Flagler's railroad provided direct access to New York City. Other factors attracting investors were the influx of motorized tourism, which brought both rich and poor visitors, and the rum runners who were able to bring in alcohol from Nassau and Grand Bahama to help visitors avoid Prohibition.

About two-thirds of all Florida real estate was sold by mail to speculators who never visited the state. Many of these real estate moguls tried to flip the land through ads in the *Miami Herald*. For those who actually went to Florida, binder boys were hired to expedite purchases. The binder boys were salesmen who got down payments with thirty-day financing and, once the checks cleared, received their commission.

When there is money to be made, people find ways to make a quick profit. What started out as an undervalued market turned into an overvalued bubble. Then reality set in. A series of events made investors realize how fragile the price increases were.

Forbes magazine warned about the overpriced real estate in early 1925. In October 1925, the "Big Three" railroad companies operating in Florida called an embargo due to the rail traffic gridlock, permitting only foodstuffs, fuel, perishables, and essential commodities to enter or move within the state. Although the railroads lifted the embargo in May 1926, disaster then followed in the shape of the September 1926 Miami hurricane, which killed over 400. A market where there were mainly buyers became a market in which there were mainly sellers and the real estate market collapsed.

The evidence for this bubble is the Land Co. of Florida, incorporated on June 16, 1924. The company was a subsidiary of Florida Western & Northern Railroad Co., and was organized to purchase upwards of 160,000 acres of land along the right-of-way of the Florida Western & Northern Railroad. The stock was a real estate investment trust trying to profit from the real estate bubble and provides a useful proxy for the Florida real estate market. After acquiring the land, the company would sell its properties when their value had been enhanced by the easy accessibility afforded it by the new railroad. Or so was the theory.

The stock traded on the New York Curb (later the American Stock Exchange) and traded in September 1925 at 93. After the train embargo was announced in October, the price fell to the 60s, and continued to fall, decreasing to the 20s by February 1926. One would expect that the hurricane of September 1926 would have caused a further collapse, but in reality, the stock price rose after September, hitting 41 in December. Perhaps the impact of the hurricane should be reevaluated, but it was downhill from 1927 on. By the time the stock market crashed in October 1929, the price had fallen to 5 and by the end of 1930, the stock was at $0.50, never to recover (Figure 22.1). The stock stopped trading on the Curb in May 1931.

The benefit of stock prices is that they provide a consistent record of market behavior. It is surprising that the stock for the Land Co. of Florida has been

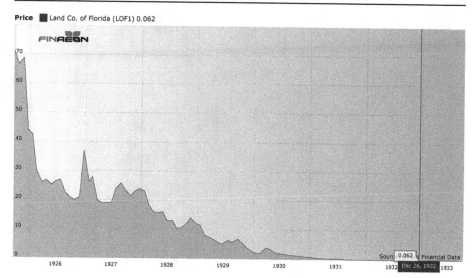

Figure 22.1 Land Co. of Florida Stock Price, 1925 to 1933.

overlooked as a proxy for the Florida real estate bubble. As could be expected, the stock was issued at the height of the bubble, otherwise the stock would have had no reason to exist as the railroad took advantage of speculators.

The stock may not have charted the rise of the bubble, but it certainly charted the collapse. The fact that the railroad was willing to market their land to investors, just as shoe shine boys were to give stock market tips at the top of the 1929 stock market bubble, should have been a clear sign to sell.

chapter twenty-three

JFK and the Great Salad Oil Swindle

John F. Kennedy was assassinated on Friday, November 22, 1963, in Dallas, Texas. The assassination not only shocked the nation, but shook the stock market as well. However, very few people have heard about the Great Salad Oil Swindle, which nearly crippled the New York Stock Exchange the weekend following the assassination. Officials at the NYSE took advantage of the closure of the exchange to keep the crisis caused by the salad oil swindle from spreading further. Here is what happened at the NYSE while the nation grieved.

Salad Oil, Cornered and Quartered

The Great Salad Oil Swindle was carried out by Anthony "Tino" De Angelis, who traded futures in vegetable oil (soybean oil), which is an important ingredient in salad oil. De Angelis had previously been involved in a swindle involving the National School Lunch Act and the Adolph Gobel Co., in which he provided food to schools for their lunches. When it was discovered that De Angelis had overcharged the government and delivered over 2 million pounds of uninspected meat, he ended up bankrupt. Con men don't stop being cons, they just try to learn from their mistakes and make more money the next time around.

Tino de Angelis had learned that government programs were a way to make easy money, so he started the Allied Crude Vegetable Oil Refining Co. in 1955 to take advantage of the US government's Food for Peace program. The goal of the program was to sell surplus goods to Europe at low prices. Initially, De Angelis sold massive quantities of shortening and other vegetable oil products to Europe, and when this worked, he expanded into cotton and soybeans.

By 1962, De Angelis was a large enough player in commodity markets that he thought he could corner the soybean oil market, allowing him to make even more money. Always the schemer, De Angelis's plan was to use his large inventories of commodities as collateral to get loans from Wall Street bank and finance companies. Buying soybean oil futures would drive up the price of his vegetable oil holdings, which would increase both the value of his inventories and allow him to profit from his futures contracts. De Angelis could use these profits not only to line his own pockets, but to pay his staff, make contributions to the community, and in one case, pay the hospital bill of a government official.

American Express had recently created a new division that specialized in field warehousing, which made loans to businesses using inventories as collateral. American Express wrote De Angelis warehouse receipts for millions of pounds of vegetable oil, which he took to a broker and discounted the receipts for cash. This proved to be an easy way to get money, so De Angelis began falsifying warehouse receipts for vegetable oil he didn't have.

American Express sent out inspectors to make sure that De Angelis had the vegetable oil that acted as collateral, but what they didn't know is that many of the tanks they inspected were filled mostly with water with a minimum of oil floating on the top to fool the inspectors, or that some of the tanks were connected with pipes to other tanks so the oil could be transferred between tanks when the inspectors went from one tank to the other.

If American Express had done its homework, they would have realized that De Angelis's reported vegetable oil "holdings" were greater than the inventories of the entire United States as reported by the Department of Agriculture. Unsatisfied with the American Express loans, De Angelis was able to get additional loans from Bunge Ltd., Staley, Proctor and Gamble, and the Bank of America. By the time the swindle collapsed, De Angelis had gotten loans from a total of fifty-one companies.

No Salad Today

As a result of attempted bribery, delivery mistakes, and other factors, the government inspectors were eventually tipped off about De Angelis's fraud. Allied Crude was supposed to have $150 million in vegetable oil as collateral, but De Angelis only had $6 million. When the inspectors found water in the tanks, and not oil, the gig was up.

The futures market crashed. Soybean oil closed at $9.875 on Friday, November 15, at $9 on Monday and $7.75 on Tuesday, November 19, wiping out the entire value of the De Angelis's loans. As you might guess, De Angelis's company had been losing money all along, and the loans were used to cover these mounting losses. De Angelis's goal was to sell out at the top and cover all of his losses, but of course, his plan didn't work out that way. The crash of the soybean oil market in November 1963 is shown in Figure 23.1.

On November 19, the Allied Crude Vegetable Oil Refining Co. filed for bankruptcy. No one should be surprised that millions of dollars were never accounted for, and fifty-one companies were stuck with bad loans from Allied Crude. Two of the brokerage houses that De Angelis had used, Williston & Beane

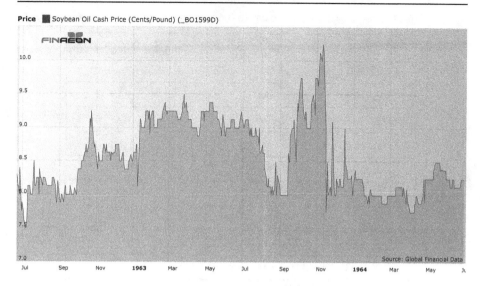

Price ■ Soybean Oil Cash Price (Cents/Pound) (_BO1599D)

Figure 23.1 Soybean Oil Cash Price, 1962 to 1964.

and Ira Haupt & Co. (which had been part of the famous Park & Tilford Distillers Corp. whiskey dividend scandal of 1946, described in Chapter 24) were suspended from trading by the NYSE. These brokerages' customers became desperate because they didn't know if they would get back the money in their accounts.

A Nation Shocked, a Market Shaken

On Friday, November 22, the NYSE organized a bail-out of Williston & Beane, and the firm was allowed to reopen at noon on Friday. Ira Haupt & Co. was a bigger problem. It collectively owned $450 million in securities and owed various banks over $37 million that it could not pay.

At 1:41 pm, word that JFK had been shot flashed on the floor of the New York Stock Exchange (NYSE), and stocks began to sell off. The Dow Jones Industrials, which was recorded at hourly intervals in 1963, was at 735.87 at 1 pm on November 22, and fell to 730.18 by 2 p.m. Over the next seven minutes, the market traded 2.2 million shares and lost an additional nineteen points, erasing around $11 billion in capitalization, before NYSE officials halted trading at 2:07 p.m. to stop the panic selling. The market rested, and the next day, JFK's body lay in repose at the White House.

On Sunday JFK's body was taken to the rotunda of the Capitol for public viewing. Over 250,000 people viewed the casket as a line stretched for forty blocks, or about ten miles. Some people waited over ten hours in the freezing cold to pay their last respects. On Monday, the casket was transferred to the National

Table 23.1 Dow Jones Industrial Average, November 22 and 26, 1963

Date	Time	DJIA	NYSE Volume
11/22/1963	10:00 AM	733.35	
11/22/1963	11:00 AM	733.61	1.46
11/22/1963	12:00 PM	732.78	1.3
11/22/1963	1:00 PM	735.87	0.86
11/22/1963	2:00 PM	730.18	0.81
11/22/1963	3:00 PM	711.49	2.2
11/26/1963	10:00 AM	738.43	
11/26/1963	11:00 AM	721.96	2.04
11/26/1963	12:00 PM	727.92	1.94
11/26/1963	1:00 PM	734.91	1.49
11/26/1963	2:00 PM	735.17	1.06
11/26/1963	3:00 PM	741.26	1.26
11/26/1963	3:30 PM	743.52	1.53

Cathedral, where his funeral Mass was broadcast to a stunned nation. Kennedy was buried in Arlington Cemetery, and the eternal flame was lit over his grave.

The stock market remained closed on Monday and reopened on Tuesday, November 26, when the market traded over 9 million shares, closing the day at 743.52, moving up 4.5 percent from the previous close. Table 5.1 provides the hourly performance of the DJIA on November 22 and 26, 1963.

Figure 23.2, based upon hourly, intraday calculations of the DJIA between October 1 and December 31 of 1963, shows both the panic sell-off on November 22, the full recovery on November 26, and the move to new highs that ultimately followed.

The closure of the NYSE gave the exchange some breathing space to address the problems De Angelis had created. If the NYSE didn't resolve this problem, not only would the collapse discourage investment by small investors, but the US Securities and Exchange Commission would intervene, reducing the NYSE's power. The NYSE solved the problem by imposing a $12 million assessment on exchange members and used the money to make Ira Haupt & Co.'s customers whole. Creditors were not as lucky. American Express and other lenders lost millions. For the first time, the NYSE had assumed responsibility for a member

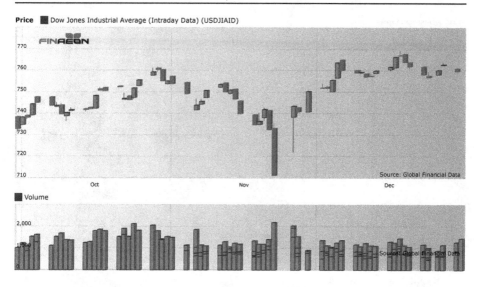

Figure 23.2 Dow Jones Industrial Intraday Average, October to December 1963.

firm's failure. When the stock market reopened on Tuesday, the market quickly recovered and moved up for the rest of the year.

Although Allied Crude was bankrupt, De Angelis wasn't, since he had stashed half a million dollars in a Swiss bank account; however, his swindle lead to charges of contempt because De Angelis had claimed he was bankrupt. De Angelis also couldn't explain the large cash withdrawals he had taken from Allied's accounts. For his fraud, De Angelis received a seven-year jail term. When he got out in 1972, he got involved in a Ponzi scheme involving Midwest cattle, but this effort collapsed before it really got going. This shows that a swindler will always be a swindler.

Warren Buffett Gets a Ten-Bagger

And what about Warren Buffett? As a result of the losses American Express suffered from funding De Angelis, American Express stock fell in price from 65 in October 1963 to 37 in January 1964. Believing the decline was temporary, Warren Buffett began buying shares and established a 5 percent stake in American Express for $20 million. As indicated in Figure 23.3, American Express recovered and made a ten-fold move between 1964 and 1973. American Express was one of the first of the many successful investments Warren Buffett made.

The differences between swindlers and investors are illustrated by Toni De Angelis and Warren Buffett. Toni De Angelis was a swindler and a con man. He was good at cheating other people and cheating the system, but not at making an honest profit. He took advantage of government subsidies and programs, provided uninspected goods, cheated on his contracts, falsified reports, covered

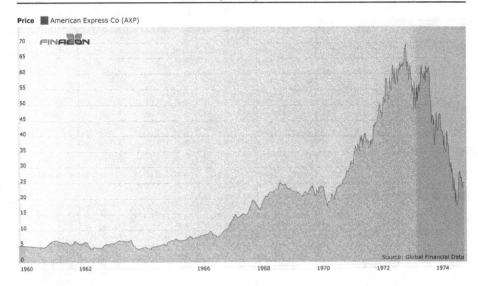

Figure 23.3 American Express Co. Stock Price, 1959 to 1974.

losses, and embezzled money. At every step he was trying to beat the system and get something for nothing, but as with any swindler, his scams eventually caught up with him. He went bankrupt twice, caused financial losses for thousands, and ended up in jail.

Contrast this with an insightful, aggressive market player like Warren Buffett. The position Buffett took in American Express was typical of the investing strategy that served him well for the next fifty years. He chose a well-established company whose stock price had temporarily declined. He took a sizeable position in the company, held onto it for many years, and profited. The Buffett method worked in 1963, and it continues to work in 2018 for savvy investors.

chapter twenty-four

Pump and Dump and Get Drunk: The Great Whiskey Dividend Scandal

Park and Tilford produced a broad line of whiskey and other products. The company had been founded in 1840, incorporated in 1923, changed its name to Park and Tilford Distillers, Inc. in 1950, and was taken over by Schenley Industries, Inc. in 1958. In 1946, however, the company and the brokerage firm of Ira Haupt & Co. ran afoul of the SEC as a result of the Whiskey Dividend Scandal they created.

War Whiskey for the Weary

In 1943, in the middle of World War II, whiskey was scarce. Most companies that produced whiskey had their factories diverted to manufacturing more important (in some people's opinion) goods. Though Prohibition had been repealed in 1933, the diversion of resources to the production of war materiel had some people worried that Prohibition was being reintroduced *de facto* if not *de jure*.

On December 15, 1943, D.A. Schulte, the president of Park and Tilford, announced that the company was contemplating a distribution of whiskey to its shareholders at cost. There was a precedent for this back in 1933, as discussed in Chapter 1 on the Famous Whiskey Dividend, when National Distillers Products Corp. distributed a dividend of a warehouse receipt for one case of twenty-four pints of sixteen-year-old whiskey for each five shares that were owned.

The announcement by Schulte had its effect. Park and Tilford stock had been at 57.625 on December 15, 1943, and advanced to 98.25 on May 26, 1944, as new shareholders tried to get access to scarce whiskey. On May 26, the company offered rights to sell six cases of whiskey for each share of stock at a reduced price.

Shareholders went crazy, but this was a classic case of sell on the news. You have to remember that this occurred in the middle of World War II, and the government had imposed price controls on consumer goods, including liquor. Upon hearing of the potential rights issue, the Office of Price Administration stepped in and

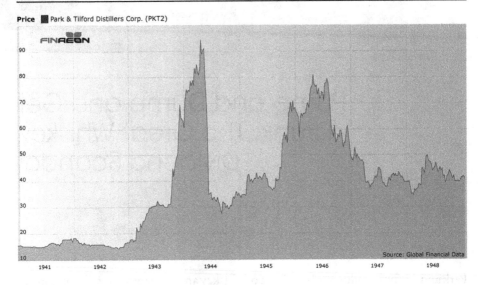

Figure 24.1 Park and Tilford Distillers Inc. Stock Price, 1941 to 1948.

limited the negotiability of the purchase rights and the maximum profit on the resale of the liquor. Obviously, some shareholders were more interested in making a quick profit than drinking whiskey.

Seeing that the profit from the whiskey dividend would be limited, the stock price collapsed, falling 10 points the next day and declined from 98.25 to 30.625 within a month. The stock price's behavior is illustrated in Figure 24.1.

Whiskey Makes the Stock Liquid

The collapse of the stock price was only half of the story. The Schulte family owned over 90 percent of Park and Tilford's stock. The Schulte family took advantage of the news of the whiskey dividend to sell their stock to the public, unloading 93,000 shares through their broker, Ira Haupt & Co. This may not seem like a large amount of stock until you realize that there were only 243,683 shares outstanding when the announcement was made. In November 1943, only 7,000 shares of Park & Tilford had traded on the NYSE, but once the announcement was made, 24,500 shares, or about 10 percent of the float, traded in the two days that followed, and 115,000 shares, or half the float, traded during the rest of the month. The whiskey announcement had made their stock very liquid.

During this period, ten representatives of Ira Haupt & Co. solicited twenty-one customers to buy shares in the company. In addition to this, the company's chief statistician prepared a written analysis of the stock for a customer. In effect, it was pump and dump so their customers could get drunk.

This was, essentially, a secondary offering of Park & Tilford stock since the company had used a brokerage firm to effectively underwrite and distribute the stock. Though Park and Tilford argued that this was not the case, the SEC saw otherwise and ruled against Park & Tilford and Ira Haupt & Co. since "[t]he only reasonable conclusion that could have been reached by respondent was that it was intended that a large block would be sold." This rule was formalized by the SEC in Rule 154, which was adopted in 1954.

If Park and Tilford's principal shareholders had only sold a few hundred shares, there would have been no violation of SEC rules, but since the company had unloaded a large block of shares, they were effectively making a secondary offering. Ira Haupt & Co. should have insisted on a registration statement for the securities being distributed and should have provided potential customers a prospectus, but it did not. As a result, Ira Haupt & Co.'s membership in the NASD was suspended for twenty days.

The next time Ira Haupt & Co. ran afoul of the SEC was during the Great Salad Oil Swindle in Chapter 23. In that case, the brokerage firm ended up bankrupt.

chapter twenty-five

John Keely and His Perpetual Money Motion Machine

Would you like to invest in the greatest invention of all time? A machine that could revolutionize the world and provide cheap energy to mankind? A machine that could overcome the first law of thermodynamics, and once perfected, would be the greatest invention of the century. What is this machine? Nothing less than a perpetual motion machine. The machine would be sold to and used by every person in the world and would make you and the inventor rich beyond your wildest dreams. If you wanted to profit from this opportunity of a lifetime, then you should have invested in the Keely Motor Co. back in the 1890s.

John Worrell Keely (seen in Figure 25.1) was born in Philadelphia in 1837. He began to attract public attention in 1873 when he claimed he had discovered a new physical force that could produce unheard-of power.

Keely's explanation of how his perpetual motion machine would work was this. Keely proposed to use the power of atoms in water to create perpetual motion. Since water covers more of the earth than land (maybe our planet should be called Aqua and not Earth), the fuel for his machine would be cheap and readily available.

Keely's idea was that atoms were in constant vibration, so all you had to do was to harness and channel the random vibrations of the atoms within water and you could produce unlimited energy. If you could get atoms to vibrate in unison, you could produce "etheric force" to run any motor of any size.

Keely went on a speaking tour to share his great discovery with the world. "How did you come to this great discovery?" someone in the audience would ask. "The discovery hit me while I was playing a few notes on the violin," he would respond. The notes on the violin had set in motion harmonic vibrations, and in a moment of serendipitous inspiration, he realized that the vibrations of atoms could be used to create energy just as the vibration of notes could be used to create music that soothed the beast.

Keely's next stop was New York, where he invited potential investors to his plush Fifth Avenue hotel room. Bankers, businessmen, engineers, lawyers, and other rich investors visited the hotel to invest in the wonder of the century. "Why shouldn't

Figure 25.1 John Ernst Worrell Keely and His Perpetual Motion Machine.

the name of John Worrell Keely stand alongside that of Thomas Alva Edison and Alexander Graham Bell in the pantheon of great American inventors?" potential investors asked.

Keely impressed visitors with phrases such as "quadruple negative harmonics," "etheric disintegration," and "atomic triplets." Through the "liberator," which was a system of highly sensitive tuning force, he would unleash the secret powers of the universe in his "hydro-pneumatic, pulsating vacuum energy" to solve the world's energy problems forever.

He demonstrated his machine to his guests, pouring water into his vacuum engine. After a little bit, the engine gurgled, then rumbled, then came alive, providing a pressure of fifty thousand pounds per square inch. As Keely put it,

> With these three agents alone [air, water, and machine], unaided by any and every compound, heat, electricity and galvanic action, I have produced in an unappreciable time by a simple manipulation of the machine, a vaporic substance at one expulsion of a volume of ten gallons having an elastic energy of 10,000 pounds to the square inch...It has a vapor of so fine an order it will penetrate metal...It is lighter than hydrogen and more powerful than steam or any explosive known...I once drove an engine 800 revolutions a minute of forty horsepower with less than a thimbleful of water and kept it running fifteen days with the same water. ("Gems from the Keely Motor," *Scientific American*, July 24, 1875, p. 57)

Even if you didn't understand Keely's theories, he was happy to demonstrate to potential investors that his machine actually worked. Keely claimed to be able to produce enough fuel from a quart of water to move a thirty-car train from Philadelphia to New York City.

On November 10, 1874, Keely demonstrated his first full-scale machine, the "vibratory generator." The motor obtained its power from "intermolecular vibrations of ether," which allowed him to create a "hydro-pneumatic pulsating vacuo-motor engine," which the press labeled a perpetual motion machine. When Keely was asked when he planned to apply to the Patent Office for his machine, he told his investors that he wasn't going to file a patent lest the secrets of his motor be unveiled and others were able to steal his ideas. The best solution was to keep every aspect of his invention secret until the etheric forces could be unleashed in a machine that made money for the company's shareholders. Otherwise, some unscrupulous and dishonest pirate could study his designs and introduce a machine similar to his, reducing the company's profits.

With the prospect of investing in the greatest invention of all time, shareholders were eager to be part of the company. Keely Motor Co. showed no profits and paid no dividends because Keely invested all of his capital and proceeds in developing mankind's greatest invention of all time. During the 1880s and 1890s, other inventions came into use, Bell's telephone, Edison's electric lights, and even automobiles, but Keely continued perfecting his machine. Investors took the long trek to his factory in Philadelphia, where he gladly demonstrated the current version of his wonder machine to visitors.

Of course, Keely would occasionally need new capital to continue developing his machine. Keely would call a board meeting, where the board would vote to issue more shares to raise additional capital. Old shareholders would purchase shares and new investors would get the opportunity to share in the creation of the world's first perpetual motion machine. After all, in the later stages of development, the machine was becoming even more complex and required even more capital. Keely himself lived well while developing the machine. Who would invest in a company whose president lived in poverty? Keely had to live a life of luxury to impress upon investors how their life would change as a result of his invention.

One of Keely's biggest supporters was a well-to-do widow by the name of Mrs. Clara Jessup Bloomfield-Moore. When others began to lose faith in Keely because of the delays, she invested more money and urged others to do the same. Ms. Bloomfield-Moore wrote articles for prominent magazines of the day, praising Keely and his invention, saying that Keely's etheric force was "like the sun behind the clouds, the source of all light though itself unseen. It is the latent basis of all human knowledge..."

When there was doubt, Keely would unveil his newest advancement in tapping the forces of nature. At one point, he showed investors the "shifting resonator," which carried seven different kinds of vibration, each "being capable of

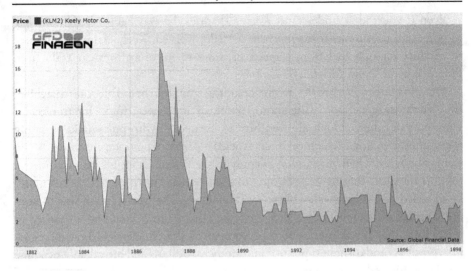

Figure 25.2 Keely Motor Co. Stock Price, 1890 to 1898.

infinitesimal division." Keely would set the whole contraption going in a variety of ways: sometimes by playing a few notes on his violin, sometimes with a zither or a harmonica, sometimes by striking an ordinary tuning fork. Whatever the method, etheric force came forth, starting the motor.

Unfortunately, there were scientists who were skeptical of Keely's claims. In 1884, *Scientific American* ran an article stating that everything Keely had done could be replicated using compressed air. Was some hidden source of compressed air the secret of Keely's wonder machine and not the etheric force? Keely dismissed these "scientists" as petty and envious men. Hadn't others scoffed at the steamship, the telephone, the telegraph and electric light? When Mrs. Bloomfield-Moore suggested Keely share his secrets with Thomas Edison to improve the prestige of the Keely Motor Co., Keely refused. He didn't need others to validate his invention.

The stock went public in January 1890 on the New York Stock Exchange, the greatest place for venture capital in the United States, with $5 million in capitalization. The stock traded steadily during the 1890s (Figure 25.2), neither shooting up in a bubble nor collapsing. With no profits and no dividends, there was no reason for the stock to skyrocket until the etheric vibrations were turned into a money-making machine.

On November 18, 1898, Keely died, twenty-six years after his company had been founded. The company had never made a profit, never paid a dividend, and never even released a product. Investors were worried. Since there was no patent, no blueprints, had Keely's great discovery died with him? Was mankind to suffer because the grim reaper had come too early?

Keely's most ardent supporter, Mrs. Bloomfield-Moore died soon after, and her son, Clarence Moore, wanted to find out whether Keely had been a scientific genius or a scam artist. He rented the building that had housed Keely's laboratory, hired two famous electrical engineers from the University of Pennsylvania, and prowled through the building. The investigators didn't find the "Hydro-Pneumo-Pulsating-Vacuo-Motor," or other mysterious engines such as the "Compound Disintegrator" and the "Sympathetic Negative Attractor," because much of Keely's machinery had been taken away by Keely's supporters as souvenirs. In the basement, however, they found a large cast iron hollow sphere, apparently a reservoir for compressed air.

The sphere was carefully hidden in the cellar floor beneath Keely's workrooms. False ceilings and floors were ripped up to reveal mechanical belts and linkages to a silent water motor in the basement (two floors below the laboratory). A system of pneumatic switches under the floor boards could be used to turn machinery on and off. Scientists seized upon the discovery to discredit Keely and claim that the *Scientific American* article had been correct. Perhaps Keely had pressed a control with his foot when he played the violin. Keely's supporters thought the revelations were lies that came from an embittered son who was angry his mother hadn't left her money to him. If only Keely had lived a few more years, the world could have enjoyed another Industrial Revolution that would have solved mankind's energy problems forever.

In the 115 years since Keely passed away, no other scientist has been able to replicate his discoveries, probably because a perpetual motion machine defies the laws of physics. Was John Keely a Nikola Tesla, whose inventions were ignored, or a Bernard Madoff, who cheated foolish investors out of their money? Just remember, if something is too good to be true, it probably is.

chapter twenty-six

Three on a Match: The Death of the Leonardo of Larcenists

Ivar Kreuger was a financial genius, for better or for worse.

Kreuger (seen in Figure 26.1) was an industrial and financial genius who sought complete control over the operations of his global match conglomerate. At the height of his power, Kreuger ran a monopoly that controlled 75 percent of all global match sales. Kreuger succeeded, in part, by introducing innovations in finance that are still being used today, but which have also been used by companies such as Enron to deceive investors. His insatiable desire for complete control and the promises Kreuger made that couldn't be kept led to the collapse of his company in 1932 and billions of dollars in losses to investors.

The Miracle Man

Ivar Kreuger got his start in the construction business, introducing new engineering techniques in Sweden that enabled him to win contracts to build the Stockholm Olympic Stadium (1912) and Stockholm City Hall (1913). Kreuger succeeded not only because he used the latest construction technology, but because he was able to complete these buildings on time and on budget. Unlike other construction companies, Kreuger promised to pay a penalty if buildings were not completed by the contract date. He also asked that he receive a bonus if the projects were completed early, which they often were. Kreuger was a wheeler and dealer from the beginning. He knew how to incentivize his clients to both win contracts and to profit from them.

Although successful in the construction business, Kreuger focused on developing the match company his family owned. He established *AB Svenska Förenade Tändsticksfabriker* (Swedish Match) in 1918 and spun off the construction business to expand Kreuger and Toll's match business. Kreuger's ultimate goal for the firm was the complete horizontal and vertical integration of the match business in Scandinavia, which he achieved.

Figure 26.1 Ivar Kreuger.

Kreuger took advantage of an innovation in the production of matches which the Swedes had introduced in order to triumph over his competitors. Kreuger and Toll replaced flammable and volatile yellow phosphorus with the safer red phosphorus. Since matches were needed to light fires, demand was inelastic, and this created huge profit opportunities for Kreuger and Toll.

Three on a Match

During the 1920s, "three on a match" was a catchphrase that warned people against lighting three cigarettes with the same match. The superstition originated during World War I when matches were scarce. Soldiers shared matches with each other in the trenches, but it was rumored that by the time the third smoker lit his cigarette, a sniper could find the group and kill the third smoker. A Hollywood movie entitled *Three on a Match* was made in 1932 in which one of three childhood friends ignored the warning and paid the price. Cynics said the superstition was a fraud, and Kreuger had spread the rumor just to increase match sales. No one would put it past him.

Kreuger took over lumber and other companies that provided the raw materials for matches. He introduced innovations to increase efficiency in production, administration, distribution, and marketing. In a few years, Kreuger had established his match monopoly in Scandinavia and prepared to conquer the rest of Europe.

Providing loans to a government in exchange for a monopoly is a European tradition. Monopoly power was the origin of the Bank of England in 1694 (see Chapter 5) and the basis of John Law's schemes in France in the 1720s (see Chapter 9). Kreuger learned the lessons of the past and used governments to build his empire.

During the 1920s, Europe was recovering from World War I. European governments were desperate for money, and just as Kreuger knew how to wheel and deal in the construction business to get contracts, he knew how to encourage cash-poor European governments to provide him with the match monopolies he wanted.

Kreuger negotiated with governments throughout Europe by offering them loans in exchange for state monopolies. It was a classic win/win. Kreuger ended up loaning almost $400 million to European governments during the 1920s and was hailed as the "savior of Europe." Loans were made to Poland, Danzig, Greece, Ecuador, France, Yugoslavia, Hungary, Germany, Latvia, Romania, Lithuania, Bolivia, Estonia, Guatemala, and Turkey.

Kreuger was able to provide funding because he owned the Skandinaviska Kreditaktiebolaget in Sweden, the Deutsche Unionsbank in Germany, the Union de Banques à Paris, the Banque de Suède et de Paris in France, and the Bank Amerykański w Polsce in Poland. He worked with banks in Europe and in America, using the assets of Kreuger and Toll with the promise of future profits and dividends to negotiate these loans. Kreuger promised everything government officials asked for, though he often didn't even know where the money for loans to Poland, Germany, or France would come from. One way or another, during the 1920s, the money always showed up.

In addition to the match business and banks, Kreuger controlled most of the forest industry in northern Sweden, planned to become head of a cellulose cartel, and attempted to create a telephone monopoly in Sweden through his ownership of Ericsson. Kreuger also had a major interest in the pulp manufacturer SCA, the Boliden gold mining company, and the SKF ball bearing manufacturer, real estate companies, movie companies, trading companies, and railroads. All of these were profitable businesses that allowed him to expand Kreuger and Toll at a rapid pace. Success bred even greater success.

Financial Innovations of the Leonardo of Larcenists

Kreuger, or the Leonardo of Larcenists as John Kenneth Galbraith referred to him, was able to achieve his rapid expansion because of his financial innovations and financial engineering. This enabled him to control how profits were reported, registering profits when none existed and shifting profits from one company or division to another to show a steady increase in profits.

Kreuger wanted complete control. He created "A" and "B" shares for Kreuger and Toll, which enabled him to raise capital while not giving up power over his company. The "B" shares had the same rights to profits and dividends as "A" shares, but not the same votes. "B" shares had 1/1000th of a voting right compared to an "A" share. Issuing different classes of shares to maintain control is commonplace today, but was new back then. In 2014, Google issued new shares that had only 1/10th of a vote of the original shares.

Kreuger was able to attract additional capital to Kreuger and Toll by consistently paying a high dividend of 15 percent to 20 percent. When Kreuger and Toll issued American Depository Receipts (another innovation) for their shares in New York, they were able to raise tens of millions of dollars. Kreuger and Toll also issued convertible gold debentures paying 6.5 percent, a high rate at the time, which could be converted into common stock if the price of Kreuger and Toll stock rose.

When Kreuger loaned money to governments, he used binary foreign exchange options to protect his company from exchange rate fluctuations. These enabled Kreuger and Toll to specify in which currency, Dutch guilders or United States dollars, governments would pay back their loans. Kreuger always demanded payment in the stronger currency.

Kreuger's real innovation, however, was in using off-balance sheet entities to expand the company's operations. Kreuger shifted losses into companies that were not included in the firm's consolidated balance sheet so the company would always appear to enjoy growing profits.

Kreuger differentiated between companies he had a majority interest in and ones he had a minority interest in. Profitable companies with a majority interest were placed on the balance sheet; companies with a minority interest were treated as investments. This enabled Kreuger to hide many of his loss-making investments from investors and competitors. The technique gave the company leverage, which meant soaring profits in a bull market. But as Enron, Bear Stearns, and Lehman Brothers were to discover decades later, this technique could also lead to large losses or even the collapse of the company when the market declined.

Kreuger and Toll was not a Ponzi scheme. Profits were reinvested in Kreuger and Toll's divisions and subsidiaries to maintain the growth and success of the company. However, because Kreuger and Toll was highly leveraged, Kreuger needed to constantly expand his operations to pay the high dividends his companies provided, to issue new loans to governments, to purchase new companies, to obtain new monopolies, to expand his conglomerate, and to show expanding profits to shareholders and stakeholders. Like a hamster on a wheel, Kreuger had to run faster and faster to maintain the appearance of success.

House of Cards

The Great Depression contributed to the collapse of Kreuger's house of cards. When revenues and profits declined, Kreuger needed loans to keep his company going. Rumors began to spread that Kreuger and Toll was facing financial difficulties and the price of the company's stock began to decline. As the graph below shows, the price of Kreuger and Toll "B" shares plummeted from 46 in March 1928 to 6 in September 1931 and traded around that level until March 1932 when the complete collapse of the company made the shares virtually worthless (Figure 26.2).

Kreuger had $650 million in capital on his balance sheet in 1932, which he used as collateral for loans and operations. Unbeknownst to anyone else, over $100 million of this was in Italian bonds, which Kreuger had personally forged. Of his $400 million in "other investments," $250 million turned out to be nothing but creative accounting.

As rumors swelled and investors and governments began to demand answers, Kreuger scheduled a meeting with Ivar Rooth, chairman of the Swedish Riksbank, to negotiate a loan to save Kreuger and Toll. The two of them were to meet in Berlin on March 13, 1932, but on March 12, Kreuger was found dead in his room from an apparently self-inflicted gunshot wound to the head.

Shares in Kreuger and Toll immediately collapsed, falling from $8 to $0.50 on the New York Curb. In the end, debenture holders did get 43 cents on the dollar, but shareholders got nothing.

Freely manipulating balance sheets was not uncommon in the 1920s and 1930s, but no one had pushed accounting to the creative levels of Ivar Kreuger. In part,

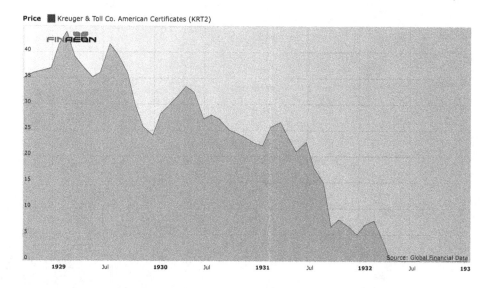

Figure 26.2 Kreuger and Toll Co. America Certificates Stock Price, 1928 to 1932.

117

it was because of Kreuger's actions that the SEC, when it was formed a few years later, introduced the concept of generally accepted accounting practices, bringing uniformity to the keeping of corporate accounts, to avoid the future fleecing of investors. This hasn't prevented the deceit and lies of an Enron or a Bernie Madoff, but it has reduced the number of frauds.

Kreuger was a flawed genius. The way he ran Kreuger and Toll, the collapse of the company seemed inevitable despite the monopolies and highly profitable businesses that made up his conglomerate. As Warren Buffett once put it, when the tide goes out in a bear market, you'll find out who is swimming naked, and Kreuger, as it turns out, didn't have a stitch of clothes to his name. Kreuger knew it, and when the game was up, he took his life, leaving investors to pick up the pieces.

chapter twenty-seven

From ZZZZ Best to ZZZZ Worst

I have written about numerous scammers who used the stock market to defraud investors of their money, but one of the towering figures of this repulsive group is Barry Minkow, whose frauds cost investors hundreds of millions of dollars. Criminal charges against him include racketeering, securities fraud, embezzlement, money laundering, mail fraud, tax evasion, bank fraud, credit card fraud, and conspiracy to defraud the United States. Minkow is currently serving a second stint in prison and has been ordered to pay over $600 million in restitution to the people and companies he defrauded. This is, essentially, a financial life sentence.

At the heart of Minkow's frauds was a desire to be recognized, literally by hook or crook, as the embodiment of the American dream of being a successful businessman. When Minkow ran ZZZZ Best, he spent $2 million on commercials that only brought in $20,000 worth of business because Minkow knew people recognized him from the commercials. He bought his fame and recognition. The sad thing is that someone like Minkow didn't learn from his failures. He tried again and again to be successful and kept reinventing himself, but inevitably fell back on fraud to achieve his ends, predestining his failure.

Birth of a Salesman

Barry Minkow wanted to achieve the American Dream of financial success. The "boy wonder" began pursuing his career when he was nine years old and got a job as a telemarketer with the carpet-cleaning business his mother worked at. Six years later, he started his own business, ZZZZ Best, out of his parents' garage with three employees and four phones. He soon became the most successful teenage businessman in the United States.

Being a successful teenage entrepreneur proved difficult. Since Minkow wasn't old enough to drive, he had to rely upon friends to transport him to different jobs. Since he was under eighteen, he did not have the legal right to write his own checks. After two banks closed his checking accounts because he was underage, he got a local businessman to provide him with money orders and cash his checks.

Minkow's business faced cash-flow problems from the beginning, so he funded his business through check kiting, stealing his grandmother's jewelry, staging break-ins at his offices to commit insurance fraud, running up fraudulent credit card charges, and borrowing money from gangsters at usurious rates.

Minkow found the secret to a successful business through "insurance restoration," in which he would file an insurance claim for the restoration of a business from flood, fire, or other damage. With the help of Tom Padgett, an insurance claims adjuster, Minkow learned how to file fraudulent insurance claims to get money from banks and insurance companies. Tom Padgett was a genius at creating a paper trail of business that didn't exist. Minkow set up a fake company, Interstate Appraisal Services, which verified the details of Minkow's non-existent restorations for the banks. ZZZZ Best received money for the insurance claims, but no work was ever done.

ZZZZ Best actually did clean carpets, but 85 percent of the company's revenues were from the fraudulent insurance restoration business. When ZZZZ Best had cash flow problems, the only way Minkow could raise more money was by promising to expand his business, but since the carpet cleaning business was losing money, this only created more losses that had to be covered up with new fraudulent activities.

The American Dream Becomes a Nightmare

In 1986, shortly after graduating from high school, Minkow took his company ZZZZ Best public. This raised over $11 million for ZZZZ Best after fees and costs, but even this wasn't enough to pay off all the debts Minkow had accumulated while building his business. Going public also created new problems. Since ZZZZ Best was a publicly traded company, Minkow had to provide audited accounts to comply with SEC rules. If the company filed truthful accounts that showed how much money it was losing, the stock price would never increase.

Minkow got around this by having Tom Padgett forge fake invoices, fake bank statements, fake business correspondence, and creating a paper trail that was impressive on the surface as long as no one investigated the actual activities of the company. Since the accountant who audited ZZZZ Best's books never visited the insurance restoration sites the company owned, the auditor never discovered these businesses were nothing more than mail boxes.

In 1986, shares issued to an officer of a company that went public could not be sold for two years. Once the two years were up, Minkow could sell his shares, cover his criminal tracks and achieve the American Dream of being a successful multi-millionaire entrepreneur. ZZZZ Best was like a Ponzi scheme in that the company had to continually get new investors to put money into the company to cover the debts Minkow had built up from previous investors. Minkow borrowed from Peter to pay Paul. Minkow just had to stay afloat until the two years were up, then he could pay everyone off and be clear of his past.

The initial public offering of ZZZZ Best stock raised $15 million, making Minkow the youngest person to lead a company through an IPO in the history of Wall Street. Flush with cash, Minkow wanted to make ZZZZ Best "the General Motors of the carpet-cleaning business." Minkow used a massive television campaign (the commercials can be found on YouTube) to expand his business across California and into Arizona and Nevada. As a result of the company's continual expansion, by 1987, ZZZZ Best had over 1,000 employees. The stock price climbed to $18 a share, giving ZZZZ Best a capitalization of $280 million and making Minkow, who was only nineteen, worth over $100 million.

Nevertheless, ZZZZ Best still had cash-flow problems since the legitimate side of the business only generated 15 percent of the company's revenues. A potential solution to Minkow's cash flow problems was to buy KeyServ, the authorized carpet cleaner for Sears, from its British parent. KeyServ's carpet cleaning business was a cash cow and would provide a much-needed cash infusion to ZZZZ Best to tide the company over until the two-year share restriction expired. KeyServ was twice the size of ZZZZ Best, but this didn't stop the company from moving forward with the $25 million purchase of KeyServ. Minkow went to Drexel Burnham Lambert to issue junk bonds to fund the acquisition.

With the KeyServ acquisition, Minkow could cover his tracks, pay off his ill-begotten debts, and become the CEO of a legitimate and successful business. Minkow's ambitions didn't end there. After absorbing KeyServe, Minkow planned to take over ServiceMaster, the leader in the industry, in a hostile takeover, and to expand into the United Kingdom. He even began discussions to buy the Seattle Mariners baseball team.

The Shakespearean Tragedy Reaches its Dénouement

Just as in a Shakespearean tragedy, with the KeyServ deal only days from being completed, Minkow's past came back to haunt him and all his dreams of success and legitimacy collapsed. In the course of a couple of weeks, Minkow went from being a multimillionaire to being both broke and a criminal.

When Minkow started ZZZZ Best, he had illegally charged people's credit cards to help his cash flow. When the clients would call in to complain about the fake charges, he would apologize and refund the money, but in the meantime this scam gave him the cash flow he needed to pay his bills.

Minkow faced charges of credit card fraud from numerous people, which he blamed on unscrupulous contractors, even though he knew this was a lie, and he paid off most of the claimants; however, one homemaker whom he had

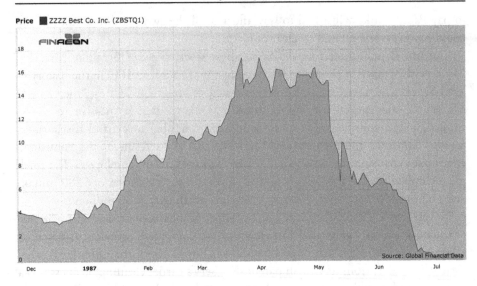

Price ■ ZZZZ Best Co. Inc. (ZBSTQ1)

Figure 27.1 ZZZZ Best Co. Inc. Stock Price, 1986 to 1987.

overcharged several hundred dollars became his undoing. That a company worth several hundred million dollars could be undone by a debt of a few hundred dollars is ironic. When Minkow ignored the homemaker's requests for repayment, she found several other people who had been cheated by Minkow. She went to the *Los Angeles Times* with her story, and the newspaper published an article about Minkow's credit card fraud days before the KeyServ deal was to close.

With that one story, the company collapsed because it uncovered all of Minkow's lies (Figure 27.1). ZZZZ Best's banks called in their loans, and Drexel postponed the issuance of its junk bonds to fund the takeover of KeyServ. Minkow tried to assuage investors by claiming record profits and sales, but when Ernst & Whitney discovered that Minkow had written fraudulent checks to help his cash flow, they resigned as the company's auditors. When it was discovered the insurance restoration business was a complete fraud, ZZZZ Best was doomed.

On July 2, 1987, Minkow resigned from the company. ZZZZ Best had retained an independent law firm to investigate allegations of wrongdoing. When its lawyers asked for the addresses of the company's nonexistent restoration jobs, which Minkow could not produce, he was forced to admit the business had been a fraud. The new board of the company sued Minkow, alleging he had absconded with $23 million in company funds, and a few days later, ZZZZ Best filed for bankruptcy under Chapter 11.

Minkow and ten other insiders of ZZZZ Best were indicted in January 1988 on fifty-four counts of racketeering, securities fraud, money laundering, embezzlement, mail fraud, tax evasion, and bank fraud. Minkow was found guilty on all charges on December 14, 1988, and was sentenced to twenty-five years in prison, was placed on five years of probation, and was ordered to pay $26 million in restitution.

Praise the Lord, I'm Released from Prison

While preparing for his incarceration, Minkow, whose family was Jewish, became a born-again Christian, and while in prison completed his theological coursework through Liberty University's School of Lifelong Learning. Minkow was released from prison in 1995, and he became the director of the Bible Institute and pastor of Evangelism at the Church at Rocky Peak in Chatsworth, California. In 1997, he became pastor of the Community Bible Church in San Diego.

Minkow, however, was unable to keep away from the world of finance. While at the church, Minkow started the Fraud Discovery Institute, which focused on finding fraud in penny stock companies. It takes a thief to catch a thief, and Minkow is alleged to have uncovered over $1 billion in fraud from the companies he investigated. His success brought him to the attention of *60 Minutes,* the *Wall Street Journal,* and Bloomberg News. Minkow began appearing on TV as a fraud expert.

Minkow realized he could profit from his reports on other companies' alleged fraudulent activities. Before releasing a report on the fraudulent behavior of a company, Minkow could short the stock and profit from the decline in the price of the stock that followed the negative news he released about the company. Minkow was accused of "short and distort," providing distorted information about a company to profit from the decline in the price of the stock that followed. Small fry bring small profits. To get a large profit, you have to catch a large fish. This was Minkow's next step.

Minkow revealed that Herbalife's president had inflated his resume, thereby questioning his leadership of the company. As a result of releasing this information, Herbalife stock declined in price, providing Minkow with $50,000 in profits from shorting Herbalife stock. As part of the process, Minkow filed a lawsuit against Herbalife for misleading investors. Minkow received a $300,000 settlement from the company to keep the lawsuit from going to court. Minkow had found a new way to make fraud profitable.

Short and Distort

Minkow's next target was the homebuilder Lennar, which he accused of massive fraud and of being little more than a Ponzi scheme. After Minkow's accusations were made public, Lennar's stock collapsed from $11.57 to $6.55, making his short position profitable. It turned out that not only had Minkow bought $20,000 worth of puts on Lennar before attacking the company, but Minkow went long the stock

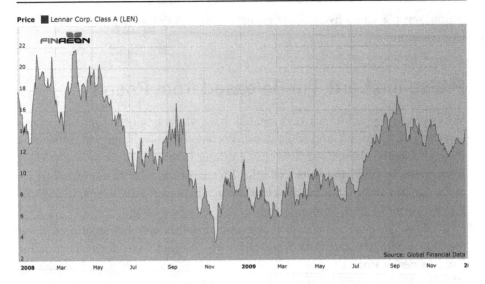

Price ■ Lennar Corp. Class A (LEN)

FINAEON

Source: Global Financial Data

2008   Mar   May   Jul   Sep   Nov   2009   Mar   May   Jul   Sep   Nov   2(

Figure 27.2 Lerner Corp. Stock Price, 2008 to 2009.

after it fell in price (Figure 27.2), anticipating that Lennar's stock would bounce back when his accusations were found to have no substance.

Accused of trying to profit from his own inside information, Minkow lied about his actions, but after the evidence was presented to him, Minkow could no longer hide his deceitful activities. Florida Circuit Court Judge Gill Freeman found that Minkow had repeatedly lied under oath, destroyed or withheld evidence, concealed witnesses, and deliberately tried to "cover up his misconduct." The judge issued terminating sanctions against Minkow, in effect revoking his right to defend himself.

Because of Minkow's purchase of puts on Lennar stock, he pled guilty to one count of insider trading on March 30, 2011. On July 21, 2011, Minkow was sentenced to five years in prison and was ordered to pay $583.5 million in restitution to Lennar. As part of his pre-sentencing evaluation, Minkow was diagnosed by Dr. Michael Brannon as having antisocial personality disorder, narcissistic personality disorder, attention deficit hyperactivity disorder, anxiety disorder, opioid dependence, and anabolic steroid abuse.

Joining Other Pastors in Prison

As a result of his criminal behavior, Minkow resigned as senior pastor of Community Bible Church. It turned out that Minkow had used church funds to fund the Fraud Discovery Institute, and he had swindled several members of his church, asking one woman for $300,000 to fund a movie about his redemption and another for $75,000 to fund a hospital in Sudan. Minkow admitted to embezzling over $3 million from the church between 2001 and 2011. During those ten years, Minkow opened unauthorized bank accounts, forged signatures, diverted church money for personal use, and charged unauthorized personal expenses to church credit cards.

As a result of his church-related activities, Minkow pled guilty to one count each of conspiracy to commit bank fraud, wire fraud, mail fraud, and to defraud the federal government. Minkow received a sentence of five years to be served after he completed his securities fraud sentence. The earliest Minkow can be released from prison for these two crimes is June 6, 2019. After he is released, he will owe over $600 million in restitution for the convictions relating to ZZZZ Best, Lennar, and the Community Bible Church.

After Prison?

From the very beginning, Minkow ran ZZZZ Best by borrowing from Peter to pay Paul, but in the worst possible way, committing credit card fraud, borrowing at usurious rates, forging documents, kiting checks, and claiming that the company was receiving huge, increasing revenues when 85 percent of his income came from fraudulent insurance claims. At every step of the way, his frauds and deceits threatened to blow up in his face, and finally they did. It is amazing that in some ways, Minkow was so incredibly brilliant, and in other ways, so abysmally stupid. No CEO in their right mind would pay 5 percent interest *per week* on a loan, but Minkow did. A con man always thinks he can avoid getting caught, but fraud is a house of cards that eventually collapses.

Like any con man, Minkow was able to transform himself to continue conning people in new ways. In his book, *Clean Sweep*, like a reformed sinner, he proudly proclaimed what a crook he was. After being released from prison, Minkow became a fraud investigator who focused on undoing other people's frauds, and he became a pastor in order to lead people to God. Minkow worked with the FBI, the SEC and police departments to uncover the frauds of others, but eventually gave into temptation and committed new frauds. Only someone who was willing to commit fraud on his level would have the audacity to use his crimes and deceits to create more fraud. Just as a lie will spin a web of bigger lies, fraud spins a web of even more fraud.

What will Minkow do when he is finally released from prison? Will Minkow try to recreate himself, as Michael Milken has done, to get the respect he needs from legitimate activities? Or will Minkow follow in the steps of O.J. Simpson and once again break the law that he feels he is above? Only time will tell.

chapter twenty-eight

Overend, Gurney and Co.: An Inspiration to Karl Marx and Bear Stearns

One of the most dramatic events in the financial history of Victorian England was the collapse of Overend, Gurney and Co. Its failure had a more severe impact on the London financial market than the collapse of Bear Stearns had on US markets over 140 years later. During the financial crisis of 1866, over 200 firms went bankrupt, including a number of banks. The failure of Overend, Gurney and Co. also led to one of the first trials for financial fraud in history, when all six directors of the bank were brought before the courts of London to answer for their alleged crimes.

Quaker Origins

Overend, Gurney and Co. was formed in 1805 by the merger of Richardson, Overend and Co., originally founded by Thomas Richardson in 1802, and Gurney's Bank located in Norwich and founded in 1770. Thomas Richardson developed the bank's business for discounting bills that became the foundation of the firm's profits.

Overend, Gurney and Co. soon became known as the banker's bank since they discounted the bills issued by other banks, held them until maturity, and made loans against bills issued by other banks. Between 1825 and 1865, Overend, Gurney and Co. was the greatest discounting house in the world. Only the Bank of England could match its resources.

Discounting was a reliable business that made consistent profits, but not content with the steady income from discounting bills, the bank wanted to expand into presumably more profitable investments. The only certain thing about a bank moving into uncertain investments is the certainty that the bank will probably end up losing money, which it did.

How to Ruin a Good Business

England was going through one of its periodic railroad booms in the 1860s with opportunities for profitable expansion also occurring in shipping, mail delivery, and other transportation activities. Between 1859 and 1862, the Quakers turned their back on the sound banking policies that had made their bank successful and managed to find speculative investments that won them the equivalent of a financial Darwin award.

It is amazing how a bank that could be so conservative in one area could be naïve enough to get involved with scammers who promoted projects that made themselves money, but were otherwise doomed to failure. The bank advanced money to invest in plantations in Dominica that grew little food, financed a railway line across the wilds of Ulster where there were few passengers, invested in the Greek & Oriental Steam Navigation Company which was unable to develop its business, failed to get the mail service for the Galway Line, and foolishly invested in the Millwall Iron Works on the Isle of Dogs which generated losses, not iron. The last three investments cost the bank around £5.2 million. As Walter Bagehot, then the editor of the *Economist* said, "One would think a child, who had lent money in the City of London would have lent it better." As a result of these investments, the bank had liabilities of around £4 million and liquid assets of only £1 million.

As the losses mounted, Overend needed capital to keep the bank solvent. The company decided to go public (Figure 28.1 illustrates the company's stock

Figure 28.1 Overend, Gurney and Company, Ltd. Stock Certificate.

certificate) and issue shares as a way of raising enough money to cover its losses and return to a profitable future. The bank converted itself into a limited liability company and offered 100,000 shares to the public at a par of £50, requiring £15 up front and reassurance that an additional call on capital would be unlikely. Of course, the prospectus never mentioned the consequences of the bank's bad investments, the excessive liabilities, and other problems, but focused on its strong reputation and the potential profits of the company.

When Limited Liability Adds Insult to Injury

Overend, Gurney & Co. stock started trading on August 21, 1865, and hit a high of 22.5 on November 16, 1865. As the price rose, investors who had missed out on the initial offering bought shares, keeping the price around 20; however, they were unaware of the rot that lay beneath the façade of the bank. By the end of February 1866, shares still traded above 20, but began to drift down, falling below 15 by late April.

In April, the investment in the Millwall Iron Works on the Isle of Dogs began unravelling, producing £500,000 in unexpected losses for the bank. The financial markets in London were reaching the heights of a small bubble, and the Bank of England responded by raising the lending rate from 6 percent to 7 percent on May 3, to 8 percent on May 5, to 9 percent on May 11, and to 10 percent on May 12. As money tightened, Overend tried to raise capital by collecting on debts owed to it by the Mid Wales Railway and others, but when the company was unable to get this money, it became evident that the bank would soon become insolvent.

Overend's only alternative was to go to the Bank of England, which, as lender of last resort, could have bailed out Overend, Gurney and Co. However, the Bank of England declined, not because allowing Overend to fail would reduce the amount of competition the Bank of England had, but because Overend was in such poor shape that no amount of money could have saved it.

On May 10, 1865, the bank announced that it was suspending payment on deposits. As can be seen in Figure 28.2, the price of the stock closed at 10 on May 10, 1866, fell to 3.5 on May 11 and to 0.5 on May 12. Until then, few had suspected that the greatest name in wholesale banking could have collapsed so suddenly. If Overend, Gurney and Co. was unsafe, could any bank be safe? A financial panic ensued, and during the next few months, over 200 companies, including many banks, failed as well.

For the shareholders, the worst was yet to come. The bank had issued shares at a par of £50, only requiring £15 of paid in capital before going public. Typically, corporations had the right to assess shareholders up to the par value of the stock. When a company needed additional funds to extend a railway, open a new factory, or expand the operations at a gold mine, they would assess shareholders for additional funds to increase the future profitability of the company. Being assessed

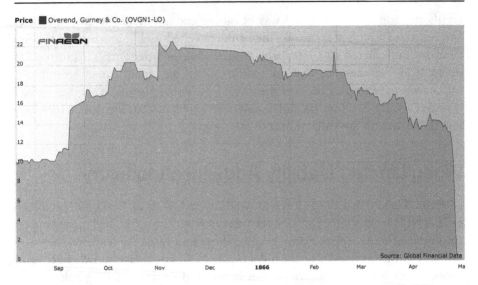

Price ■ Overend, Gurney & Co. (OVGN1-LO)

Figure 28.2 Overend, Gurney and Co. Stock Price, 1865 to 1866.

for the losses of a bankrupt company was not something Overend's shareholders would have predicted.

Since the bank still had many outstanding liabilities, the shareholders were liable for these, though only to the extent of the par value of the shares. Still, this meant that not only had shareholders lost all they had invested in Overend, Gurney and Co., but now they would be required to pay an additional £35 to a bankrupt company to help cover outstanding liabilities.

Although some shareholders made legal challenges to this demand, the courts said a contract was a contract and shareholders had to pay the additional £35 (equivalent to about $7,500 in today's money) even though they would never get anything back. Can you imagine how shareholders in Bear Stearns would have reacted if, after losing everything, they had been required to send in an additional $7,500 for each share they owned even though the company was already bankrupt?

Many felt the directors of Overend had committed fraud by issuing a prospectus to raise money for the firm while failing to mention the true state of the bank. Of course, in 1866 there was no SEC to review prospectuses before shares were issued, and there were few legal precedents for financial fraud, but after the collapse of the company, the demand for justice became so overwhelming that on January 26, 1869, the directors of Overend & Gurney Co. were committed to trial for fraud.

In December 1869, all six of the Overend, Gurney & Co. directors were acquitted. As during the 2008 financial collapse, although the directors had obviously made some very bad decisions, and were less than transparent, they were found not guilty of having conspired to defraud investors and were allowed to go free.

The End of Overend

The failure of Overend, Gurney and Co. inspired writers for years to come. Trollope used one of the swindlers involved in the collapse for his novel, *The Way We Live Now*, Bagehot frequently referred to the Overend fiasco in his book *Lombard Street*, and Marx used the Overend collapse as a symbol of all that was wrong with capitalism.

Just as no one from Wall Street went to jail as a result of the collapse of Bear Stearns, other companies, and the billions of dollars in losses that occurred during the 2008 financial meltdown, no one from Overend, Gurney and Co. was convicted of any crimes. In fact, the Norwich Gurney bank continued to operate even after shareholders had been fleeced of their money since the bank had been legally separated from Overend, Gurney and Co. when it became a limited liability company.

As the French say, *plus ça change, plus c'est la même chose*. The more things change, the more they stay the same. Today, banks may pay billions in fines to the government for their misdeeds, but no banker goes to jail. If only criminals worked for billion-dollar corporations, we wouldn't have to build any prisons.

part III

Stock Corners

chapter twenty-nine

The Panic of 1792

Speculators can short a stock to make money when it declines in price. In essence, the short borrows the stock from a brokerage firm and sells it. If all goes well, the stock declines in price. The short then buys the stock at the lower price, repays his loan by returning the shares to the broker, and pockets the difference between the price he originally sold the stock at and the price he bought the shares back at.

This assumes that the short is able to buy back the shares he has borrowed. If someone owns all the outstanding shares in the company and there is no one else to buy the shares from, the stock has been cornered. The short must pay whatever price the owner of the shares demands because he is the only source for the stock that is needed to repay the loan. The corner reaps the profits while the short can suffer immense losses.

The first attempt at a stock corner in the United States came at the birth of the American stock market, occurring even before the New York Stock Exchange had been established. In 1792, Philadelphia was both the capital and the financial center of the United States, and it was on the Philadelphia Stock Exchange that shorts first faced their worst nightmare: a stock corner. Consequently, politics and finance intermixed to create the nation's first financial panic and the first time the United States government stepped in to save the markets from themselves.

Alexander Hamilton and the Bank of the United States

Alexander Hamilton, the first Secretary of the Treasury, laid the foundations of the American financial system. When Hamilton became Secretary of the Treasury on September 11, 1789, the nation's finances were in a mess. Government 6 percent bonds were trading at 25 since they were in default and hadn't paid interest in years. Hamilton decided to follow in the footsteps of John Law, who had reduced the amount of government debt in France by allowing it to be converted into equity in the Bank of the United States.

The President, Directors and Company of the Bank of the United States, or the First Bank of the United States, as it is more commonly known, was chartered for a term of twenty years, by the United States Congress on February 25, 1791. The bank was part of Alexander Hamilton's plan for stabilizing and improving the nation's credit by establishing a central bank, a mint, and introducing excise taxes. Opposition to the bank was led by Thomas Jefferson and James Madison, who thought the bank was unconstitutional and created an unnecessary centralization of power, but Hamilton had convinced Washington of the benefits of establishing sound finances for the fledgling nation.

Hamilton modeled the Bank of the United States on the Bank of England. The bank would be a depository for collected taxes, make short-term loans to the government, and could serve as a holding bank for incoming and outgoing money. Nevertheless, Hamilton saw the main goal of the bank as a way of promoting commercial and private interests by making sound loans to the private sector. Most of the bank's activities were commercial, not public.

The Bank of the United States was established with $10 million in capital, of which $2 million was subscribed by the US government. $8 million in shares were sold to the public (20,000 shares at $400) in July 1791. To understand how large the Bank of the United States was, the revenues of the federal government were only $4.4 million in 1791, so the capitalization of the Bank of the United States was over twice that of the federal government's revenues.

The Bank Scrip Bubble

Scrip on the Bank of the United States, which represented rights to buy full shares of stock, initially sold for $25 on July 1, 1791. To complete ownership, payments of $75 were due on December 31, 1791, $100 on July 1, 1791, $100 on December 31, 1792, and $100 on July 1, 1793. One-quarter of the payment had to be in gold, but the remaining three-quarters could be made in US government bonds. By allowing three-fourths of the payment to be made in United States debt securities, the prices of US government bonds immediately rose in price.

US government debt had been reorganized in October 1790. The federal government assumed all the debts of the individual states and refunded the outstanding debt with new bonds. Someone owning $1,000 in old 6 percent bonds received $455 in new 6 percent bonds, $333 in new 3 percent bonds and $222 in deferred 6 percent bonds that didn't pay any interest for ten years. By July 31, 1791, 6 percent bonds, which had traded at 25 when Hamilton became Secretary of the Treasury, were trading at 100.

Fully-paid shares in the Bank of the United States were issued in August 1791, and they rose in price from 530 to 740 by the end of August, only to fall back to 524 by early October. Trading also occurred in the scrip of the Bank of the United States. The scrip represented shares that had not been fully paid for (these later

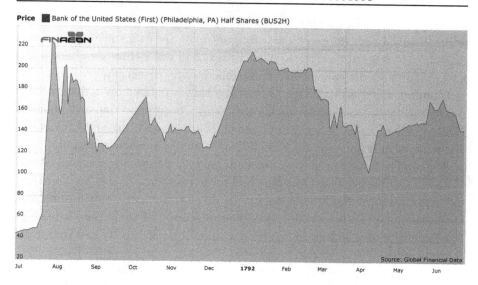

Figure 29.1 Bank of the United States Scrip and Half-Shares, 1791 to 1792.

became half shares and three-quarter shares as payments became due) and were more volatile than fully-paid shares.

As is illustrated in Figure 29.1, the scrip rose from 25 at the beginning of August to 249 on August 12, 1791, falling to 165, rising again to 207 on August 22, then sliding back to 121 by September 16. The speculation became known as the Bank Scrip Bubble of 1791. Within weeks of the issuance of bank shares, the nation had gone through its first stock market bubble and crash.

The charter creating the Bank of the United States had set up the Sinking Fund Commission composed of Vice President John Adams, Secretary of State Thomas Jefferson, Attorney General Edmund Randolph, Chief Justice John Jay, and Secretary of the Treasury Alexander Hamilton, charged with resolving financial crises. The Bank Scrip Bubble provided the Commission with its first test.

In September 1791, Hamilton met with fellow members of the Treasury's Sinking Fund Commission and persuaded them to authorize purchases of government securities in the market place to keep the prices of stocks and bonds from collapsing. Hamilton worked with William Seton, the cashier of the Bank of New York, to authorize the purchase of $150,000 of public debt in New York to be covered by government revenues. By September 12, Hamilton's intervention had not only stabilized the market, but had also laid the groundwork for his cooperation with the Bank of New York, which would later be crucial in ending the Panic of 1792.

Duer and the "Six Percent Club"

The Society for Establishing Useful Manufactures (SUM) was established in 1791 to promote industrial development along the Passaic River in New Jersey, founding the city of Patterson in the process. The goal was to use the Great Falls of the Passaic River as a power source for grist mills. The company was the idea of Assistant Secretary of the Treasury Tench Coxe and was chartered in New Jersey under Hamilton's direction as a type of public-private partnership.

Hamilton asked William Duer, who had sided with Hamilton in the *Federalist Papers*, writing in support of the United States Constitution under the alias of "Philo-Publius," to become governor and chief salesmen for the SUM. Duer was instrumental in helping to raise $500,000 in capital for the new company.

William Duer was not only a master salesman, but a speculator as well. When Hamilton discovered that Duer had been a driving force in the "scripomania" that had driven the Bank Scrip Bubble, he sent Duer a letter admonishing him for speculating in bank scrip. Like any plunger, Duer's failure in the Bank Script Bubble only motivated him to invest on a larger scale and to try to have greater control over the market to ensure success.

Duer organized a pool along with Alexander Macomb, a wealthy land speculator who had purchased the largest piece of property from the state of New York, and with other owners of shares in the Bank of the United States. They were known as "The Six Percent Club" since shares in the Bank of the United States paid a 6 percent dividend. Their goal was to try to corner the market before the next distribution of shares in July 1792 and sell the shares to European investors at a profit. Duer and the others bought the shares on time, in essence buying options, rather than buying full shares, so they could maximize their profit through leverage.

The Bank of the United States finally opened in December 1791 and made use of its capital by making loans and issuing banknotes. This increased the money supply and helped to feed new speculation in bank shares and US 6 percent bonds. The wild ride in shares of the Bank of the United States continued, as is illustrated in Figure 29.2. Shares rose in price from 524 to 680 on October 26, 1792, fell back to 528 on December 17, 1791, and rose to 712 on January 4, 1792. Since the US government 6 percent bonds could be used to buy shares, their price rose in sympathy with the increase in the price of the Bank of the United States. The bonds rose in price from a par of 100 to 129 on March 5, 1792 (Figure 29.3).

Duer got others to invest with him, reportedly including a madam from one of the city's brothels, who probably kept the money hidden in one of the well-worn beds, and cosigned notes with merchants to raise capital. Duer even withdrew $292,000 from the treasury of the SUM for personal investments and expenses to allow him to buy even more shares, an act that would later lead to his downfall.

With the shares overvalued, a number of shorts formed a bear raid to push the stock price lower. The bears were led by Governor George Clinton of New York, an ally of Thomas Jefferson who was opposed to the Bank of the United States and to Alexander Hamilton. Anything Clinton could do to embarrass the bank or cause it to fail would help Jefferson and his cause. Clinton and his clique sold short all the stock they could to Duer.

Price ■ Bank of the United States (First) (Philadelphia, PA) (BUS2)

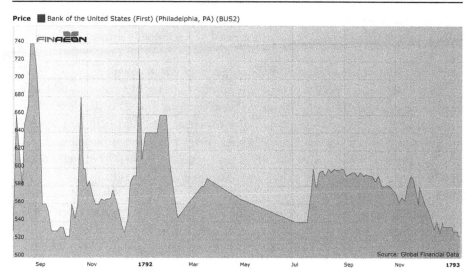

Figure 29.2 Bank of the United States Stock Price, 1792.

Price ■ United States 6% Bonds (BGUSA6S)

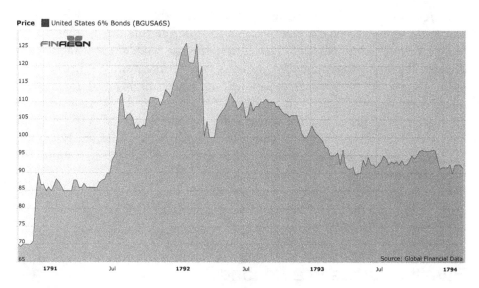

Figure 29.3 United States Six Percent Bonds, 1790 to 1794.

The Panic of 1792

By March, the banks started to face a credit crunch. Clinton and his clique began to withdraw large amounts of money from the city's banks to create a credit shortage. Moreover, it was springtime when farmers began withdrawing money from the banks to pay for the crops they were planting.

Oliver Wolcott, the comptroller of the currency, discovered a deficiency of $292,000 at the SUM, which Duer acknowledged, and demanded repayment.

When he failed to pay, Wolcott called upon the US attorney in New York to sue Duer for the long overdue debt. Duer appealed to Alexander Hamilton to intercede on his behalf, but Hamilton refused, and on March 9, 1792, Duer failed to meet payments on some of his loans and Duer's paper pyramid collapsed.

With Duer and his pool no longer able to buy shares in the Bank of the United States, the price of the stock began a precipitous decline. On March 23, Duer took refuge in the New York city jail. Duer was soon joined in jail by two other members of the "Six Percent Club," Walter Livingston (who is buried at Trinity Churchyard near Wall Street), who had cosigned over $200,000 of notes signed by Duer, and Alexander Macomb, who defaulted on $500,000 in stock he had purchased from the bears.

By mid-April, with the Six Percent Club defaulting and the price of Bank of the United States stock collapsing, the country suffered its first financial panic. This delighted Secretary of State Jefferson, Governor Clinton, and his allies, who were opposed to Hamilton's attempt to centralize the finances of the United States. They wanted to turn the panic into political capital that they would use to undercut Alexander Hamilton.

In response to the crisis, many banks tightened their credit, and in March and April, money began flowing to farmers to provide funding for their crops. From December 29 to March 9, cash reserves for the Bank of the United States decreased by 34 percent, prompting the bank to not renew nearly 25 percent of its outstanding thirty-day loans. In order to pay off these loans, many borrowers were forced to sell securities they had purchased, which caused the price of stocks to fall sharply. The price of Bank of the United States half shares collapsed from 203 on March 3 to 146 on March 21 while the price of US Sixes fell from 129 to 95. The price of stock in the Society for the Establishment of Useful Manufactures fell from 136.5 on February 8 to 30 on March 13, 1792.

Duer had perpetrated the young nation's first financial panic and stock market crash, and he paid the price. Duer spent the rest of his life in debtor's prison, where he died on May 7, 1799.

Hamilton Steps in a Second Time

For a second time, Hamilton and the Sinking Fund Commission authorized the government to buy up government bonds to support their price and slow the collapse in prices. On March 26, and with only Jefferson dissenting, the commission authorized $100,000 in open-market purchases of securities to offset the credit crunch.

To get out of the financial crisis, Hamilton had the Bank of New York take several measures. Hamilton encouraged the bank to take loans collateralized by government securities, but to lent at seven percent instead of six. Hamilton promised that the government would buy from the bank up to $500,000 of securities should the Bank of New York be stuck with excess collateral. Hamilton also supported lending by the Bank of Maryland and Hamilton authorized an additional $150,000 of open-market purchases by the Bank of New York. In essence, Hamilton followed Bagehot's dictum, given eighty years later in his book *Lombard Street* to "lend freely, against good collateral, at a penalty rate," acting as the lender of last resort for other banks.

Nevertheless, in the congressional elections of 1792, Jefferson and his allies benefitted as voters expressed their disgust with Duer and his financial shenanigans. After the collapse was over, the United States began its first bull market, with stocks rising in price until 1802.

The outline of every financial panic that has happened over the past two hundred years occurred in the Panic of 1792: the wild speculation, the financial frenzy, the collapse that followed, and the intervention of the government to keep the rot from spreading. Despite everything the Federal Reserve, Congress, president, stock exchanges, and other agencies may do to make sure that financial panics are a thing of the past, this pattern will no doubt be repeated many times over in the century to come. Speculators as a species will never die.

chapter thirty

Jacob Little and the First Stock Corner

Jacob Little was the first and one of the greatest speculators on Wall Street. He engineered the first successful stock corner on the New York Stock Exchange in 1835. William Duer had attempted to corner the stock in the Bank of the United States in 1792, but he had failed. Jacob Little was known as "Ursa Major," or "the Great Bear of Wall Street." Like any bear, he was loathed by the bulls, but through his stock operations, he became one of the richest men in the United States. Although Little is now mostly forgotten, his speculative expertise laid the foundation for Jay Gould, Daniel Drew, Jesse Livermore, and others who followed in his footsteps.

Jacob Little (seen in Figure 30.1) was born in 1794. His father was a man of large wealth and distinction who was ruined financially in the War of 1812. Little's father helped Jacob get a position with Jacob Barker, one of the leading merchants of New York. In 1822, Little started his own business as an exchange specie broker, dealing in banknotes issued by private banks, where he gained a "reputation as an honest, energetic, and successful broker." Jacob Little opened his own brokerage house in 1834 in the old Exchange Building in Wall Street, and for the next twenty-five years, Jacob Little & Co. dominated Wall Street.

Railroads Transform the Stock Market

When Little entered the stock market in 1834, it was going through tremendous changes. Until the 1830s, most of the listed stocks were in insurance companies and banks. Most finance companies were small, had a limited number of shares outstanding, and their shares traded infrequently. Speculative activity was limited.

In the 1830s, shares in railroads began to dominate the stock market since they needed large amounts of capital to fund their operations. The first exchange-listed railroad, the Baltimore and Ohio Railroad, started trading in 1828. Whereas railroads weren't even represented on the New York Stock and Exchange Board, as

Figure 30.1 Jacob Little.

it was then known, in 1825, by the 1840s, they represented around 90 percent of the volume of the exchange. With the growth in share size and volume, speculators like Little were able to jump into the market and seize opportunities that didn't exist until the 1830s.

Little had a fanatical obsession with the market. He often worked twelve hours at his office speculating on stocks, only to spend another six hours at night buying and selling banknotes issued by private banks. Little played both sides of the market, shorting stocks he felt were overpriced, trying to corner stocks the shorts were selling, or going long during a bull market. Little could remember every transaction he made and attended to every detail of his transactions. He even delivered stock he sold personally to make sure there was no mistake in the transaction.

Until Jacob Little arrived on the scene, most speculators used inside information to make their fortunes, but Little relied upon predicting the future direction of stocks and manipulating stocks to reap his fortune. Little was an inveterate gambler, but one who wanted the cards stacked in his favor. The spirit of Jacob Little was summed up when he said, "I don't care what happens, so long as I am in it."

To understand Little's involvement in the stock market, you have to understand how the stock market of the 1830s differed from the market today. Of course, there was no CNBC or ticker tape, telegraph or telephones, no computers trading stocks in milliseconds...all trading was done on the floor of the exchange in person.

Shares were not traded all day long as they are today. Instead there was a morning session and an afternoon session. During each session, a representative of the exchange would run through each of the listed stocks. Traders could only buy and sell when a stock was announced. When the representative of the Exchange arrived at Erie, for example, he would offer to buy or sell shares at set prices. Traders would respond by offering to buy and sell shares. Then the exchange moved on to the next stock.

Continuous trading in stocks did not exist. You had two chances each day to trade a stock. That was it. Each and every transaction was written down and published in the *New York Times,* the *New York Herald,* or another newspaper the following day. If you go to a copy of the *New York Times* from the 1850s, you can see a record of every transaction that took place on the stock exchange.

Shares were sold short either through borrowing shares directly from an owner, or more often through selling options on the stock. In the 1830s, options were not derivatives that relied on mathematical formulae calculated on computers to set their price. Instead, someone would offer a customer the opportunity to buy or sell the stock to them at a fixed price to be delivered at the request of the buyer at any point in the next six months. If you look at the record of transactions published in the *New York Times*, you can see the notation of the time period the buyer had the option to buy or sell the stock as well as the agreed upon price. Since this was how foreign exchange transactions and moving money between cities were carried out, this methodology seemed natural to people on the floor of the exchange.

Little and Morris: The First Corner

Little's first coup occurred in his corner of the Morris Canal and Banking Company in 1835. The Morris Canal was a 107-mile canal, established in 1822, that stretched across northern New Jersey from Phillipsburg on the Delaware River to Jersey City on the Hudson River. The canal lowered the cost of moving coal from Pennsylvania to New Jersey and iron ore from New Jersey back to Pennsylvania. It took only four days to move goods from one end of the canal to the other, but when railroads were able to move goods the same distance in five hours, the canal could no longer compete.

Rather than make a tender offer for outstanding shares, as is done today, raiders had to buy up all existing shares of a company to own it. Little determined to do this for the Morris Canal, and in the process, he cornered shares of the company. Little and his group of New Jersey traders ended up owning all of the outstanding shares, and shorts had to buy their stock from Little in order to cover their short positions. The price of Morris Canal stock went from $20 in February 1834 to $185 in January 1835. Little could have asked for more from the cornered shorts, but if he had, the shorts would have had to sell shares in other companies to raise the capital to cover their shorts, which could have destabilized the market as a whole. The spike in price caused by the corner is visible in Figure 30.2.

Little followed up this coup with a corner on Harlem Railroad in September 1835. There were reportedly 60,000 shares of Harlem sold short, but only 7,000 shares outstanding. Little drove the price of Harlem stock up from $40 per share in March 1835 and to $195 a share in September 1835. Of course, the shorts did

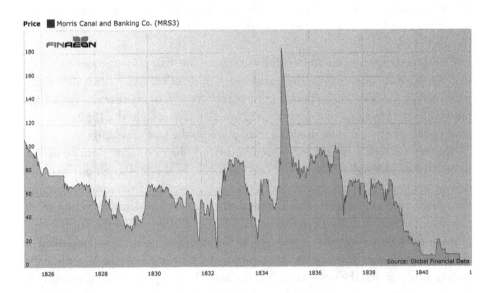

Figure 30.2 Morris Canal and Banking Company Stock, 1825 to 1841.

Price ■ New York and Harlem Railroad Co. (HAR1)

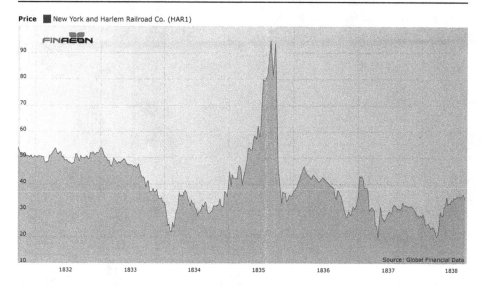

Figure 30.3 Harlem Railroad stock, 1831 to 1838.

not want to fulfill their contracts and lose heavily, so they went to the Board of the Exchange to find out if there was any flaw in the contracts that would allow them to get out of them. The Board ruled that contracts had to be fulfilled, and the price of $160 was settled upon to close out the short positions. This decision set a precedent for future corners on the Exchange, and shorts knew they would have to pay if they were caught in a corner. The effect of the corner can clearly be seen in Figure 30.3.

With these two corners, Jacob Little became known as the "Napoleon of the Board." Little foresaw Andrew Jackson's campaign against the Bank of the United States and the Panic of 1837 that followed. Little went short on the market and profited from its decline, whence his other nickname, the "Great Bear of Wall Street." By one count, Little's fortune reached $30 million by the 1840s, making him one of the richest men in the United States.

Two Failed Corners

Jacob Little also participated in an attempt to corner the stock of the Norwich and Worcester Railroad in 1846. He organized a pool with several Boston operators to secure control of the railroad. Each member put up a $25,000 bond pledging not to sell any stock below $90 (Figure 30.4). The pool drove the stock price up, but Little thought the corner would fail. He sold his stock while it was in the 80s to cut his losses, and as promised, delivered a check for $25,000 to his co-conspirators. Little made a similar mistake in 1847 when he was given a chance to invest in the telegraph by Samuel Morse, but declined, a decision he later regretted.

Price ■ Norwich and Worcester Railroad 8% Capital Stock (NWR1)

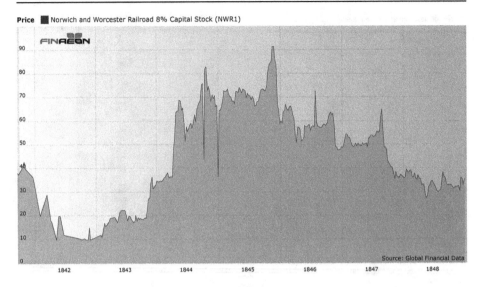

Figure 30.4 Norwich and Worcester Railroad Stock, 1841 to 1848.

There was one case where Little himself almost suffered the fate of being cornered. Little regularly shorted shares in the Erie Railroad Co., and in 1855, a syndicate of rival brokers that called themselves "the Happy Family" laid a trap for Little. They allowed Little to sell shares short, buying up the shares themselves. When they thought they had Little cornered, the family issued its one-day notice that they expected delivery of shares. Certain they had tripped up Little, the Happy Family estimated that Little had lost over $1 million on Erie and now he would pay as they had done.

The next day the Happy Family went to the floor of the NYSE and Nelson Robinson called out the list of stocks for trading. When he got to Erie, he offered 62 cash for Erie, then 63, 64, 65. There were no takers and Robinson and the others realized there was no float left. Although they knew they had him caught, Jacob Little sat placidly nearby, still offering to sell shares.

In 1855, shares weren't delivered by certificate and power of attorney, but had to be formally transferred at the office of the company. Knowing a showdown was at hand, Robinson and almost every operator on the Street went to the Erie office the next day to watch Jacob Little squeal when he failed to deliver the shares. Little showed up a few minutes before closing and Robinson said to him, "Well, we've got Erie locked up tight enough, every share of it. Now, stand to the rack like a man and acknowledge that the jig is up."

What Robinson and his clique didn't know was that Little had purchased convertible bonds on Erie in London, and that morning he had converted the bonds into shares of common stock. Little not only delivered all the shares that were demanded of him, but had shares left over, which he offered for sale. Little

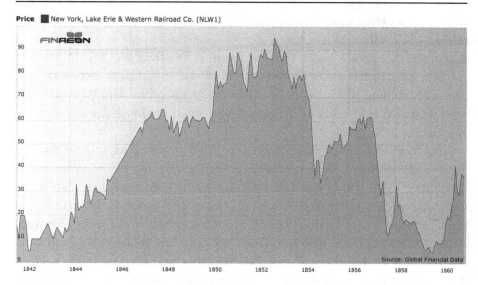

Price ■ New York, Lake Erie & Western Railroad Co. (NLW1)

Figure 30.5 Erie Railroad Stock, 1842 to 1860.

cleared over $100,000 from this operation. From there, the price of the stock quickly fell into the teens as is seen in Figure 30.5.

The Mystery of Jacob Little

Over the course of the twenty-five years he operated on Wall Street, Jacob Little made several fortunes and went bankrupt three times. He wasn't always bearing stocks, but also invested in state bonds and railroad bonds when he was unable to find good shorts. In the 1850s, Jacob Little & Co. was the largest brokerage house on Wall Street. That didn't occur just because Jacob Little was a bear. Jacob Little may have speculated in railroad stocks, but he was also known as the "Railroad King" because of his large ownership of rail shares.

It is hard to tell the truth about Jacob Little because much of the information about him is taken from reminiscences that are erroneous when you check the facts. Having the actual stock market data proves that some of the stories about Jacob Little are wrong. The examples below illustrate how the stories differ from reality.

In relation to the Erie story, one source said this occurred on November 12, 1855, but by then the stock had already fallen from the 60 range where the attempted corner occurred. Another source said this happened in 1838, but this was before the Erie railroad had even issued any shares. The data do confirm the stock corners in Morris Canal and Harlem Railroad, but leaves the stories about Erie in terms of amount and timing in question.

According to one source, Jacob Little went bankrupt on December 5, 1856, after a reversal in Erie stock in which he was short 100,000 shares, and his

149

position went from a profit of $2 million to a loss of $10 million. The problem is that a $12 million reversal on 100,000 shares could only occur if the stock had moved 120 points, but in 1856 the range on Erie stock was only 15 points. I found another article in *The Economist* from 1856 that said Jacob Little was short about $10 million in Erie, New York Central and Reading, and his total losses were estimated at $1 million. The contemporary account in the *Economist* makes more sense.

The *New York Times* of December 6, 1856, reported that the failure of Jacob Little & Co. had been announced at the opening of the exchange on December 5. The article said Little had reportedly been a seller of "two-thirds the outstanding contracts registered at the Board for the past sixty days or ninety days." In other words, Little had taken a bear stance against the entire New York Stock Exchange. The article mentioned not only Erie, but Reading and New York Central among the stocks he had been shorting. On December 5, 1856, Erie closed at 62. The stock remained above 60 until February when it began its descent to 8 in October 1856.

Jacob Little was certainly correct to be bearish, but his timing was off and he gambled too much. Had he waited a few more months or gambled less, he could have made another fortune off the Panic of 1857. Although the suspension left Little free of any liability, he eventually distributed $1 million to his creditors, paying every creditor in full with interest.

When the Panic of 1857 hit on October 13, 1857, twenty brokerage firms failed or were suspended when the market crashed and banks suspended specie payments. Among the suspended firms was Jacob Little & Co. Although Jacob Little is central to the painting entitled "Wall Street, half past Two O'clock, October 13, 1857," which represented the scene when banks suspended specie payments, Jacob Little & Co. was allowed to resume its seat on the board three days later. As one newspaper put it, "It is said that the Stock Board cannot get along well without Jacob."

In the May 13, 1859, issue of the *New York Times*, the newspaper reported that Jacob Little was suspended from trading on the NYSE because once again he was unable to meet his engagements, though the amounts were smaller than the suspension of 1856. In this case, Little was bullish, hypothecating bonds and shares of the Delaware and Hudson Railroad, Illinois Central Railroad and Panama Railroad, as well as the Sixes of Missouri, Tennessee and Virginia. When these stocks and bonds declined in value, Little was unable to meet the margin calls. Again, Little promised to make good on the basis of the average market price of the day once he determined his overall financial condition. Little apparently paid his contracts in full, for as one source put it, "Jacob Little's suspended paper was better than the checks of most merchants."

Jacob Little: Penniless Pauper or a Trader to the End?

Some sources say Jacob Little never recovered from the Panic of 1857 and died penniless, but did he? According to the *Merchant's Magazine*, Little lost most of his fortune as a result of the Civil War rather than the Panic of 1857. Though his fortune was reduced, Little continued to trade in the 1860s. I personally own a stock transfer certificate, signed by Jacob Little on August 26, 1864, assigning twenty-five shares to H. J. Morgan and Co. (see Figure 30.6).

If Jacob Little had been so penniless and forgotten, why would the *Merchant's Magazine* devote the lead article in their June 1865 issue to the passing of Jacob Little, who died on May 28, 1865? According to the article in the *Merchant's Magazine*, "The news of his death startled the great city. He had long been one of its most remarkable men. Merchants congregated to do him honor. Resolutions of enduring respect were adopted, and the Stock Board adjourned for his funeral." The New York Stock Exchange didn't adjourn to honor paupers.

Jacob Little was a generous man. He knew what it was like to face a stock market reversal and lose everything. When other traders lost a fortune and went to him for help, he never turned them down, but freely loaned them money. He never called in the loans, and by the time he was suspended from the exchange, Jacob little was owed hundreds of thousands by the people he had helped.

Although Jacob Little was the first stock market tycoon, the first to corner a stock, and the first to make millions and lose millions over the course of a lifetime, he is barely known today. What little we do know about him are stories drawn from reminiscences of his fellow traders. Even if you assume that the stories about the Morris Canal, Harlem Railroad, Erie Railroad, and others are true, it still

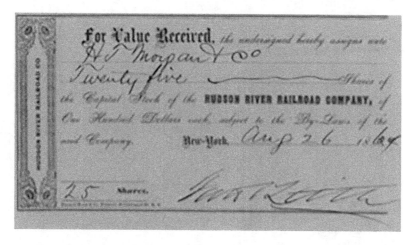

Figure 30.6 Hudson River Railroad Co. Transfer Certificate Signed by Jacob Little.

makes you wonder what he did the rest of the time he spent twenty-five years on Wall Street. Little didn't create the largest brokerage firm on Wall Street in the 1850s by shorting a few stocks. He had to be a consistent market trader who went bullish and bearish, who probably traded bonds more than he did stocks, and dealt with everyone on Wall Street successfully, despite his reputation. Perhaps it is the untold stories of Wall Street that are more interesting than the ones that are told.

chapter thirty-one

Northern Pacific: The Greatest Stock Squeeze in History

The Northern Pacific Railway was a transcontinental railroad that operated across the northern tier of the western United States stretching from Minnesota to the Pacific Coast (Figure 31.1). The purpose of building the railroad was to connect the Great Lakes with the Puget Sound. Along with the Southern Pacific and the Union Pacific (originally the Central Pacific, but renamed during the Civil War), it was to be the northernmost of three transcontinental railroads.

The Northern Pacific Railway was approved by Congress in 1864 and given nearly 40 million acres (160,000 km^2) of land grants, which it used to raise money in Europe. Construction began in 1870, and for the next thirteen years, workers labored to complete the railroad, pushing eastward from the Pacific and westward from the Great Lakes so they could complete the 6,800 miles of track. The main line opened when former president Ulysses S. Grant drove in the final "golden spike" in western Montana on Sept. 8, 1883.

The cost of building the Northern Pacific was much greater than Jay Cooke and other investors anticipated. As a result, the Northern Pacific was pushed into bankruptcy in 1873, along with many other companies that failed during the Panic of 1873. The railroad succeeded in escaping bankruptcy through austerity measures designed to control costs, but its finances remained unsound, and the company had to reorganize again in 1879. The Northern Pacific again fell into bankruptcy during the Panic of 1893 because the Northern Pacific was earning insufficient revenues to cover its costs. The railroad reorganized for a third time in 1896.

Chicago, Their Favorite Town

One of the primary reasons the Northern Pacific faced continual financial difficulties was that the railroad lacked a direct link to Chicago, which was the economic center of the Midwest. Instead the Northern Pacific went to Port Huron

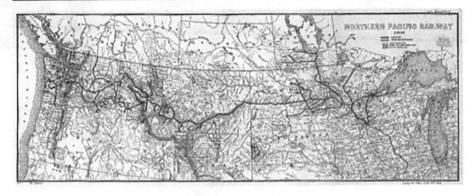

Figure 31.1 Northern Pacific Railroad Line in 1900.

on Lake Superior. Not only did Villard, who ran the Northern Pacific, lack a direct link to Chicago, but James J. Hill, who controlled the Great Northern Railroad, and Edward Harriman, who controlled the Union Pacific Railroad, also needed a direct link to Chicago. Without a direct link, it was difficult to transport freight efficiently from the Pacific Ocean to Chicago.

One railroad that did offer a direct link was the Chicago, Burlington and Quincy (CB&Q). Each of the railroad magnates set out feelers to purchase the CB&Q. Charles Perkins, owner of the CB&Q, realizing the value of his direct link, demanded $200 per share for the CB&Q railroad, and although Harriman balked at the price, Hill was willing to pay it. The merger was negotiated, and the Chicago, Burlington and Quincy Railway was purchased with 48.5 percent going to both the Great Northern and the Northern Pacific.

Not content with this jewel in his crown, Harriman decided to buy out the Northern Pacific as well. Harriman initiated a raid on Northern Pacific stock and was able to obtain all but 40,000 shares, a portion of which were owned by J.P. Morgan. Because Harriman was paying a large premium for the shares, and some doubted he would succeed, some traders went short Northern Pacific stock. By selling the shares short, they sold shares they did not own with the promise that at some point in the future they would obtain actual shares and buy back the shares they had borrowed, but as Daniel Drew once put it: "He who sells what isn't his'n, must buy it back or go to prison."

The Shorts Are Squeezed

Harriman had essentially cornered Northern Pacific stock. Harriman's goal was simply to own the company and to do so by buying up all the available shares. He was oblivious to the speculative activity of the shorts and his corner of the stock was unintentional. There were almost no Northern Pacific shares left to buy back to cover the shorts. Because there was demand, but virtually no supply, the stock

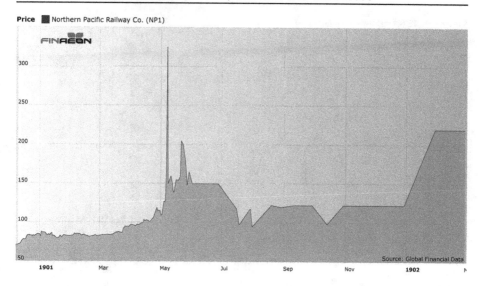

Price ■ Northern Pacific Railway Co. (NP1)

Figure 31.2 Northern Pacific Stock, 1901.

price exploded. Northern Pacific stock had been at 95 in April 1901 and hit 150 on May 6, 1901. Thence, the price of the stock went straight up.

The corner reached its highest level on May 9, 1901, when the share price hit 1,000 (Figure 31.2). The *New York Times* reported on May 10, 1901 that:

> A "corner" more complete and more disastrous in its results than any that Wall Street has ever before known came to its culmination yesterday. The enormous purchases of the Harriman syndicate and the Hill-Morgan syndicate had completely cleared the market of all floating stock, so that the "shorts" were placed in the position of having to deliver stock that they did not own, and which they could neither buy nor borrow.

> The first sale of Northern Pacific common was at 170, an advance of 10 points over the previous day's final transaction. Then by tremendous strides, jumping as much as 200 or 300 points between sales, the stock rose to 1,000, many sales being made cash for yesterday's delivery. At this point a little help came to the panic-stricken "shorts" in the form of an announcement by J.P. Morgan & Co. and Kuhn, Loeb & Co. to the effect that they would not at once demand delivery of the stock due to them yesterday.

> The effect of these announcements was immediate and marked. The next sale after the one made at 1,000 was made at 600, a decline of 400

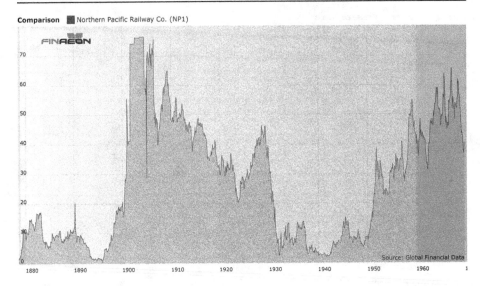

Figure 31.3 Northern Pacific Railroad, 1879 to 1970.

points. Three hundred shares sold at this price; then there was a sale of 700 shares at 500, and this was followed by a sale of 100 shares at 450.

Then came another jump in the stock which carried it to 700, but the price soon fell off again 200 points, and from that time on the quotation worked its way to a lower level. Upon the return of Mr. Schiff to his office it was announced there that Kuhn, Loeb & Co. would notify all those who owed Northern Pacific stock that they would settle with them at 150.

Hill and Morgan formed the Northern Securities Company with the aim of tying together their three major rail lines, the Burlington Route, Northern Pacific, and Great Northern. The Supreme Court ordered the Northern Securities Company dissolved in 1904, and regular trading of Northern Pacific stock resumed on the stock exchange in 1905.

Anyone who is interested in the Northern Pacific Corner is encouraged to read *Reminiscences of a Stock Operator* by Edwin LeFèvre, who documented the intricate dealings of the Northern Pacific Corner.

Northern Pacific Railroad stock began a slow, but steady decline in price until 1941 when the stock hit a low of $3.75 (Figure 31.3). Ironically, the Northern Pacific merged into Burlington Northern Inc. on March 2, 1970. By doing so, the Burlington Route, Northern Pacific, and Great Northern, which had been the three original railroads in the Northern Securities Company, were joined into a single railroad.

The Burlington Northern merged with the Santa Fe to form the Burlington Northern Santa Fe Corp. in 1995, which was acquired by Berkshire Hathaway on February 12, 2010, at $100 a share. In this convoluted way, William Buffett inherited the remnants of the most famous stock corner in the history of the New York Stock Exchange.

chapter thirty-two

High Noon at the NYSE: Stutz vs. the Shorts

Corners are a battle to the finish between shorts and the owner of a company. A stock is cornered when shorts have sold more shares in a company than are available in the outstanding float, and one shareholder owns the floating stock. Since the shorts must cover their positions by buying back the shares they have borrowed, if one person owns all the shares, he can set the price and the shorts have no choice but to pay the price the owner demands.

There were only four stock market corners in the United States in the twentieth century: Northern Pacific in 1901, Stutz Motor Co. in 1920, Piggly Wiggly in 1923, and RCA in 1928. Although the Northern Pacific short was settled amicably because the short squeeze was a byproduct of the attempt to take over Northern Pacific, the Stutz corner turned into a war between the shorts and Allan A. Ryan, who owned Stutz Motor Co. and who cornered the shorts. Unfortunately, as detailed in John Brooks' article in the *New Yorker*, "A Corner in Stutz," the corner ended in a disaster for both sides.

In today's electronic stock market, the battle between bulls and bears is usually impersonal, one computer algorithm trading against another computer algorithm, but in 1920, it was man vs. man, bull vs. bear, and as in the Stutz corner, the conflict got personal. In 1920, the New York Stock Exchange was still overseen primarily by "old school" financiers who ran the NYSE more as their personal fief than as a corporation that served its customers. This affected the outcome of the corner in ways that could not have been predicted beforehand.

Ryan Races to Produce Roadsters

Thomas Fortune Ryan, Allan A. Ryan's father, helped his son to get his start on Wall Street. Thomas Ryan opened a brokerage firm in 1873 and bought a seat on the NYSE in 1874. Ryan made his fortune by consolidating public transportation in New York City, amassing personal wealth estimated at $50 million in the process.

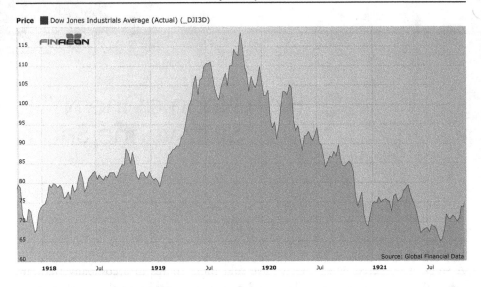

Price ■ Dow Jones Industrials Average (Actual) (_DJI3D)

Source: Global Financial Data

Figure 32.1 The Dow Jones Industrial Average, 1917 to 1921.

Ryan built the Metropolitan Traction Company out of street railroads that ran through New York City. Ryan also formed the Union Tobacco Co. in 1898, which consolidated with James Duke to form the American Tobacco Co. Together, Ryan and Duke developed the British-American Tobacco Co. to protect their American tobacco interests. Ryan also owned Royal Typewriter and backed the maker of the Thompson submachine gun. At the time of his death in 1928, Ryan's fortune was estimated at over $150 million, making him the tenth wealthiest man in the United States.

Thomas Ryan tutored his son, Allan Aloysious, in the intricacies of finance, and in 1905, when he was twenty-five, he turned over his seat on the NYSE to his son. Three years later, Charles M. Schwab, first chairman of U.S. Steel, befriended Allan Ryan after Ryan's father introduced him to Schwab. His son formed a brokerage firm, Allan A. Ryan & Co.

The stock market boomed after America's entry into World War I in 1917, with the DJIA almost doubling in price by October 1919. Ryan and his brokerage firm were successful during this period of time because Ryan was one of the primary bulls on the exchange and enjoyed profiting from squeezing the shorts.

Ryan also invested in the Stutz Motor Car Co. of America, Inc., which he gained a controlling interest in and became president of in 1916. The company was incorporated in New York and took control of the Stutz Motor Car Co. of Indiana. Stutz Motor Car Co. is best remembered for making the Stutz Bearcat at its factory in Indianapolis, an expensive and high-performing roadster that became synonymous with the roaring twenties. While a Model T cost $500 in the 1920s, a Stutz Bearcat cost $2,000.

Stutz stock participated in the bull market rally, moving up from 40 at the end of 1918 to 144.875 in October 1919 (Figure 32.1). The DJIA peaked at 118.63 on November 1, 1919, as inflation cut into post-war demand, but Stutz stock remained strong in the face of the post-war bear market. On February 28, 1919, the DJIA hit 91.31, a 23 percent decline from the top and, by definition, a bear market. Nevertheless, Ryan still thought the bull market had strength left in it.

The Bear Raid Begins

Ryan interpreted the decline in his stock as a bear raid designed to push the price of Stutz down so the shorts could profit from the decline in the stock. In March 1919, Stutz stock diverged from the rest of the market, making a spectacular rise. The stock had closed in February at 110, but by March 23, the stock was at 245, on March 24 it was at 282, and by the end of March, the stock stood at 391.

Other Stutz shareholders took their profits, but Ryan continued to buy Stutz stock while the shorts, even more certain that the price of the stock would ultimately collapse, shorted even more shares. Ryan borrowed millions of dollars to support the price of his stock, and by the end of the month, Ryan was almost the sole owner of shares in the Stutz Motor Co.

The Shorts Are Cornered

Confident that he could break the back of the bear raid, and owning virtually all the outstanding stock, Ryan continued to loan shares to the shorts so he could squeeze them until they faced either financial ruin, or if they were unable to buy the shares back, potentially face prison for breach of contract.

Since Ryan was the sole lender, he knew who the borrowers were, and he knew they were primarily fellow members of the NYSE, including members of the Exchange's Board of Governors. The men he worked with on the floor on a daily basis were shorting his company's stock, trying to ruin him financially. During the week ending March 27, Stutz stock moved up from 220 to 318 on 73,900 shares. Stutz stock closed at 329 on March 29, at 370 on March 30, and at 391 on March 31 when only 930 shares were traded because no stock was available. The shorts had clearly underestimated Ryan's resolve.

Ryan was called before the Exchange's Business Conduct Committee on March 31 to explain the wild gyrations in Stutz stock. As the *New York Times* put it,

> It was clear enough before noon that offerings of the stock had practically disappeared and the Governors acted through a moratorium to protect those speculators who had worked themselves into this

untenable position. A single group was found to own more stock and contracts for delivery of stock than the full outstanding Stutz shares. The ruling prevents Stock Exchange members from participating in further dealings in Stutz stock until the ban is lifted.

Ryan told the Committee that he would settle with the shorts, some of whom were on the Committee he faced, and allow the shorts to fulfill their contracts at $750 a share. The offer probably made the shorts sick to their stomachs. Ryan knew there were more shares short than there were shares outstanding, and that he owned all the outstanding shares. Ryan could have asked $1,000 or $5,000 per share. The shorts had put themselves in this position, and they had only themselves to blame. Ryan had cornered Stutz stock, and he wanted the shorts to pay for their bear raid. The shorts in the Northern Pacific corner had paid the price that Harriman had set, so why shouldn't Ryan set the price for Stutz stock and force the shorts to pay up?

The NYSE Tips the Scales

Ryan may have cornered the stock, but the shorts were determined to use their power at the NYSE to destroy Ryan and save their skin. The Committee threatened to strike Stutz from the stock exchange list, and Ryan responded by threatening to demand $1,000 a share. Nevertheless, the NYSE decided to suspend all trading in Stutz stock. When a reporter said there was no precedent or rule for the suspension of trading in shares, a NYSE spokesman replied, "The Exchange can do anything."

On April 5 came the most amazing announcement of all when the Law Committee of the NYSE announced, "The Exchange will not treat failure to deliver Stutz Motor stock, due to inability of the contracting party to obtain same, as a failure to comply with his contract." Essentially, the NYSE sanctioned breach of contract by the shorts, putting them under no legal obligation to cover their shorts. The NYSE told Ryan he was free to challenge their ruling in court. In response, Ryan demanded that the NYSE obtain a settlement price for all the shorts to avoid the trouble of Ryan having to negotiate with each of the shorts.

When nations don't agree, they go to war; when companies don't agree, they call in the lawyers and go to court. The shorts hired the Dos Passos Brothers, who were the leading experts on stock exchange law. John Randolph Dos Passos had written the standard work on stock exchange law, *Treatise on the Law of Stock Brokers and Stock Exchanges* in 1882, and he had rigorously opposed the Sherman Anti-Trust Act in his book, *Commercial Trust*, written in 1901. His son, John Roderigo Dos Passos, later wrote his socialist trilogy, *U.S.A.*, in rebellion against his father's defense of capitalism. Interestingly enough, by the 1950s, Dos Passos had changed his political views dramatically and campaigned for both Barry Goldwater and Richard Nixon.

Ryan hired the firm of Stanchfield & Levy, the lesser firm in this David vs. Goliath battle. Realizing it was Ryan vs. the NYSE, Ryan resigned his seat in the NYSE because he felt the Exchange was changing the rules to benefit the shorts. Ryan's resignation freed him to act independently. He was no longer bound by the NYSE's restriction on members selling shares since he was no longer a member of the Exchange. Ryan gave a reporter of the *New York World* the names of the NYSE governors, some of whom were on the committees that had sat in judgment on Ryan, whom he said were caught short in Stutz stock. The obvious conflict of interest led some to demand that the NYSE come under state or federal regulation, something members of the NYSE definitely wanted to avoid.

The NYSE backed down from its position that shorts could violate their contracts and left the resolution of the issue up to Ryan and the shorts. On April 20, the protective committee capitulated and said it was ready to accept impartial mediation on a negotiated settlement price between Ryan and the shorts. There were fifty-six firms that held shares short in Stutz involving 5,500 shares. On the other hand, the banks that had loaned Ryan millions to defend Stutz stock also became involved to ensure there were sufficient funds for Ryan to repay his loans.

Negotiations dragged on for several days, and with no resolution, Ryan indicated that he planned to buy in all the stock on April 24, a Saturday, on the Curb Stock Exchange, which operated literally on the curb of the New York Stock Exchange on Broad Street. Traders on the Curb didn't move into their own building until 1921 when the New York Curb Exchange Building was built on Greenwich Street. Brokers made trades on the street in the open air, then signaled to the clerks in the office windows above to carry out their trades. This was where the High Noon shoot-out between Ryan and the shorts was to take place.

High Noon on the Curb

Hundreds showed up that Saturday morning just for the spectacle of seeing Ryan place his order to close out his position on the shorts. Colonel John W. Prentiss, who had become the principal spokesman for the shorts, said they should come to terms with Ryan before the Curb opened for its half-day of operations that Saturday. The shorts agreed to act in unison, and slips of paper were passed around where the shorts could write down what they thought would be an appropriate settlement figure. Prentiss then took the average of the numbers that had been written down.

A delegation went to the office of Allan A. Ryan & Co. at 111 Broadway, arriving at 9:40 a.m. The delegation offered Ryan $550 per share, which Ryan unhesitatingly accepted, and at two minutes before ten, Colonel Prentiss announced to reporters that the Stutz matter had been settled at $550 per share. Everyone was happy except the spectators on Broad Street who were deprived of viewing the showdown. This appeared to be a great victory for Ryan since he had made almost $1.5 million in the transaction and remained the sole owner of Stutz Motor Co., which was worth, on paper, over $100 million.

Unfortunately, for Ryan, this was a Pyrrhic victory. Ryan still owed millions to the banks, and the only way he could raise the money to cover his debts was by selling shares in Stutz Motor Co. With trading in Stutz stock still suspended on the NYSE, Ryan lacked a liquid market to sell large blocks of shares to the public. Unless he could raise sufficient funds to cover his loans, Ryan could become bankrupt.

Ryan's Victory Ends in Bankruptcy

Though defeated, the shorts were still determined to have their pound of flesh. The NYSE refused to accept Ryan's resignation from the Exchange, and the Board of Governors adopted a resolution saying Ryan's conduct had been "inconsistent with just and equitable principles of trade," because he had created "an arbitrary and fictitious price" for Stutz stock. Ryan was called to appear at a closed hearing at the NYSE to defend his actions. Ryan refused to appear before the "star chamber" and he was tried *in absentia*. Ryan was found guilty as charged and was voted unanimously to be expulsed from the NYSE. The NYSE sold his seat in July 1920 for $98,000, but by November, the Exchange was still withholding the proceeds from Ryan on a technicality.

Ryan's main problem remained the banks he had borrowed from, which were pressing him for their money. The stock market had continued to decline and the prices of the other companies Ryan owned shares in, including Stromberg Carburetor, Continental Candy, Chicago Pneumatic Tool, and Hayden Chemical, were falling in price dramatically.

By November, Ryan was "cleaned out" and Ryan's creditors turned to the Guaranty Trust Company, of which Ryan's father was the largest shareholder, to see if his father would support Ryan. Unfortunately, Ryan and his son had been at odds for several years, and Ryan showed no interest in helping his son. In November, the banks formed a committee to take charge of Ryan's affairs. Ryan fought a losing battle until he was forced to declare bankruptcy on July 21, 1922. It turned out that Ryan owed over $1 million to Harry Payne Whitney, son of his father's old partner, about $3.5 million to the Chase National Bank, and $8.66 million to the Guaranty Trust Co.

Ryan's salvation lay in the shares he owned in Stutz Motor Co., which were to be sold at auction. A lawyer for Guaranty Trust estimated that if Stutz stock sold above $60, Ryan would probably be able to cover his debts and avoid bankruptcy. Stutz stock traded on the Curb, since it was not permitted to trade on the NYSE, and the stock had fallen in price dramatically in the intervening two years. The stock, which had been at $180 at the end of 1920, had fallen to $50 at the end of 1921 and was trading at $15 when Stutz declared bankruptcy (Figure 32.2).

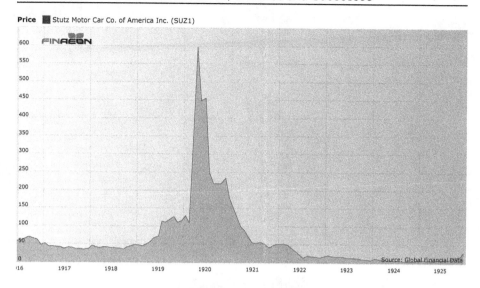

Figure 32.2 Stutz Motor Co. of America, Inc. Stock Price, 1918 to 1925.

In the auction, Stutz's holdings were sold at $20 a share to Charles A. Schwab, his erstwhile mentor. Schwab failed to turn Stutz Motor Co. into a profitable enterprise, despite the popularity of the Bearcat automobile. In December 1930, the company had to institute a 1-for-10 reverse split, and in 1932, the company was reduced to making grocery-delivery vans rather than luxury cars and roadsters. The company went bankrupt in 1938.

Ryan never recovered from the collapse of Stutz Motor Co. and he died in 1940. Unfortunately, Ryan never made up with his father, and when Thomas Fortune Ryan died in 1928, although he left millions to Allan Ryan's siblings and sons, the only thing Allan Ryan received out of his father's estimated $150 million estate was his father's white pearl shirt studs.

chapter thirty-three

The Piggly Crisis

The next time you go to the grocery store, pull out a shopping basket, and walk down the aisles, you should think about the fact that the modern grocery store is a result of the innovations of one man: Clarence Saunders.

Saunders' Self-Shopping Innovation

Until the 1920s, customers did not pick up their own groceries. Instead, they went to clerks who stood behind a counter and put together their purchases for them. Think of the way an old country store was set up.

Saunders was obsessed with the idea of efficiency and thought that customers wasted a lot of time waiting on clerks. Saunders wanted to free customers from the tyranny of clerks by letting them do their own shopping. Saunders also developed a just-in-time delivery system to get food to his Piggly Wiggly stores. This system later inspired Toyota to apply the same concept to automobiles, which helped Toyota to control costs and conquer the globe.

Saunders opened up his first Piggly Wiggly store on September 6, 1916, at 79 Jefferson Ave. in downtown Memphis, Tennessee. Each store had a turnstile at the entrance. Every item in the store had a price on it, another innovation, and Saunders provided shopping baskets so customers could take their items to a check-out stand in front. Saunders patented the idea of self-service stores in 1917.

Saunders incorporated the Piggly Wiggly Stores Corp. in 1918. The stores were an immediate success. By 1922, there were over 1,200 Piggly Wiggly Stores, of which about 650 were owned by Saunders, and by 1932, there were 2,660 Piggly Wiggly stores with sales of $180 million.

Unfortunately, in 1923, Saunders lost control over his Piggly Wiggly stores.

Saunders vs. the Shorts

Clarence Saunders also became part of the last stock corner on the New York Stock Exchange in 1923. The corner became so prominent that the whole affair became known as the Piggly Crisis. Clarence Saunders was generous, determined, stubborn, and well-known in Memphis. Saunders became known as the home boy who faced off the financiers of Wall Street, who were using a bear raid to try to profit from a decline in Piggly Wiggly stock.

The goal of shorting a stock is to borrow shares from someone who owns them and sells them. When the stock declines in price, the shorts buy the shares back at a lower price, make a profit, and then return the stock to the person they borrowed it from. In a bear raid, several shorts make a concerted effort to drive the price of a stock down so they can profit from the decline.

The bulls, on the other hand, can try and beat the shorts by forcing the price of the stock up, squeezing the shorts and forcing them to sell at a loss. If the bulls can buy up the existing float, the stock is cornered. The shorts have no choice but to buy the stock from the bulls at whatever price they demand. Of course, creating a corner is risky for the bulls as well because it takes a lot of resources to buy up the float in the stock. Once the corner is completed and the shorts have covered their positions at the inflated price, little demand is left for the stock. The price of the stock can collapse, leaving the bulls with a burdensome load of debt. The whole process can end up bankrupting both the shorts and the bulls.

Piggly Wiggly shares started trading over-the-counter in July 1920 and listed on the New York Stock Exchange (NYSE) in June 1922. In November 1922, several of the independently owned Piggly Wiggly stores in New York, New Jersey, and Connecticut failed and went into receivership. Although Saunders's corporation operated independently of these stores and was profitable, some Wall Street operators saw this as a reason to begin a bear raid on Piggly Wiggly stock.

The bear raiders began selling PIggly Wiggly short and spread rumors that the company was in poor shape. Saunders took this challenge personally. He had created Piggly Wiggly stores, created the concept of self-shopping, was spreading his stores across the country, and some bears were trying to create profits by spreading lies about his stores. Saunders decided to "beat the Wall Street professionals at their own game."

Saunders not only used his own money to battle the shorts, but he borrowed $10 million from a group of bankers in Memphis, Nashville, New Orleans, Chattanooga, and St. Louis to buy up the existing float. In the Wall Street of the 1920s, bear raids came and went. Companies didn't go bankrupt because of bear raids, and if the fundamentals of the company were sound, the stock would bounce back after the bear raid was over. Nevertheless, Saunders refused to give in to the Wall Street city slickers.

Saunders hired Jesse L. Livermore, the most famous bear on Wall Street, to help him break the back of the bear raiders. Within a week, Livermore had bought 105,000 shares of Piggly Wiggly, over half the float of 200,000 shares. The bears had shorted Piggly Wiggly stock in the 40 range, but by January, Saunders's bull campaign had pushed the price of shares past 60. The shorts were losing money.

The Shorts Are Cornered

Piggly shares were traded on both the Chicago and New York Stock Exchanges. In January, the Chicago Exchange announced that the stock had been cornered, though the NYSE denied that a corner existed. So Saunders decided to try a new tack. He announced that he would issue 50,000 shares of Piggly Wiggly shares at $55 each. Saunders regularly advertised his stores in the newspapers, and he used some of these ads to offer shares to small investors. Saunders pointed out that Piggly Wiggly stock paid a $1 per quarter dividend, yielding 7 percent to investors. Because this occurred before the S.E.C. came into existence, Saunders could promise that this was a "once in a lifetime opportunity" and get away with it.

Since Piggly stock was then trading at 70, why would Saunders offer shares at 55, leaving 15 on the table for each of the 50,000 shares? The reason is that Saunders knew that once the shorts had been cornered, the demand for Piggly stock would dry up. Saunders's stock distribution created a market where he could distribute his shares to new investors. Saunders even allowed investors to buy new shares on the payment plan, put $25 down and pay $10 a month for three months. Since the new shareholders couldn't sell their shares until they were paid for, this would keep the shorts from obtaining these newly minted shares to cover their positions.

On March 19, Saunders let it be known that he controlled all but 1,128 shares of Piggly Wiggly's outstanding shares. He had cornered the shorts. On Tuesday, March 20, Saunders called on the shorts to deliver their shares to him. By the rules of the exchange, the shorts were required to produce the shares by 2:15 on March 21. The stock opened on the March 20 at 75½, moved up to 124 by noon, but then dropped to 82 on the rumor that the Exchange planned to suspend trading in Piggly and postpone the delivery deadline for the shorts.

It was no rumor. The NYSE did suspend trading in the stock. Saunders responded by saying that he expected settlement on Thursday the 22nd by 3 p.m. at $150 per share. Thereafter, his price would be $250 per share.

The exchange permanently halted trading in Piggly and gave the shorts until 5 p.m. on Monday the 26th to settle with Saunders. With this ruling, the NYSE saved the shorts. This postponement tipped the scales in favor of the shorts because it gave them several extra days to find some of the 1,128 outstanding shares to settle their accounts without having to come begging to Saunders.

Was it right for the Exchange to change the rules in the middle of the game to prevent a corner similar to the one that had occurred in Northern Pacific in 1901? Or should the Exchange have left the shorts to their fate? The NYSE justified its actions on the grounds that the demoralizing effect of the corner could have spread to the rest of the market.

Saunders Comes Up Short

On Friday the 23rd, Saunders offered to settle at $100 per share. In the meantime, the shorts were able to find enough shares floating around in Iowa or New Mexico to cover their positions. Shareholders in Sioux City who knew nothing of the Piggly Crisis were happy to double their money by selling to the shorts while the shorts were happy to get the shares at a mere $100. Saunders now had complete control of Piggly stock, but he was also deeply in debt.

It is estimated that Saunders made half-a-million dollars out of his corner, but that proved insufficient to cover his costs. After Saunders paid off the banks with his proceeds, he found that he was $5 million short, half of which was due on September 1, 1923, and the balance on January 1, 1924. Since Piggly shares could no longer trade on the NYSE, Saunders was forced to sell shares directly to the public and advertised in the newspapers once again, offering Piggly Wiggly shares at $55.

Although the public was sympathetic toward Saunders and his battle against the Wall Street bears, the public was unwilling to put their money where their sympathies lay. Saunders took out another newspaper advertisement saying that if Piggly Wiggly were ruined, it would "shame the whole South." Memphis's newspaper, the *Commercial Appeal*, aligned itself behind Saunders and helped lead a campaign to convince Memphians to buy Piggly Wiggly shares and save their local boy. The newspaper planned a three-day campaign to sell 50,000 shares to Memphians at $55 a share. This was to be an all-or-nothing proposition. If they were unable to sell all 50,000 shares, none would be sold.

The campaign began on May 8, and soon 23,698 shares had been subscribed. Despite this, skeptics began to raise questions about who was the true beneficiary of this campaign, Saunders or the public. They asked for a spot audit of Piggly Wiggly to reassure potential investors that the company was a good investment. Saunders refused the audit, but offered to step down and let a committee run the company.

Skeptics also asked why Saunders was still building his million-dollar Pink Palace when Piggly Wiggly was possibly in its last throes. The Pink Palace was a huge house built using pink Georgia marble. The Palace was to include a pipe organ, Roman atrium, indoor swimming pool, ballroom, bowling alley, its own golf course, and other luxuries. Saunders promised to board up the Pink Palace and stop construction.

Unfortunately, the campaign was unable to sell even 25,000 shares, and the attempt to save Saunders soon fizzled. Saunders responded by selling Piggly Wiggly stores, rather than stock, to raise money. Despite selling stores in Chicago, Denver, Kansas City, and elsewhere, Saunders failed to raise enough money to meet the September 1 payment of $2.5 million. After defaulting, Saunders turned over his Piggly Wiggly stock, the Pink Palace (which was sold to the city of Memphis for

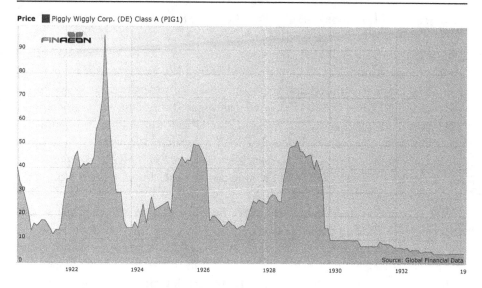

Figure 33.1 Piggly Wiggly Stores, Inc. Stock Price, 1920 to 1934.

$150,000 and opened as a museum in 1930. Today, it includes a replica of the first Piggly Wiggly store, a planetarium, a natural history museum, and a museum of twentieth-century Memphis) and other property to his creditors. By spring, Saunders was in formal bankruptcy proceedings. The gyrations in Piggly Wiggly Stores, Inc. stock is illustrated in Figure 33.1.

If Saunders had never launched his campaign against the shorts, he would not have had to borrow the money that drove him into bankruptcy. Pride went before the fall.

Life After Piggly Wiggly

Although Saunders was bankrupt, he got those who believed in him to help finance new ventures. He incorporated a new company, Clarence Saunders Corp., in 1924 and made plans for a new chain of grocery stores. In 1928, Saunders started a new grocery chain called Clarence Saunders, Sole Owner of My Name Stores, Inc., about as bizarre a business name as has ever been created. Stock in Clarence Saunders Corp. stock traded on the New York Curb from November 1928 to January 1930.

Initially, the stores, known as Sole Owner Stores, were hugely successful. A millionaire once again, Saunders was able to buy a million-dollar estate just outside Memphis. Saunders also organized a professional football team called the Sole Owner Tigers, which beat the NFL champion Green Bay Packers in 1929 by the score of 20–6. In 1930, the Tigers were invited to join the National Football League, but Saunders declined because he didn't want to go to away games.

When the Depression hit, the Sole Owner Stores went bankrupt in 1930. Still, Saunders was able to find backers for his next venture, Keedoozle ("Key Does All") stores, which were completely automated. Goods were placed behind glass as in an Automat. Customers would turn a key in front of the item they wanted to buy. Their purchases were placed on a conveyor belt, delivered to the front, assembled, and boxed. The system eliminated shopping carts, stocking by employees, and queuing at the checkout stand. The stores embodied Saunders's obsession with increasing efficiency. Two Keedoozle stores were opened up in Memphis and in Chicago, but the machinery was too complex and expensive to compete with the quaint fashion of having people push shopping carts around the store. The stores failed.

When Saunders died in October 1953, he was still trying to perfect his idea, this time with the Foodelectric system, which did everything the Keedoozle did, including adding up the bill. Today, there are over 600 independently-owned Piggly Wiggly stores located in seventeen states, mainly in the southern United States.

It is easy to see why the S.E.C. banned stock manipulation, not only for corners, but for pools and other schemes that were used to profit from unsuspecting investors in the 1920s. The corner game ended up destroying both the bulls and the bears and benefitted no one. Had Saunders never borrowed $10 million to challenge the shorts, he never would have lost control over his stores.

Since the Piggly Crisis, there has been only one stock corner in the United States, in E. L. Bruce stock in 1958. That is another story.

chapter thirty-four

Eddie Gilbert: The Boy Wonder of Wall Street

Eddie Gilbert died on December 23, 2015, four days shy of his ninety-third birthday, though few people outside of Albuquerque noticed his passing.

This is surprising. Gilbert was once known as the "boy wonder of Wall Street" for his successful stock market trading and his takeover of E. L. Bruce, in which he created the last corner on a US stock exchange. Gilbert also went to prison twice, was friends with Jack Kerouac, John Dos Passos, and other luminaries, made and lost fortunes, and finally succeeded with his real estate business in New Mexico, becoming a multi-millionaire. Despite having one of the most colorful histories of anyone in the financial world, Eddie Gilbert doesn't even have an entry in Wikipedia, though a cricketer, wrestler, and hockey player of the same name do.

Eddie Gilbert was one of those driven individuals who was a born salesman and deal-maker with plenty of chutzpah. He always had to make a deal, and no matter what the circumstances were, Gilbert could always find a way to make money. He would leverage his transactions, get others involved, and oversaw and coordinated his market transactions. Like a general at war, Gilbert was determined to win, and usually did, but sometimes the deals blew up in his face.

The Shorts Get Cornered, but Who Owns Bruce?

Gilbert began his business career in the 1950s working for Empire Millwork, which had been founded by his grandfather and which was then headed by his father. By the 1950s, Gilbert had already spent years trading stocks and commodities, and he had produced two plays on Broadway, including a production of *Peter Pan* with Jean Arthur and Boris Karloff.

Between 1955 and 1957, largely due to Eddie Gilbert's determination, sales at Empire increased from $5 million to $30 million. Eddie demanded that his pay be increased from $15,000 to $50,000, the same as the officers of the company. When they refused to raise his salary, he quit, but he was soon hired back at $50,000 when they realized how much the company needed him.

Gilbert discovered that one of their competitors, E. L. Bruce, was poorly run, and he felt he could run it much more efficiently. Bruce's sales had been stagnant for the previous ten years while Empire's sales were increasing. Gilbert began buying up shares of Bruce in February 1958 at $16.875 to acquire majority ownership of the company. As Gilbert bought more and more shares, Bruce's stock price rose, and short sellers entered into the market, believing that an underperforming company like Bruce wasn't worth the price it was trading at.

In the process, Gilbert was acquiring all the float in Bruce's stock. As the price of Bruce stock rose further, the shorts were forced to cover their positions. On June 12, 1958, the American Stock Exchange suspended trading in E. L. Bruce stock when the stock soared to $77 a share. Shares were in short supply because the management of E. L. Bruce owned 50 percent of the outstanding shares and Gilbert had taken control over the remaining 50 percent of Bruce stock.

The shares that were sold short represented the balance between Bruce and Gilbert. Typically, in a situation like this, the exchange would step in, negotiate a fair price for the shorts to cover their position, and settle outstanding short contracts for cash, but Gilbert didn't want to do this. Gilbert wanted the shares the shorts had borrowed because getting those few extra shares would determine who owned E. L. Bruce Corp.

Although the American Stock Exchange required that all shorts cover their positions, the stock no longer traded on the ASE, and the shorts had to find shares over-the-counter. This led to a mad scramble among the shorts, and the stock reportedly traded as high as $190 as shorts desperately tried to cover their positions (Figure 34.1). Short interest in the stock gradually declined from 16,134 shares on May 15 to 6,440 shares by August 15 and to 3,500 shares by September 4.

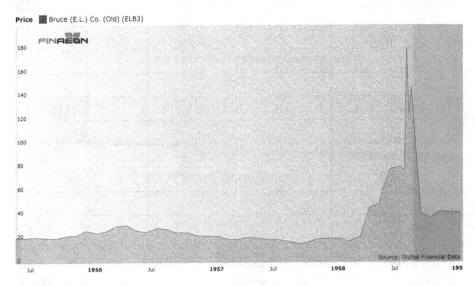

Figure 34.1 E. L. Bruce (Old) Stock Price, 1955 to 1959.

The remaining shorts simply could not find the shares to cover their position, so they filed suit to avoid having to cover their positions, claiming there was no "fair market" in the stock, and refused to have their shares bought in until a fair market was established; however, in *Aronson v. McCormick*, the court denied their preliminary injunction and the shorts were required to cover their shares.

The real question was, who controlled E. L. Bruce? Gilbert had invested over $5 million in his attempt to take over E. L. Bruce, and the outstanding short shares could determine whether Gilbert had control of the company. It was important to have this issue resolved by September 18, 1958, when shareholders of record would be contacted for the corporate meeting at which Gilbert wanted to take over the company. Gilbert's group demanded delivery of the shorts' shares in the hope that it would give them 50.1 percent ownership in the company.

On September 22, the Gilbert and Bruce factions met at the Waldorf-Astoria hotel in New York. Gilbert arrived in a limousine followed by an armored truck. Inside the armored truck were the actual certificates for all the shares Gilbert owned. He had the shares taken up to the suite in the Waldorf-Astoria and had them dumped on the floor. Gilbert told the Bruce board members that he had over 50 percent of the outstanding shares and if they didn't believe him, they could count them. Gilbert said he would allow the Bruce management to still be on the board, but he would have control of the company. Gilbert said he was going out to lunch and when he came back, he wanted to know if they would accept his offer. When Gilbert returned from lunch, the piles of stock lay untouched on the floor, and the Bruce management acceded to Gilbert's demands. Gilbert later confessed that they were a bit short of the full 50 percent, but he was happy his bluff had worked. With this coup, Gilbert became known as "the boy wonder of Wall Street."

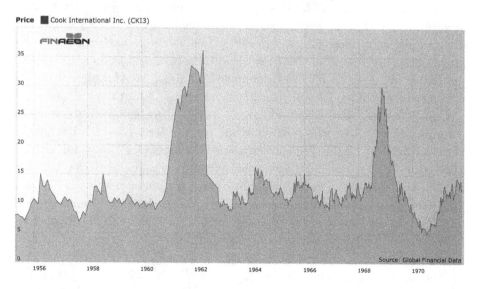

Figure 34.2 Empire Millwork Corp.-E. L. Bruce Corp. (New) Stock Price, 1955 to 1971.

Empire Millwork Corp. (Figure 34.2) changed its name to Empire National Corp. in 1960 and to E. L. Bruce in 1961. By 1962, Bruce had $60 million in sales and Gilbert began eyeing Celotex, with sales of $80 million, as his next takeover target. In 1962, Gilbert began buying up shares of Celotex, both on his own account and through E. L. Bruce. The market was in the midst of a bull market, and by March 1, Celotex had risen from around 26 to 41 5/8.

Blue Monday for Bruce and Celotex

Gilbert had also gotten André Meyer from Lazard Frères involved in the Celotex takeover. In 1960, Gilbert had sold Lazard Frères $2 million in convertible debentures, which could either be paid off or converted into shares of E. L. Bruce. Meyer approved of the takeover, and he and Gilbert agreed that Meyer would buy up shares of Celotex, then sell the shares to Gilbert at a profit when the takeover was consummated. Meyer redeemed half of the convertible debentures in early 1962, but since Bruce stock had doubled in price since 1960, redeeming half the convertible debentures meant that this cost E. L. Bruce $2 million, which was provided through a loan from Union Planters Bank.

Meyer bought 87,000 shares of Celotex, but demanded that Gilbert redeem the rest of the debentures in order that Meyer could buy an additional 163,000 shares of Celotex. Gilbert asked that the funds be held in escrow to be paid when the Celotex deal was completed, but instead Meyer withdrew the funds from the escrow account, nearly wiping out Gilbert's cash reserves.

Gilbert had bought shares on margin, and when the stock market crashed on Blue Monday, May 28, 1962, Gilbert received margin calls on his Celotex shares (Figure 34.3). Gilbert now was cash poor, and the $500,000 in cash he had left was insufficient to meet the margin calls. If Gilbert were unable to cover the margin calls, not only would his holdings in Celotex be sold, making the merger impossible, but the prices of both Celotex and E. L. Bruce would crash. E. L. Bruce Corp. would also suffer because the company owned 77,300 shares of Celotex.

Gilbert directed that $1.953 million of corporate funds be used to cover his margin calls to prevent the collapse in the price of Celotex and Bruce shares. Unfortunately, he did this without first getting the approval of the board. Gilbert knew that the Ruberoid Co. was also interested in acquiring Celotex, so he contacted a friend at Ruberoid to see if they would buy out his position in Celotex. This would provide sufficient funds for Gilbert to cover the $1.953 million.

Gilbert called a meeting of the E. L. Bruce board met on June 12 to discuss how he and the company would handle the $1.953 million he had taken. Since Meyer had taken out the $2 million from the escrow account, Gilbert had insufficient funds to cover the $1.953 million, but he pledged all of his resources as collateral to guarantee he would return the sum. As Gilbert had become successful, he had built

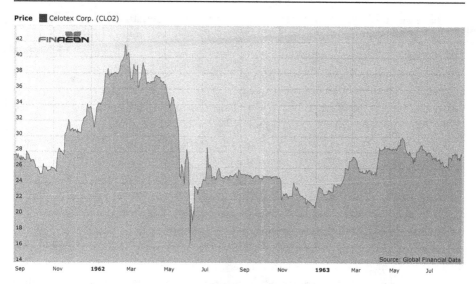

Figure 34.3 Celotex Stock Price, 1961 to 1963.

up a sizeable stamp collection, purchased antiques and paintings for his home, had acquired a villa on the Riviera where he entertained, and regularly went to Monte Carlo, where he would win or lose hundreds of thousands. In fact, John Brooks referred to Gilbert as "the Last Gatsby."

Unfortunately, Ruberoid called back and said they would not be interested in acquiring the block of Celotex shares. Gilbert knew he was sunk. He had ample resources, just very little cash. Not wanting to face the consequences of his actions, when Gilbert left for lunch, he booked a flight to Rio, and after resigning his position at E. L. Bruce, fled the country.

The Fugitive Playboy

When Gilbert arrived in Brazil, he left behind a spacious apartment on Fifth Avenue in Manhattan, a villa on the French Riviera, a $3.5 million tax lien, and $14 million in debts. When news of his flight to Brazil broke, the press went wild, and Gilbert became known as the "fugitive Playboy." The story followed him to Brazil. Gilbert was featured in a nine-page spread in *Life Magazine* and was the subject of a half-hour "Eyewitness Reports" feature on CBS entitled "Refuge in Rio." Gilbert also became the basis of a character in Louis Auchincloss's novel *A World of Profit*. This was not how Gilbert had wanted to become famous.

Even though Gilbert had left the United States with almost no money, Gilbert traded stocks on the Rio stock exchange and speculated in United States dollars. By the time Gilbert returned to the United States five months later, he had made $100,000.

One huge problem Gilbert faced was that the IRS demanded that Gilbert pay taxes on the $1.953 million he had taken from the Bruce treasury. Instead of treating the money as a loan Gilbert would repay, the IRS treated it as income to be taxed. The IRS put a lien on Gilbert's assets, putting the IRS first in line. Until the IRS matter was resolved, Gilbert was unable to pay any of his creditors, putting him in an even worse position. It also didn't help that his wife Rhoda had purchased $732,000 of jewelry from Cartier's shortly before the stock market collapsed.

Given all the publicity relating to his case, Gilbert feared that the trial might not go his way. Two years after returning to the United States, Gilbert pled guilty to three counts of grand larceny and securities violations in the hope that he would get a suspended sentence. Instead, Gilbert was sentenced to two years in prison by the federal government and two years by the state of New York.

Gilbert served two years in prison, where he reportedly cornered the cigarette market, and was released in 1969. In 1977, the US Court of Appeals ruled that Gilbert was not guilty of any of the crimes he had pled guilty to, but that he had "tripped over a legal technicality while risking his own fortune in a sincere effort to save his company's interests," since he had planned to repay the money taken from the treasury. Though this saved Gilbert's name, it didn't give him back the two years he had spent in prison.

The Conrac Conspiracy

Unfortunately, Gilbert got into more trouble a few years later. In 1975, he was investing in a stock called Conrac, a communications equipment manufacturer, which he had recommended to several friends. One of his fellow traders, James Couri, bought shares on margin, and when Couri received margin calls, 20,000 shares were sold by his brokers, driving the price of the stock down from $28 to $23.375. Consequently, on December 18, 1975, the NYSE suspended trading (Figure 34.4).

This led to a civil suit by the SEC against Gilbert, Couri, and seventeen others, alleging they had obtained over 100,000 shares of Conrac to profit from manipulating the stock. Gilbert had been involved in about 75 percent of the transactions. No action was taken by the SEC in 1976, but in 1980, Gilbert was indicted on thirty-four counts of stock manipulation, along with traders James Couri and John Revson and stock broker Harvey Cserhat.

In order to convict Gilbert, the prosecution had to prove that Gilbert and the others had conspired to manipulate the price of the stock and had coordinated their actions through wash sales, in which someone sells a stock to himself in another account at a higher price, or through match sales in which one person sells the stock to another co-conspirator at a higher price.

The four admitted they were all trying to profit off the stock, but contended they did not coordinate their activities to manipulate the stock. James Couri made an agreement with the prosecutor to plead guilty and testify against Gilbert in

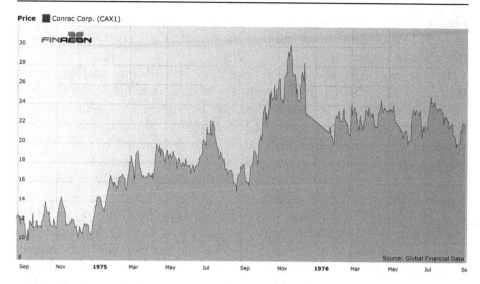

Price ■ Conrac Corp. (CAX1)

FINAEON

Source: Global Financial Data

Sep   Nov   **1975**   Mar   May   Jul   Sep   Nov   **1976**   Mar   May   Jul   Se

Figure 34.4 Conrac Stock Price, 1974 to 1976.

exchange for a suspended sentence. Revson and Cserhat had their trial severed from Gilbert.

The prosecution put together charts to show the jury how the trades were interrelated and coordinated, but the key to the trial was the credibility of Couri. After the trial was over with, it turned out that Couri was facing criminal indictments for fraud and related charges in another case, but the jury and Gilbert didn't know this. Gilbert was found guilty on thirty-four counts of stock manipulation.

When Couri testified at the trial of Revlon and Cserhat, the jury did not find Couri credible, and the two defendants were found not guilty. Of the four, Gilbert was the only one found guilty, and he went to prison for two years. This case makes you realize exactly why it is so hard to prove criminal intent in securities cases.

Gilbert Becomes a Real Estate Mogul

After being released from prison, Gilbert was forbidden from the securities market. He moved to New Mexico in 1989 and started the BGK Group in 1991, along with Ed Berman and Fred Kolber, to profit from investing in real estate. By the early 1990s, commercial real estate prices had collapsed from their levels in the 1980s, in part because of the fallout from the savings and loan crisis.

Gilbert, of course, was the deal maker for BGK. He scoured the market for underpriced office buildings and made an offer for them. If the offer was accepted, Gilbert put together a limited partnership to raise money from investors. Gilbert negotiated the terms of repayment to maximize the return up front. Gilbert made sure that investors always got a 20 percent return in their first year, whether the funds came from profits or from the investors' own capital. When BGK sold the property, the company would return all the capital to investors and keep half of the profits for themselves.

For example, BGK bought an Albuquerque, New Mexico, shopping center (Plaza at Paseo del Norte) for $5.9 million in 1993. BGK raised $1.8 million and borrowed $4.3 million. The property was sold in 1998 for $17.8 million, netting a $11.4 million profit split between BGK and investors. This and other properties were bought on leverage, with BGK usually borrowing around 75 percent of the purchase price. This time, the leverage did not blow up in Gilbert's face.

In 2010, Gilbert cashed out when BGK sold a majority stake to Rosemont Capital. Gilbert died a multi-millionaire.

It is a tribute to Gilbert that he never gave up, and though he was forbidden from dealing in securities after the Conrac conviction, he was able to succeed in real estate even more than he had in the stock market. Was Gilbert a criminal, or the victim of zealous prosecutors? Was he a great salesman and a financial genius who could make money wherever he went, or did he manipulate markets in his favor?

Gilbert kept his word and repaid all his debts. Most people would have given up after what Gilbert went through, but he persevered and finally ended up on top. Eddie Gilbert wasn't just the "boy wonder of Wall Street," but he was a wonder all around.

part IV

Stock Markets

chapter thirty-five

A Brief History of the Dow Jones Utility Average

The Dow Jones Utility Average (DJUA) is both the youngest of the three averages calculated by S&P Dow Jones Indices and the least volatile. During its ninety-year existence, there have only been three major reorganizations of the index, and only forty-five companies have been part of the Utility Average since it was introduced in 1929. This is quite a contrast to the Industrial and Transportation Averages, which have included over 100 companies each since they were founded and change their constituents every two or three years.

Why an Average?

It should be remembered that the DJUA is an average rather than an index, based upon the average price of the member stocks rather than their capitalization. When the Dow Jones Average was first calculated back in 1885, using an average was the logical way to calculate an index. Few people realize it, but until October 13, 1915, stocks on the NYSE were quoted as a percent of their par value. Most stocks were issued at $100 par, but others had par values of $50 or $25. If a stock were issued at a $50 par, a quote of 120 meant the stock sold at 120 percent of its par value, or $60. Consequently, including stocks with different par values had no impact on the calculation of the average.

Since all stocks were quoted in percentage terms, an average was the easiest way to calculate the index. If a stock reduced its par from $100 to $50, in effect a two-for-one split, the stock would continue to be quoted at 120 percent, so there was no need to change the calculation of the index. This also made it easier to substitute stocks in the average since their quoted prices were similar in value.

The introduction of trading based upon the dollar value of stocks created problems for both the Dow Jones and *New York Times* averages when stocks split. The *New York Times* chose to count stocks twice if they split, in effect ignoring the split, while Dow Jones chose to introduce a divisor and adjust it when splits occurred. Originally, the divisor would be equal to the number of stocks in the index. If there were 30 stocks in the index and they all had a two-for-one split, the index would be divided by 15 instead of by 30. Since no DJUA companies split until the 1950s, there was no need to change the divisor until then.

Today, computers make it simple to calculate capitalization-based indices of stocks, but the revival of equal-weighted indices for the S&P 500 and other indices shows the value of this approach.

The Introduction of the Dow Jones Utility Average

The DJUA was introduced in the December 25, 1929, issue of the *Wall Street Journal,* a Christmas present, if you will, to Wall Street data buffs. The index was calculated back to July 1, 1929, to provide some history, and in April of 1930, the average was extended back to January 2, 1929. The average only included eighteen stocks before July 1, 1929, because daily quotes could not be found for two of the components, Commonwealth & Southern and Niagara Hudson Power (later Niagara Mohawk Holdings, Inc.) before July 1929.

The original index included twenty utility companies, broadly defined to include telephone companies, electric utilities, and natural gas utilities. Of the original twenty companies, four remain in the average today: Edison International (originally Southern California Edison Co.), PG&E (originally Pacific Gas & Electric), American Electric Power (originally American Gas & Electric Co.), and Consolidated Edison. Here is a list of the original components as introduced in December 1929.

American & Foreign Power	Electric Power & Light Co.
American Gas & Electric Co.	Engineers Public Electric
American Power & Light Co.	International Telephone & Telegraph
American Telephone & Telegraph	National Power & Light
American Water Works & Electric Co.	North American Co.
Brooklyn Union Gas	Pacific Gas & Electric
Columbia Gas System	Public Service Co. of N.J.
Consolidated Gas System	Standard Gas & Electric Co.
Consolidated Edison	Western Union Telegraph

Niagara Hudson Power (later Niagara Mohawk Holdings, Inc.)
Southern California Edison (now Edison International)

The DJUA remained unchanged until June 1, 1938, when the average was reduced to fifteen companies and the telephone companies were removed. One interesting consequence of this change was that American Telephone & Telegraph was moved to the Dow Jones Industrial Average (DJIA) on March 14, 1939, and replaced IBM. IBM was not added back to the DJIA until June 29, 1979. During those forty years, IBM was one of the best-performing stocks on the New York Stock Exchange, and if it had been kept in the DJIA during those forty years, the average would be 22,000 points higher than it is today (See Chapter 43).

The Public Utility Holding Company Act of 1935

The next major change in the DJUA resulted from the Public Utility Holding Company Act of 1935 (PUHCA). Until the 1930s, many utilities were owned by holding companies that stretched across state lines. The purpose of this legislation was to force utility holding companies to divest themselves of multi-state utilities so they could be regulated by individual states. The importance of the holding companies to investors was reflected in the fact that up until the 1930s, Standard Statistics kept separate indices for utility operating companies and utility holding companies.

Another reason for the passage of the law was Samuel Insull, whose holding company owned a number of Chicago-area public utilities as well as railroads. It was both the monopolistic influence of his companies and the repercussions caused by the collapse of his holding company that contributed to the passage of the PUHCA. The Energy Policy Act of 2005 repealed the PUHCA, effective February 8, 2006.

Several members of the DJUA were holding companies. The problem not only was that the holding companies were shrinking in size and became completely different firms, but that the utility holding company stocks were quite volatile due to leverage and the uncertainty over the companies' future.

Six holding companies in the DJUA Average (Commonwealth & Southern Corp. Preferred, American Water Works & Electric, Electric Bond & Share, Electric Power & Light, Engineers Public Service, and North American Co.) were removed in 1938. These companies either distributed shares in the new companies that were spun off to shareholders (Engineers Public Service Co.), sold their interest in other utilities (North American sold its interest in St. Louis County Gas Co.), or ceased operations as a domestic utility (Electric Bond & Share Co.) After this reorganization, the DJUA included four natural gas companies, three electric utility holding companies (which had direct control over their subsidiaries and did not have to reorganize under the PUHCA) and eight operating electric utilities.

The Utility Average Modernizes

No further changes were made in the DJUA for the next thirty-eight years! It would be hard to conceive of the all of the components of the DJUA in 2017 still being in the average in 2055, but that's the way things used to be. The change in

1986 only occurred because the Cleveland Illuminating Co. (a member of the DJUA) and Toledo Edison merged into Centerior Energy. So in one sense, it wasn't really a change at all.

In 1991, ARKLA, Inc. (later NorAm Energy) replaced Columbia Gas when Columbia Gas filed for protection under federal bankruptcy law, making it the first real change to the DJUA in forty-three years.

The third big change in the DJUA occurred in 1997 when the editors of the *Wall Street Journal* made an attempt to "revitalize" the DJUA by adding "some of the largest, most actively traded and innovative utilities in the country." Given the fact that the country was in the middle of the Dot Com Bubble, these changes were in keeping with the spirit of the times. The change also tried to make the index more geographically diversified, with less of an emphasis on east coast utilities, and to increase the number of natural gas companies represented in the index. Consequently, Columbia Gas, which had been replaced by ARKLA, Inc., was added back into the average. The changes left the DJUA with ten electric companies and five natural gas companies.

Three mergers in 2000 led to changes in the DJUA. Dominion Resources was added when it acquired Consolidated Natural Gas, and NiSource, Inc. was added when it acquired Columbia Energy. When PECO Energy acquired UniCom and reorganized as Exelon, the change necessitated the addition of a new company since both PECO Energy and UniCom had been in the DJUA. This led to the addition of AES Corp. Though located in Virginia, AES Corp. is a global company providing electricity and natural gas to customers on five continents, giving the DJUA a global presence.

One of the additions to the DJUA in 1997 was Enron, which certainly qualified as an innovative utility, but not to the benefit of its shareholders. It was removed from the DJUA on December 2, 2001, when it collapsed into bankruptcy. Enron was replaced by First Energy Corp. On October 9, 2007, when TXU Corp. was taken private, it was replaced by NextEra Energy, Inc. (formerly Florida Power & Light Co.) The most recent change in the DJUA occurred on September 30, 2014, when American Water Works, Inc. replaced The Williams Companies because the utility had evolved into an energy company. This change also enabled the Utility Average to add a water company as one of its components.

A graph of the performance of the Dow Jones Utility Average from 1929 until 2018 is provided in Figure 35.1.

The DJUA in the 21st Century

Will the DJUA remain as stable in the 21st century as it did in the 20th century? Probably not, but the average will have fewer membership changes than the DJIA and DJTA. There were only three major changes in the Dow Jones Utility Average

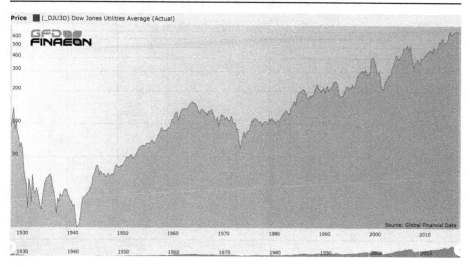

Figure 35.1 Dow Jones Utility Average, 1929 to 2018.

in the 20th century, in 1938, 1946, and 1997. All of the other changes resulted from a merger/acquisition or bankruptcy. In some ways, the DJUA is a relic of the past, but in an era when the components of the S&P 500 change almost every month, having such a stable index is quite reassuring.

chapter thirty-six

Los Angeles During the 1929 Stock Market Crash

The Stock Market Crash of 1929 had a dramatic impact on the primary stock market indices as share prices collapsed. The Dow Jones Industrial Average declined from 381.17 on September 3 to a low of 198.69 on November 13, a decline of 48 percent. The S&P Composite declined from 31.92 on September 7, to 17.66 on November 13, a decline of 45 percent. Was the decline universal throughout the United States?

In the 1920s, there were a number of regional exchanges where local stocks were listed. If a stock does an IPO today, it usually lists on the NYSE or NASDAQ, where the shares can be traded electronically throughout the United States, but in the 1920s, there were still regional exchanges that primarily listed local stocks. A stock from Illinois would list on the Chicago Stock Exchange, and one from Massachusetts on the Boston Stock Exchange.

In California, you had exchanges in both Los Angeles and in San Francisco. The San Francisco Stock Exchange was formed in 1882, and the Los Angeles Stock Exchange was formed in 1889. The two exchanges merged to form the Pacific Stock Exchange in 1957. The Pacific Stock Exchange was bought out by Archipelago Holdings on September 27, 2005, which was in turn acquired by the New York Stock Exchange in 2006.

We recently discovered that the Los Angeles Stock Exchange had a stock exchange index in 1929. We only found two articles on the index, but we were able to obtain the values for the index for 1929 to see how stocks on the West Coast performed relative to stocks in New York.

In a 1930 article in the *Commercial and Financial Chronicle*, John Earle Jardine, President of the Los Angeles Stock Exchange, noted that "the speculative attention soon was attracted to the nationally known industrial and utility issues which were vigorously sponsored by certain groups, of which issues only a few are listed on our Exchange." Consequently, stocks on the Los Angeles Exchange failed to rise as much as the New York stocks and, consequently, declined less.

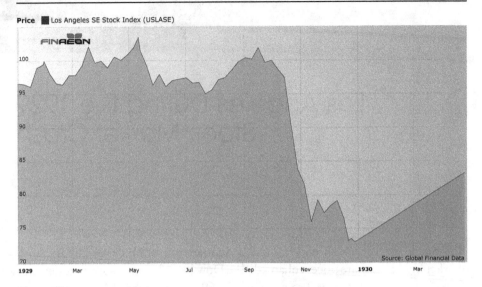

Price ■ Los Angeles SE Stock Index (USLASE)

Figure 36.1 Los Angeles Stock Exchange Index, 1929 to 1930.

The Los Angeles Stock Exchange calculated a general index of thirty common stocks, as well as sector indices of ten oil stocks, ten industrial stocks, and ten financial stocks. The indices had a base of January 31, 1929, equal to 100.

The timing of the decline in stocks in Los Angeles differed from New York. The Los Angeles Stock Exchange Index reached its high point on May 13 at 103.5 and declined to 73.1 on December 30, declining a little less than 30 percent. The oil stocks were hit the hardest by the crash, falling to 65.6, losing over 35 percent of their value. The ten industrials fell to 75.8 and the financials fell to 77.6.

The recovery from the December 30 low also varied from one group to the other. The index of thirty common stocks recovered to 83.3 by April 26, 1930, the ten oils to 78.2, the ten industrials to 90, and the ten financials to 81.2. Of the three groups, the industrials recovered the most quickly, and the financials were the laggards.

Among individual stocks, utilities apparently bounced back the strongest, including Edison, Pacific Lighting, and Pacific Gas. Standard Oil of California and Union Gas had also fully recovered their losses by April 1930.

Unfortunately, we could not find any additional information on the indices. We were unable to determine either which stocks were included in the index, who calculated the index, whether it was price-weighted or capitalization-weighted, and what happened to the index after April 1930.

Nevertheless, the index provides an interesting insight into the 1929 stock market crash. A graph of the index is provided in Figure 36.1.

chapter thirty-seven

America's First Bull Market in the 1700s

Global Financial Data has extended the S&P Composite back to 1791. This effort has revealed something new: America's first bull market. Between September 1791 and April 1803, GFD's index of US equities increased by 47 percent, a stunning vote of faith by investors in the new country.

GFD has incorporated the groundbreaking work of Sylla, Wilson, and Wright in their "Price Quotations in Early US Securities Markets, 1790–1860" into the Global Financial Database. They collected prices on over 2,000 securities from the Revolutionary War to the Civil War traded on nine domestic exchanges and on the London Stock Exchange. Accessing old newspapers on microfilm, they recorded and organized this archived weekly data.

Financial Companies in the New Republic

With this information, GFD has been able to extend the data for the S&P Composite back to 1791. We used data from seven banks (Union National Bank of Boston, Massachusetts National Bank of Boston, the First Bank of the United States, Bank of the State of New York, Bank of Pennsylvania, Bank of South Carolina, and the Bank of America), three insurance companies (New York Insurance Company, Insurance Co. of Pennsylvania, Insurance Co. of North America), and two transport companies (Philadelphia and Lancaster Turnpike Company and Schuylkill Permanent Bridge Company) to create this index.

The graph in Figure 37.1 illustrates the progress of America's first bull market between 1791 and 1802. You could easily draw a ten-year-trend line from the start of the bull market in 1791 to its peak in 1802.

It should be noted that most of the stocks that were listed in Philadelphia, Boston, and New York in the 1790s were banks and insurance companies. Although we have no data on the profitability of these companies during the 1790s, we have some data on dividends.

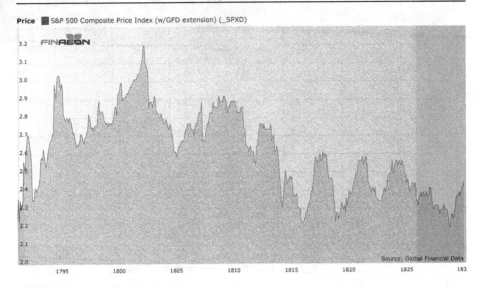

Price ▪ S&P 500 Composite Price Index (w/GFD extension) (_SPXD)

Figure 37.1 United States Stock Market, 1791 to 1830.

The Union Bank of Boston paid $12 in dividends in 1793, $16.50 in 1803, and $10.50 in 1807. The Bank of the United States paid $30.50 in 1793, $34 in 1803, and $32 in 1805. The Bank of Pennsylvania paid $8 in 1793 and 1803, but $9 in 1808. Dividends at the Massachusetts National Bank fell from $45 in 1785 to $35 in 1789, rose to $82 in 1792, then stabilized at $40 to $45 between 1793 and 1805.

It should be remembered that the yield on United States government bonds declined during this period of time, allowing yields on stocks to decline. Investors bid up the prices of individual stocks to get a higher return on company dividends than they could receive on United States government bonds.

Alexander Hamilton Reforms the Nation's Finances

What made investors optimistic about their new country? Alexander Hamilton. Not only was Hamilton a ground-breaking politician, he was a businessman who founded the Society for the Establishment of Useful Manufacturers, a profitable corporation that manufactured textiles.

Hamilton was appointed the first Secretary of the Treasury on September 11, 1789. He played a fundamental role in stabilizing the young nation's economy. Hamilton reorganized government debt to convince foreign investors that the US would repay its obligations, once again making the United States attractive to investors. Hamilton had a unified vision of how the government could work together with the banks and the private sector to promote the national economy.

Hamilton helped to establish a currency based upon silver and gold so the phrase "not worth a continental" would never be heard again. He helped to found the First Bank of the United States, introduced excise taxes on whiskey to fund the federal government, and helped Thomas Jefferson to succeed George Washington as president in 1800.

Alas, all bull markets must come to an end. From 1803 until 1830, stocks followed a slow, gradual decline back to the levels of 1791. Technicians would be happy to know that the 1791 levels provided support to the market in 1816, 1819, and 1829.

It is important to remember the impact of the sound financial policies of Hamilton. Before he became Secretary of the Treasury, the government paid for its expenditures with worthless paper after running ruinous deficits. The continental currency fell in value until it was worth only 0.1 percent of its value in bullion. Banks were unwilling to lend because of the financial chaos, and government finances were in disarray. Alexander Hamilton's reforms eliminated these concerns.

The twenty-first century can still learn from the eighteenth century. Sound fiscal and monetary policies provide the foundations for a bullish stock market.

chapter thirty-eight

The Death of Equities

Equity markets across the world continue to struggle. The indices of some developed countries remain below the level they were at in 2000 when the 20th century ended. Many investors are worried that stocks will continue to provide inferior returns for years to come. Unfortunately, they may be right.

Historical Returns to Stocks and Bonds

Equities reflect the present value of future earnings and free cash flow to corporations. If investors anticipate that future earnings will increase, stock prices rise, but if investors anticipate a decline in future profits, share prices will fall.

As shown in Figure 38.1, during the 19th century, the average share price of equities changed little over a period of decades because there was little inflation. Investors did not have to consider the trade-off between income taxes and capital gains taxes, and most profits were returned to shareholders as dividends.

This changed in the 20th century. As countries abandoned the gold standard and allowed their paper currencies to inflate, share prices rose (often accompanied by numerous stock splits). As governments grew in size, so did taxes, and in countries where income taxes on dividends exceeded capital gains taxes, investors benefited from allowing corporations to reinvest profits that generated capital gains. As illustrated in Figure 38.2, anticipation of future capital gains led to price/earnings (P/E) expansion as investors anticipated rising earnings. Finally, as central banks manipulated interest rates to influence the economy, lower interest rates made equities more attractive, contributing to the rise in equity prices.

At the same time, returns to fixed-income investors today are at unprecedented low levels. In some countries, yields on government bonds are even negative. Short-term treasuries yield 2 percent in the United States while a ten-year bond yields less than 3 percent. Generally speaking, the long-term yield to fixed-income investors equals the coupon when the bonds are issued, so fixed income investors should expect no more than a 3 percent annual return for the next decade, and if inflation

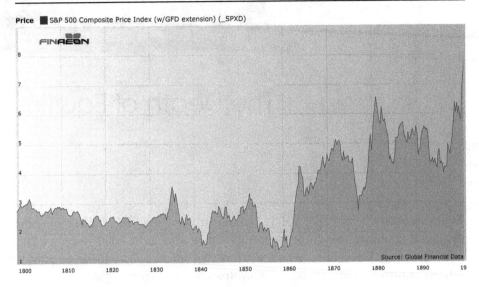

Figure 38.1 United States Stock Market, 1800 to 1900.

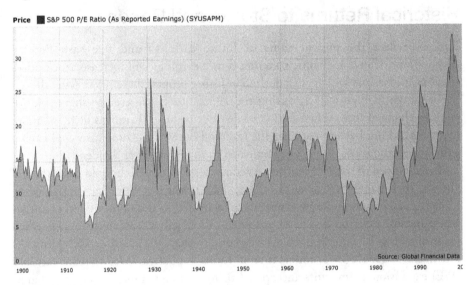

Figure 38.2 S&P 500 Price/Earnings Ratio, 1900 to 2000.

were to pick up, real returns after inflation could be negative. If yields stay at these low levels, fixed-income investors get little or no return, and if yields fall, the situation becomes even worse. If inflation or other factors drive yields up, fixed-income investors face capital losses that reduce their total return.

Could the 21st century be reverting back to the condition of stock markets in the 18th and 19th centuries, when the capital gains on stocks were minimal or non-existent? Unfortunately, the answer to this question could very well be yes.

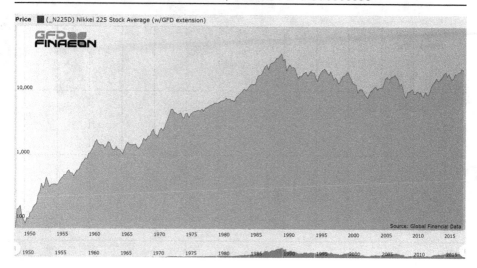

Figure 38.3 Nikkei 225 Stock Average, 1950 to 2018.

Japan's Two Lost Decades

Japanese stock investors saw little or no return between 1990 and 2018. As illustrated in Figure 38.3, from 1950 to 1989, Japan had one of the best-performing markets in the world, when the annual return to stocks and bonds was 14.24 percent per annum. The phenomenal growth in equity returns occurred as Japan's economy caught up with the rest of the world after the devastation of World War II.

Since 1989, stock prices have declined dramatically, showing an annual decline of 0.3 percent between 1989 and 2017. In 2016, the Japanese stock market traded at levels it had been at in 1986, thirty years before. With the yield on Japan's ten-year bond actually turning negative in 2016, bonds provide a poor alternative to equities, which provide a 2 percent dividend yield. With the yen appreciating against other currencies, the return from foreign investments to Japanese investors is reduced. Is this the fate of investors in the rest of the world in the century to come?

The No-Growth Economy

What went wrong? Why did stocks perform so poorly in Japan between 1990 and 2018? Part of the explanation is the bubble in stocks that occurred in Japan in the late 1980s, pushing share prices to unsustainable levels, just as Internet stocks increased in value in the 1990s. However, while other indices may stabilize after the bursting of an equity bubble, Japan remains in a downward trend. But why would it take over twenty-five years to recover from an asset bubble?

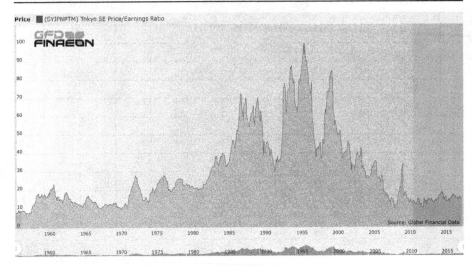

Figure 38.4 Japan P/E Ratio 1956 to 2018.

The more important long-term factor is Japan's nominal GDP, which in 2018 was little changed from 1992. No increase in GDP meant no increase in profits and no increase in stock prices. Whereas GDP had been rising in Japan from the end of World War II until 1990, allowing profits to increase and stock prices to rise, the end to rising GDP not only kept profits from growing but led to a compression in the P/E ratio and lower stock prices.

This is illustrated in Figure 38.4. The price/earnings ratio for Japanese stocks was between 10 and 15 during the 1960s, but rose after that to 70 in 1989 when stock prices peaked, and to almost 100 in 1995. This allowed the price of stocks to increase faster than earnings. Since then, this trend has reversed. Once again, the P/E ratio lies in the 10 to 15 range, as it did in the 1960s. This at least means that the prices of Japanese stocks are unlikely to decline further unless the earnings of Japanese companies decline.

In addition to enduring a stable nominal GDP, the Japanese population declined between 2003 and 2018 and only increased by 3.5 percent between 1990 and 2018 The Japanese population has been aging, reducing the number of people of working age and in the labor force, further reducing the ability of GDP to grow. As the dependency ratio between workers and non-workers increases, the cost of supporting retirees rises, further limiting the growth in profits and thus share prices. This trend is reflected in the fact that labor force participation in Japan has fallen from 64 percent in 1970 to 59 percent in 2018.

Although the size of the government in Japan is smaller than it is in the rest of the developed world, government expenditures still represent about 40 percent of GDP, leaving only 60 percent of the economy for the private sector to generate the growth needed to provide the future corporate profits that will allow share prices to increase.

Could Japanese share prices be the same in 2050 or 2100 as they were in 2015? Yes. If the profits of Japanese corporations fail to grow, then stock prices will stay where they are now. With no inflation, no growth in population, a shrinking labor force, a low dividend yield, a low yield on government bonds, rising government debt, an increase in the dependency ratio as the population ages, and a stronger yen, stagnant stock prices remain not only a possibility but a probability.

People talk of Japan's two lost decades. Could it be a lost century? More importantly, is this the fate that awaits the rest of the developed world?

America's and Europe's Lost Decade

Most of the factors that have kept share prices from rising in Japan are also present in Europe and in the United States. Europe's population is shrinking in some countries and stagnant in others, though population in the United States is rising due to higher birth rates and immigration. However, both the United States and Europe face aging populations with rising dependency ratios. Labor force participation peaked in the United States in 2000 and has declined since then, while labor force participation in Europe has been declining since the 1990s. A large portion of the increase in labor force participation at the end of the 20th century came from women joining the workforce, but women's share of the labor force has stabilized since the 1990s.

Many governments have tried to spend their way out of stagnant economies by running large budget deficits caused by increases in government spending and declining government taxes; however, the deficits these policies have produced are unsustainable and have led to austerity programs in countries facing fiscal crises.

A second response has been to expand the central bank's balance sheet as a way of providing liquidity to the private sector. These policies have also sent interest rates to unprecedented historical lows, even to negative rates in some cases, reducing returns to fixed-income investors. Low interest rates may encourage corporations to borrow but hurt investors saving for the future.

One important fact to remember about fiscal and monetary policy is that they can help the economy reduce the impact of economic and financial crises, but it is more difficult for them to create real growth. Growth occurs because more resources are made available or because there is greater productivity, not because of changes in fiscal or monetary policy.

Fiscal policy can redistribute income to avoid large drops in aggregate demand, but true GDP growth comes from increasing productivity and the amount of resources allocated to economic activity. Monetary policy can be used to control inflation, or the central bank can act as a lender (or bond purchaser) of last resort to prevent a financial meltdown, but monetary policy cannot generate changes in productivity or the amount of economic resources that are used in the economy. Only the private sector can generate the economic growth needed to increase corporate profits and equity prices. As the size of the private sector shrinks, it becomes more difficult to generate growth in the economy.

In one important way, Europe and the United States are in a worse position than Japan. In many European countries, the government represents half of GDP. Although the government—federal, state, and local—represents about 40 percent of GDP in the United States, if you add in the health and education sectors, which are largely state-provided in Europe, the government, health, and education sectors represent about 50 percent of GDP in the United States as well.

This leaves only 50 percent of the economy to the private sector. At the beginning of the 20th century, government represented around 10 percent of the economy when countries were not at war, leaving 90 percent of the economy in the for-profit sector to generate profits for investors. That is no longer true. In addition to government expenditures, the cost of transfer payments and the impact of government regulations must also be considered as factors that limit the growth in corporate profits.

So in a world where the non-profit government sector represents half of GDP, where populations are stable and labor force participation is shrinking, where populations are aging and the dependency ratio of non-workers to workers is rising, where inflation is low or stable, where nominal GDP is stable, where the "catch-up" growth that occurred in Japan and Europe after World War II has come to an end, where governments have built up large debts, sometimes exceeding GDP, where these governments have even larger future liabilities in terms of pension and health care for retired workers, how can investors anticipate the increase in profits necessary to generate higher stock prices? Good question.

On the contrary, it would be quite easy to argue that it is because of these conditions that expectations of future corporate profitability have fallen and that equities have shown no increase in price in many countries over the past decade. This also means that unless the conditions cited above change, equity prices could be the same at the end of the 21st century as they were at the beginning.

The problem this creates is obvious. Workers directly or indirectly through their pension plans save for their retirement. Providing a sufficient amount of money to cover personal expenses after retirement has become dependent on high returns to equities and fixed income. However, if equities once again become like bonds and show little capital appreciation, and dividends and bonds only return 2 percent to 3 percent per annum, there will be less money available for retirees. The fact that many people retire earlier and live longer will only exacerbate this situation.

When people save for the future, they set aside money they can use after they retire. This has worked well until now because GDP has grown over time; however, if GDP remains stagnant, retirees will not see an increase in their standard of living. Unless the size of the pie grows, there will not be enough resources available for those who are no longer working.

Many governments have created pension plans and retirement income dependent upon rising government revenue generated by a rising workforce and/or high returns on their investments. If either of these events fails to materialize, governments will have to cut back on the benefits they provide. Less money available to retirees means fewer expenditures, which means lower profits for corporations, which creates a vicious circle sustaining the absence of capital appreciation in equities.

The Death of Investing

Investors in the 21st century may face the worse of all possible worlds. Fixed income provides little or no returns, and if yields rise, fixed-income investors will face capital losses. Equity investors may also face a similar situation.

Rising equity returns depend on rising corporate profits. But if government represents 50 percent of GDP and provides substantial transfer payments, the share of the economy that allows corporate profits to grow becomes limited. Even within the for-profit sector, the opportunity for growth is limited. Increases in profits depend on productivity increases due to innovations, not applying existing technology to benefit from "catch-up" growth, or increasing labor force participation either through an increase in the working age share of the population, bringing more women into the workforce, or shifting workers from agriculture into industry and services. In most developed countries, services represent two-thirds of GDP, making productivity increases more difficult. If nominal GDP remains stagnant and labor force participation declines, it is difficult to see how investors can anticipate the rising profits necessary to sustain capital gains in equities. What profits are generated will be transferred to the aging population instead of being reinvested to increase future profits.

If the returns to equities fall, investors could focus on timing the market, but this is a zero-sum game. Investors in the developed world could move more of their investments to developing countries where these conditions are not yet present, but such a move would create problems of its own. Many developing countries have their own barriers to or controls on foreign investment. Although there are still many opportunities for "catch up" growth in emerging markets, these markets also face the problems of lower population growth, rising dependency ratios, and growing populations dependent upon pensions and other retirement benefits. Because of China's one-child policy, which was only recently repealed, the country is aging quickly, and by the 2020s, the median age in China will be higher than in the United States. Most Asian and Latin American countries have already reached the point where population growth has stabilized.

The Lost Century

Will the 21st century be a "lost century" for investors in which capital gains are rare and investors live off of the dividends and interest payments provided by the shares and bonds that they own, as occurred in the 18th and 19th centuries?

If the 21st century is one in which populations are stable or declining and growing older, and the labor force participation is declining, the dependency ratio between workers and non-workers will increase. Government, health, and education represent a substantial and rising portion of GDP, leaving less opportunity for corporations to grow profits. If nominal GDP remains stagnant as the service sector dominates the economy and the opportunities for productivity growth are limited, then the opportunities for growth in the 21st century will be extremely limited.

Some of the solutions are non-starters. Demographics are unlikely to improve. The trend of an aging population with a rising dependency ratio is unlikely to change. Higher inflation would only change nominal not real returns, and trying to trade the market's fluctuations is difficult and ignores the fact that this is a zero-sum game. Shifting investments to emerging markets may provide some short-term relief, but may only delay the inevitable day of reckoning.

Is there anything that can be done to avoid having finance join economics as a "dismal science"? The only way to allow future profits to increase at a higher rate is to allow the private sector more opportunities to generate profits. This would mean shrinking both the size of the government and the role of government in the economy at every level. This would include reducing the level of government expenditures, eliminating the corporate income tax and tariffs, simplifying the tax system, reducing government regulation, eliminating activist monetary policy, and allowing the role of the private sector to increase at every level of the economy. What is needed is more private-sector stimulus and public-sector austerity rather than the other way around.

The 21st century need not necessarily be a lost century, but unless the role of government in the economy changes, it very well could be.

chapter thirty-nine

Are You Ready for the Bubble of the 2020s?

Long-term data allows you to make long-term predictions. Given the performance of the stock market over the past 300 years, there appears to be a high probability that the next roaring bull market for equities will occur in the 2020s. If you look back at the stock market over the past 350 years, you'll find that in each century, the twenties have always enjoyed bull markets in equities. This is true for the 1720s, the 1820s, and the 1920s. Unfortunately, as we've seen with each of those bull markets, these dramatic bubbles came crashing down by the end of the decade.

Although there is no reason why events 100 years ago should determine events 100 years forward, similar situations can produce similar results. As the saying goes, history doesn't repeat itself, it rhymes. What were the situations that produced the bull markets of the 1720s, 1820s, and 1920s? Could this pattern repeat itself in the 2020s?

Figure 39.1 shows the growth in UK government debt from 1691 to 2010. The rise in debt through 1720 that resulted from the War of the Spanish Succession is quite visible, as is the quadrupling of government debt during the Napoleonic Wars, the increase in debt during World War I and World War II, as well as the increase in debt that has occurred in the UK since 1970. Debt drives bubbles, and government debt creates the biggest bubbles of them all.

The Bubble of the 1720s

The 1720s are best known for the South Sea Bubble in London, but in fact, there were simultaneous bubbles in both Amsterdam and in Paris. The War of the Spanish Succession (1701 to 1714) was a European-wide war fought over whether Spain and France should be united under a single monarchy. This war added to the government debts of all the European countries, and after the war was over, governments wanted to find a way to eliminate the debt they had created.

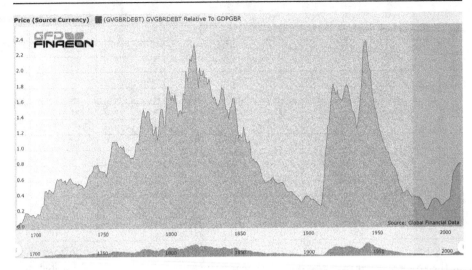

Figure 39.1 United Kingdom Government Debt, 1691 to 2016.

In both Paris and London, governments found ways to convert outstanding government debt into equity in trading companies whose monopolies would supposedly produce large returns to shareholders, but instead the debt conversions created bubbles for the *Compagnie du Mississippi* in Paris (see Chapter 9) and the South Sea Company in London (see Chapter 6). Although the South Sea Bubble is the more famous of the two, the *Compagnie des Indes* stock was the bigger bubble, with share prices going from 282.5 in November 1718 to over 10,000 by November 1719 (Figure 39.2). The South Sea Stock's increase from 116 to 1,045 seems small by comparison (Figure 21.3).

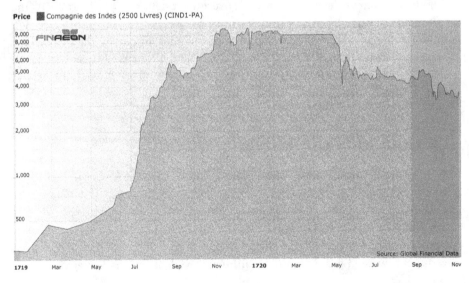

Figure 39.2 Mississippi Company Stock, 1718 to 1723.

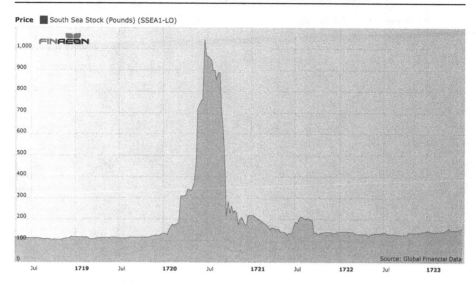

Figure 39.3 South Sea Co. Stock, 1718 to 1723.

In both France and Great Britain, the causal factor of the first global stock market bubble was the government trying to rid itself of excessive debt load and stimulating the economy through inflation and a debt/equity swap. The government benefitted because it reduced its debt, while many speculators benefitted from the resulting sharp rise in equity prices. But the long-run costs outweighed the short-run benefits. As a result of these bubbles, the stock market was seen as a speculative trap that hurt investors, and The Bubble Act that was passed in England in 1720 stifled investment in legitimate companies until the canal stocks became a source for capital at the end of the century.

The Bubble of the 1820s

Stock markets in both London and Paris remained quiescent for the rest of the century. The French Revolution of 1789 led to the Napoleonic Wars, which not only engulfed Europe in war, but as always, produced huge debts. After the Napoleonic Wars ended in 1815, London was awash in liquidity. During the wars, the South American colonies declared their independence from Spain while Spain was ruled by Napoleon's brother, Jose Bonaparte.

Since South America was one of the primary sources of gold, silver, and other metals, the newly born countries used this fact to borrow money from Europe, using the anticipated future revenues from gold and silver as a guarantee for the bonds and equities that were issued, just as the South Sea Co. and Mississippi Co. had used their expected monopoly trade revenues to justify the bubble of the 1720s. The end result was the same, liquidity flowed into the new government

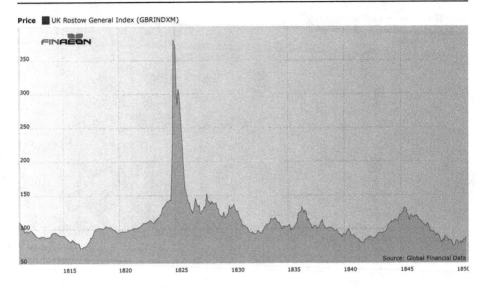

Figure 39.4 United Kingdom Stock Index, 1811 to 1850.

bonds and stocks, and having forgotten about the bubble of the 1720s, the bubble of the 1820s ensued (Figure 39.4).

Most of the price changes occurred in mining stocks. Real del Monte of Brazil (Figure 39.5) lost over 90 percent of its value very quickly once it was realized the mining revenues that were anticipated would never occur.

Of course, countries like Spain, Portugal, and Greece in Europe (sound familiar?) and Chile, Brazil, Argentina, and others in South America all defaulted

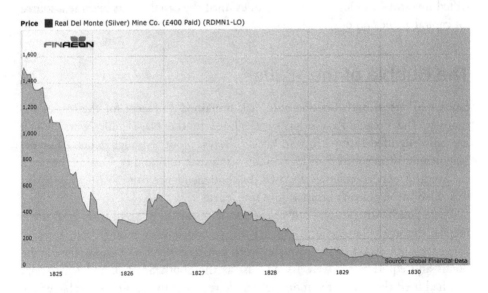

Figure 39.5 Real del Monte (Brazil) Stock, 1825 to 1830.

on their debts. Countries that never existed, such as Poyais, could no longer issue debt to gullible investors (see Chapter 19 "The Fraud of the Prince of Poyais on the London Stock Exchange").

As in the 1720s, excessive government debt led to excessive liquidity. The prospect of large profits abroad encouraged new investments. As money flowed into South America, a bubble was created that inevitably crashed. After two such misadventures, you would think that investors would have learned their lesson.

The Bubble of the 1920s

Between 1914 and 1918, Europe again fell into war. World War I generated large debts for all countries involved, brought an end to the gold standard, along with *de facto* defaults on government debts through inflation. Germany's hyperinflation wiped out investors in government debt and created severe losses for shareholders (Figure 39.6).

Although we think of the Roaring Twenties as a period when stock markets were booming worldwide, this simply wasn't the case. Northern European stock markets and Japan didn't participate in the bull market of the 1920s at all.

Americans pulled their money out of Europe and invested it in the United States, and the great bull market of the 1920s ensued (Figure 39.7), only to come crashing down by the end of the decade. As with any bubble, since the fundamentals made the bubble unsustainable, a crash was inevitable. However, the global economic community was unable to address the financial dislocations created by World War I. The combination of poor monetary policy, economic dislocation, the inability

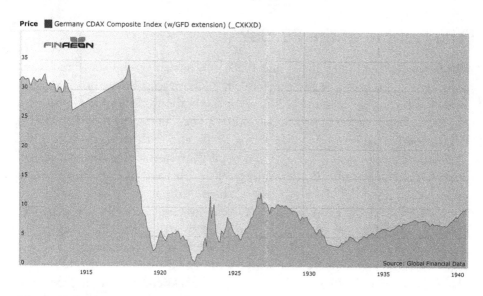

Figure 39.6 Germany Stock Market Index, 1911 to 1940.

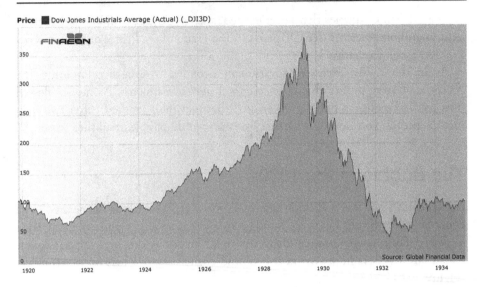

Figure 39.7 The Dow Jones Industrial Average, 1920 to 1934.

of the international community to work out solutions to these problems, and the unwillingness of the isolationist United States to take leadership on these global economic issues, contributed to the problem. The global economy went into a death spiral from 1929 to 1932 and pulled financial markets down with it.

As in the 1720s and in the 1820s, government's unwillingness to deal with the debt it had created, and its inability to reach a political solution, meant that the markets were forced to deal with the consequences of the government's failures.

The Bubble of the 2020s?

The bubbles of the 1720s, 1820s, and 1920s were amazingly similar. In each case, wars had created excessive government debt. Governments inflated their way out of their debts in France in the 1720s, in Austria in the 1820s, and in Germany in the 1920s. Investors found new opportunities abroad, in trading companies in the 1720s, South American companies in the 1820s, and in the United States in the 1920s. Both government debt holders and equity investors lost money as a result of these bubbles as governments defaulted on their debts and share prices collapsed. In each case, it was decades before markets began to recover.

In addition to the century cycle we have discussed here, there is a pattern covering several decades that would also point to a significant move up in the markets in the 2020s. Since 1900, the S&P 500 has had three major moves up and three plateaus (Figure 39.8). The first plateau existed from 1900 to 1920 before the bull market of the Roaring Twenties began. Stocks collapsed during the Great Depression, and then sank back until the next bull move began in 1941. A second

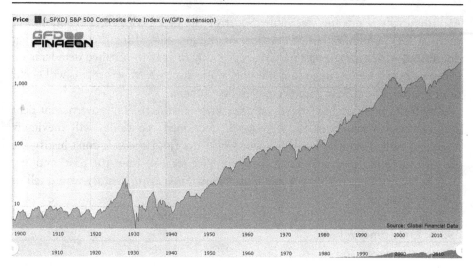

Figure 39.8 S&P 500 Index 1900 to 2018.

plateau occurred between 1966 and 1982 before the bull market of the 1980s and 1990s. Stocks have been stuck in another plateau since 2000. Could the market break out for a similar bull market after another twenty-year plateau?

Could a similar bubble occur in the 2020s? There certainly are some similarities between now and then. Government debt has been piling up in Europe, Japan, and the United States at unprecedented rates. Government bonds pay extremely low rates, so investors are looking for alternatives. Central Banks in Europe and the United States have expanded their balance sheets to absorb the debt the private sector abhors. Emerging markets provide higher growth rates than the developed world, as well as opportunities that are unavailable in the more mature economies. Finally, equities have provided low or negative returns in Japan between 1990 and 2018 and in Europe between 2010 and 2018.

Governments could try to reduce their debt burden through inflation or some other form of default. Money might pour out of the trillions of dollars of government debt that have accumulated and go into equities, especially if new technological innovations occur, or changes in developing countries make investments there more attractive. As stocks rise in price and more money pours in, a new bubble could develop.

Government debt has increased throughout the world and Central Banks have expanded their balance sheets to absorb it. Many countries are able to avoid the problems of excessive debt because interest rates remain low, but there is no guarantee that interest rates won't rise at some point. If they do, the cost of servicing the debts that countries have built up could become excessive. At that point, investors might abandon government debt of the developed countries as they did in the past and invest their money in foreign growth stocks. This could be either "established" emerging markets such as the BRICS, or frontier markets in Africa. A bubble in

African stocks is not inconceivable. Some of the best performing economies of the past few years have been in Africa. As the growth-stifling dictatorships that dominated Africa for the past fifty years give way to growth-oriented democracies, investors may seize on "once-in-a-lifetime" opportunities. Whether this will occur or not remains to be seen, but the possibility is there.

Any flight to emerging stocks out of reaction to the risks of government debt and underperformance of the debt-laden developed economies will inevitably lead to a crash. Financial bubbles occur where the fundamentals don't justify the changes in equity prices. Perhaps investors have learned from the past, and any such bubble will be snuffed out before it begins. Then again, history would tell us a different story.

Will a bubble in the roaring 2020s mimic the bubbles of the 1720s, 1820s and 1920s? Only time will tell...

chapter forty

The Complete Dow Jones Industrial Average

The Dow Jones Industrial Average (DJIA) is both the oldest stock index for industrial stocks in the world and a benchmark for stocks in the United States. When someone says "the market" was up 100 points today, they are referring to the Dow Jones Industrial Average. Most people are unaware of the history of the DJIA and that Global Financial Data provides a unique version of the DJIA that extends the series on a daily basis back to 1885 by combining all four versions of the DJIA into a single index.

The Four Indices

The Dow Jones averages were introduced by Charles Dow (Figure 40.1) in 1885. The historical data for the DJIA is a combination of four separate indices. On February 16, 1885, an index of twelve railroads and two industrial stocks was first calculated (Dow Jones 14 Stocks) by Charles Dow and Edward Davis Jones, the originators of the Dow Jones averages. On January 2, 1886, the 1885 index was replaced by an index of ten railroads and two industrial stocks (Dow Jones 12 Stocks). On May 26, 1896, the index was revised to include twelve industrial stocks, but no railroad stocks (DJIA 12 Stocks). This twelve industrials index was calculated until September 30, 1916, when a new index was introduced that included twenty industrial stocks (DJIA 20 Stocks). The new index was calculated back to December 14, 1914, the day the NYSE reopened after closing in August 1914 because of World War I. The index of twenty industrials was expanded to include thirty stocks (DJIA 30 stocks) on October 1, 1928, and has remained at thirty industrials since then.

The DJIA is not a capitalization-weighted index; rather, it is an equally weighted average. The reason for this is that, in the 1800s, stocks were not quoted at their cash price as they are today, but were quoted as a percentage of their par value. Most stocks had a par value of $100, but some had par values of $50, $25, or even

Figure 40.1 Charles Henry Dow, originator of the Dow Jones Industrial Average.

$5. In Germany in the 1800s, several versions of a stock, each with a different par value (500 marks, 200 marks, 100 marks), traded side by side. If a stock were quoted as a percentage of par, then you could simply multiply the percentage quote times the par value to get the cost of the stock. This practice was discontinued on October 13, 1915, when the NYSE began quoting all stocks in dollars.

Complications Begin

Because stocks were quoted as a percentage of par, calculating an index was relatively easy. You simply added up the quote for each stock and divided by the number of stocks in the index. The result was an equal-weighted index of stocks. This also made the process of substituting one stock for another stock simple because you didn't have to worry about the impact on the index of replacing a stock quoted at $25 with one quoted at $500 or vice versa, since all stocks were quoted as a percentage of par rather than at their cash value. Even if a stock split or paid a stock dividend, it continued to be quoted as a percentage of par, so no adjustments to the divisor for the index were ever needed.

On October 13, 1915, the exchange started quoting stocks in cash prices, not as a percentage of par value. This created problems. A stock split or dividend meant that the quoted price for a stock fell, so on October 1, 1928, when the DJIA expanded to thirty stocks, Dow Jones introduced a divisor as a way of adjusting for changes in the price of stocks due to stock splits, dividends, distributions, recapitalizations, or substitutions. The divisor, which stood at 16.67 when it was introduced on October 1, 1928, was equal to 0.14523 in March 2018, implying that the DJIA had "split" over 200 times since it was introduced in 1914.

Global Financial Data's Complete Version of the Dow Jones Industrial Average

GFD's version of the DJIA includes several unique adjustments (Figure 40.2). First, GFD has combined the four versions of the DJIA into a single index by providing adjustment ratios when new indices were introduced in 1886, 1896, and 1914. We were able to accurately do this by going back to the *New York Times* in 1886 and in 1896 to calculate the prices of the stocks in the new and the old averages on the day the new index was introduced. Once we found the ratio of the value of the stocks in the old and new indices we used this adjustment factor to chain link the series together.

Calculating the adjustment in 1914 was easier because Dow Jones provides data for both the DJIA 12 Stock Average and the DJIA 20 Stock Average between December 1914 and September 1916. Unfortunately, this has led to an oft-repeated error.

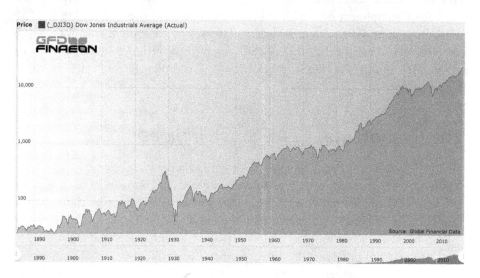

Figure 40.2 The Dow Jones Industrial Average 1885 to 2018.

The Missing Link in the Dow Jones Industrial Average

Many other sources use the DJIA 12 Stock average through July 30, 1914, and the DJIA 20 Stock average from December 12, 1914 on, not realizing that they are using different indices that are not comparable. The DJIA 12 Stock average closed at 71.42 on July 30, 1914, and closed at 74.56 on December 12, 1914, meaning that stocks actually rose in price during the closure of the NYSE. The new DJIA 20 Stock average closed at 54.63 on December 12, 1914. Sources that combine the 12 Stock and 20 Stock averages incorrectly state that the DJIA declined by 23.5 percent, from 71.42 to 54.63, during the closure of the exchange, when in fact, the DJIA increased in value while the NYSE was closed.

Global Financial Data has provided another unique feature to the DJIA. Although the NYSE was closed between July 30 and December 12 of 1914, stocks were quoted by brokers and traded off the exchange. GFD has gone back and collected stock data during the closure of the NYSE to recreate the DJIA while the NYSE was closed. We collected the data for the twenty stocks in the new DJIA 20 Industrials and calculated the average of the bid and ask prices on these twenty stocks from October 14, 1914, to December 12, 1914. This enabled us to determine that the 1914 bottom for stocks occurred on November 2, 1914, when the DJIA hit 49.07, a level the DJIA wouldn't revisit until the Great Depression in 1932. Few people realize that stocks in the US had already bottomed out and were heading into a new bull market even before the NYSE reopened on December 14, 1914.

Any research on the historical performance of the DJIA should include an analysis of the individual stocks that comprise the Dow Jones Industrial Average. Global Financial Data is the only company that has data on every security that has been a component of the Dow Jones Averages from their beginning in 1885 until the present. GFD also provides a full history of the components of the DJIA over the past 125 years. The only stock that was in the DJIA in 1896 and was part of the DJIA in 2017 was General Electric whose complete history is illustrated in Figure 40.3.

The Grandfather of All Stock Indices

The Dow Jones Industrial Average is the grandfather of stock market indices, with a history stretching back to 1885, providing over 130 years of daily data on US stocks. The index has been substantially revised three times by changing the number of stocks or components within the index.

GFD provides three unique features to help investors understand the history of the DJIA. First, it provides adjustment factors that enable users to chain link each of these indices together and provide a more complete picture of the DJIA and

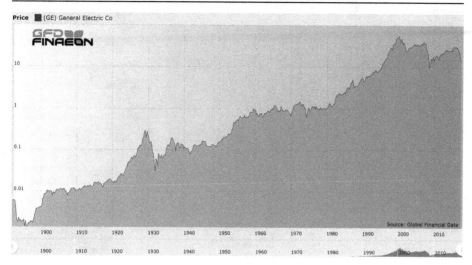

Figure 40.3 General Electric Co. Stock Price 1892 to 2018.

US stocks over time. Second, it has recreated the index during the NYSE's closure in 1914 to provide users information on US stocks unavailable anywhere else. Although few realize it, US stocks had already started moving higher a month before the NYSE was reopened in December 1914. Finally, Global Financial Data provides historical data on every security that has been in the Dow Jones Averages, including the Dow Jones Transport Average and Dow Jones Utility Average, since 1885.

Today, 133 years after it was introduced, the Dow Jones Industrial Average remains one of the most important benchmarks for the US stock market.

chapter forty-one

Seven Years of Famine for Emerging Markets?

How much of an investor's portfolio should go into developed markets and how much should go into emerging markets? This is a question that has befuddled investors since the South American mining bubble emerged in the 1820s. Developed markets generally provide more stable returns and outperform emerging markets in times of uncertainty. Emerging markets, on the other hand, have a higher potential for long-term growth than developed markets, but they can also be riskier. Emerging stocks have stronger bull markets, but deeper bear markets. Can historical data help investors to allocate money between developed and emerging markets?

The chart in Figure 39.1 shows the long-term relative performance of emerging markets to developed markets. Global Financial Data has extended the MSCI Developed and MSCI Emerging Market indices back to the 1920s so their long-term interaction can be analyzed in detail.

As can be seen in Figure 41.1, the emerging-developed market equity cycle lasts around seven to ten years. Developed markets outperformed emerging markets from 1945 to 1968, 1979 to 1986, 1994 to 2001, and since 2010. Emerging markets outperformed developed markets from 1968 to 1979, 1986 to 1994, and from 2001 to 2010. Based upon past patterns, you would expect the current underperformance of emerging markets to continue until 2020 at the latest, when emerging markets might begin outperforming developed markets.

How far can emerging markets fall relative to developed markets? If the trend follows the pattern of the past, quite a lot. Whether the relative performance of emerging to developed markets continues down to the levels of 1985 or of 2000, or even 1968, remains to be seen, but this chart does not bode well for emerging markets over the rest of the decade.

This technical analysis is backed up by the fundamentals. The end of the zero interest rate policy in the United States will attract more money to developed markets. Assuming the worst of the Eurocrisis is over, growth may soon return to Europe. Wages have risen significantly in China, and countries like India struggle

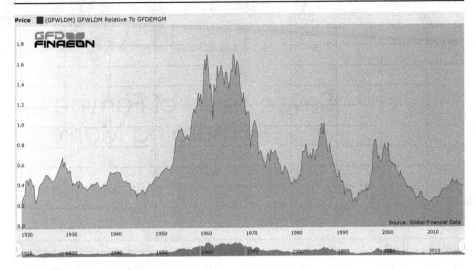

Figure 41.1 Emerging Market Index Relative to the World Stock Index, 1920 to 2018.

with providing the infrastructure necessary for economic growth. Many emerging markets will have to see their exchange rate decline to make their labor markets more competitive. Commodity prices rose significantly in the 2000s, but they have been declining in the 2010s.

In short, the chart and the fundamentals suggest that you should not see the current weakness in emerging markets as a buying opportunity. Instead, it probably foreshadows continued weakness for several years to come. Don't try to catch a falling knife, because you are likely to get hurt.

chapter forty-two

Cyprus and Its
Equity-Destroying Disaster

Which country has the dubious distinction of suffering the worst bear market in history?

To answer this question, we ignore countries where the government closed down the stock exchange, leaving investors with nothing, as occurred in Russia in 1917 or in Eastern European countries and China after World War II. Instead, we focus on stock markets that continued to operate during their equity-destroying disaster.

There is a lot of competition in this category. Almost every major country has had a bear market in which share prices have dropped over 80 percent, and some countries have had drops of over 90 percent. The Dow Jones Industrial Average dropped 89 percent between 1929 and 1932, the Greek Stock market fell 92.5 percent between 1999 and 2012, and adjusted for inflation, Germany's stock market fell over 97 percent between 1918 and 1922.

The only consolation these losses could bring to investors is that the maximum possible loss on their investment is 100 percent, though one country almost achieved that dubious distinction. Cyprus holds the record for the worst bear market of all time. Investors who bought at the top would have lost over 99 percent of their investment! Remember, this loss isn't for one stock, but for all the shares listed on the stock exchange.

The Cyprus Stock Exchange All Share Index hit a high of 11,443 on November 29, 1999, and fell to 938 by October 25, 2004, a 91.8 percent drop (Figure 42.1). The index then rallied back to 5,518 on October 31, 2007, before dropping to 691 on March 6, 2009. Another rally ensued to October 20, 2009, when the index hit 2,100, but collapsed from there to 63.85 on February 16, 2016. Figure 40.1 makes any roller-coaster ride look boring by comparison.

The fall in the index from 11,443 to 64 means that someone who invested at the top in 1999 would have lost 99.4 percent of their investment by 2018. That places the index over 76 percent below where it had been in 1983 when the Cyprus Stock Exchange Index was introduced. And remember, this is for *all* the shares listed

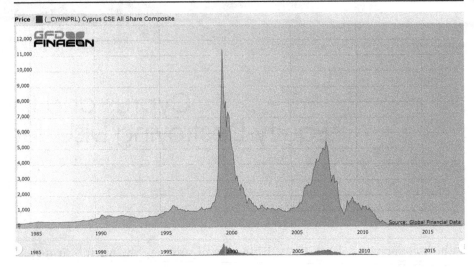

Price ■ (_CYMNPRL) Cyprus CSE All Share Composite

Figure 42.1 Cyprus CSE All-Share Composite, 1985 to 2018.

on the Cyprus Stock Exchange. By definition, some companies underperform the average and have done even worse, losing their shareholders everything.

For the people in Cyprus, this achievement has only added insult to injury. In March 2013, Cyprus became the fifth Euro country to have its financial system rescued by a bail-out. At its height, the banking system's assets were nine times the island's GDP. As was the case in Iceland, this situation proved unsustainable.

Since Germany and other paymasters for Ireland, Portugal, Spain, and Greece were tired of pouring money down the bail-out drain, they demanded from Cyprus not only the usual austerity and reforms to put the country back on the right track, but they also imposed demands on the depositors of the banks that had created the crisis, creating a "bail-in." Cypriots would help bear the cost of the collapse of their financial system.

As a result of the bail-in, debt holders and uninsured depositors had to absorb bank losses. Although some deposits were converted into equity, given the decline in the stock market, this provided little consolation. Banks were closed for two weeks and capital controls were imposed upon Cyprus. Not only did depositors who had money in banks beyond the insured amount suffer losses, but depositors who had money in banks were restricted from withdrawing their funds. The impact on the economy was devastating. Real GDP declined by 9 percent between 2011 and 2015, and real GDP is below where it had been at in 2006. Unemployment rose from 6 percent in 2010 to 16.8 percent in 2013, declining to 10 percent in 2018 (Figure 42.2).

Unfortunately, several years after the collapse of the Cyprus economy in 2012, the outlook remains grim. Stock markets usually rise before an economy recovers, anticipating future growth, but by the end of 2016, the Cyprus stock market still showed no signs of recovery.

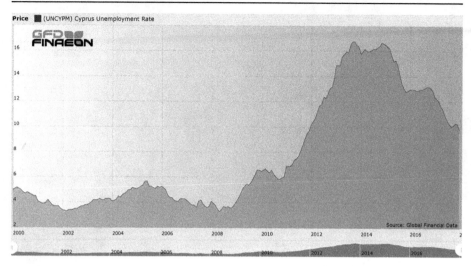

Figure 42.2 Unemployment Rate in Cyprus 2000 to 2018.

chapter forty-three

The Dow Jones Industrial Average's 22,000-Point Mistake

One of the long-term components of the Dow Jones Industrial Average has been IBM. The company was originally added to the Dow Jones Industrials on March 26, 1932, in a reshuffle involving eight stocks including Coca-Cola, Nash Motors (later American Motors), and Proctor & Gamble. On March 13, 1939, however, both IBM and Nash Motors were removed from the average and replaced by American Telephone & Telegraph and United Aircraft Corporation (now United Technologies).

AT&T had been in the Dow Jones Utilities Average until June 1, 1938. When the DJUA was created, the Dow committee interpreted utilities in a broader sense to include electric, gas, and communications companies. In 1938, the Dow Jones committee decided to restrict membership in the Utilities Average to power utilities.

The resulting reshuffle removed nine stocks, including AT&T, International Telephone & Telegraph, and Western Union, all of which were communications utilities, from the Dow Jones Utilities Average. Since AT&T was such a huge company, it was moved over to the Dow Jones Industrial Average, which required that another stock be removed to make room for AT&T. Thus, IBM was kicked out of the Dow Jones Industrial Average. By 1979, IBM had become the largest company in the world.

What if the Dow Jones committee had not redefined the Utilities Average to only include power utilities? What if IBM had stayed in the Dow Jones Industrial Average between March 13, 1939, and June 29, 1979, when IBM replaced Chrysler in the Dow Jones Industrials? Obviously, the Dow Jones Industrials would be higher than it is today, but how much higher?

International Business Machines incorporated on June 16, 1911, as The Computer-Tabulating-Recording Co., a merger of The Computing Scale Company of America, The Tabulating Machine Company, and The International Time Recording Company of New York. The company listed on the NYSE in November 1915, and on February 14, 1924, the company acquired the old International Business Machines and changed its name in a reverse acquisition.

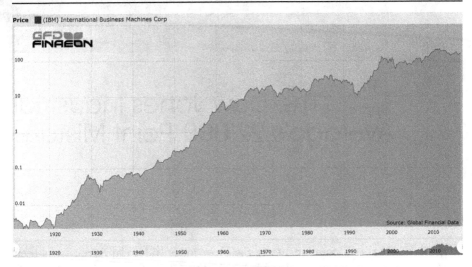

Price ■ (IBM) International Business Machines Corp

GFD
FINAEON

Source: Global Financial Data

Figure 43.1 IBM Stock Price 1911 to 2018.

Since its founding, IBM has been one of the best performers on the stock exchange in history. If you had invested $1 in IBM when it started trading OTC in August 1911, your investment would have grown to $33,000 by the end of 2017, even ignoring dividends. If you had reinvested your dividends back into IBM, your $1 investment would have grown to $1,000,000 by the end of 2017. In the past 100 years, IBM has given over a million-fold return. How many other stocks can boast of that? Figure 43.1 shows the performance of IBM stock over the past 100 years.

AT&T incorporated in New York on March 3, 1885, and began trading on the NYSE in May 1900 after it had acquired the American Bell Telephone Co. in March 1900. The company was forced to split up into "Ma Bell" and the "Baby Bells" by the US government on December 31, 1983. On November 18, 2005, AT&T Corp. ("Ma Bell") was acquired by one of the Baby Bells, SBC Communications, which then changed its name to AT&T Inc. in a reverse acquisition.

AT&T has not performed as well as IBM over the past 100 years. As you can see in Figure 43.2, if you had invested $1 in AT&T in May 1900, your investment would have grown to only $4.26 ignoring dividends, or $639 if you had reinvested all of your dividends back into the company by the time AT&T was broken up in February 1984.

So, what if the Dow Jones Committee had kept IBM in the Dow Jones Industrial Average between March 1939 and June 1979 and had never added AT&T, keeping it in the Utilities Average? What would the result have been? IBM closed at 187.25 on March 14, 1939, while AT&T closed at 166.125. IBM closed at 73.375 on June 29, 1979, while AT&T closed at 57.875 (Figure 43.2). Pricewise, the results appear to be similar.

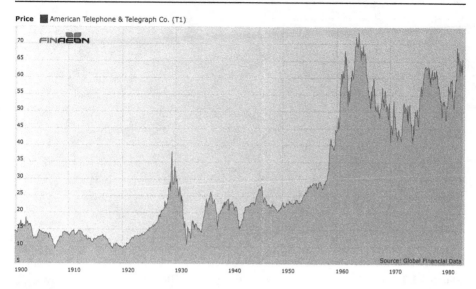

Figure 43.2 American Telegraph and Telephone Co. Stock Price, 1900 to 1984.

The difference is that both companies had stock splits as well as several rights offerings in the intervening forty years. The cumulative effect of these stock splits and rights offerings is significant. You would have to adjust the stock price of AT&T by 7.15 to allow for the impact of stock splits and rights offerings during the intervening forty years, meaning that one share of AT&T in 1939 would have grown to become 7.15 shares in 1979; however, you would have to adjust IBM stock by a factor of 562.48. If neither stock had split or provided rights offerings in those intervening forty years, as Berkshire Hathaway has refused to do, AT&T stock would have been at 414 in June 1979, but IBM would have been at 41,272. IBM increased almost 100 times more than AT&T during those intervening forty years.

The DJIA stood at 151.1 on March 14, 1939, and 841.98 on June 29, 1979. Since the DJIA is price weighted, you can remove the impact of AT&T on the DJIA by subtracting out the price of AT&T and replacing this amount with the value of IBM stock. If you do this, you would find that the DJIA would have been at 23,582 in June 1979, not 841.98. In other words, IBM would have added 22,740 points to the DJIA had it never been removed, more than doubling the present level of the Dow Jones Industrial Average.

The DJIA closed 2017 at a value of 24,719 (Figure 43.3). If you add 22,740 points to this value, you would arrive at a DJIA close to 46,000. If IBM had stayed in the DJIA, CNBC and the *Wall Street Journal* would be proclaiming the DJIA's approaching the 50,000 barrier. However, since the Dow Jones Committee removed IBM from the Dow Jones Industrial Average in 1939 and kept it out for forty years, we will have to wait several more decades before we can celebrate reaching that milestone.

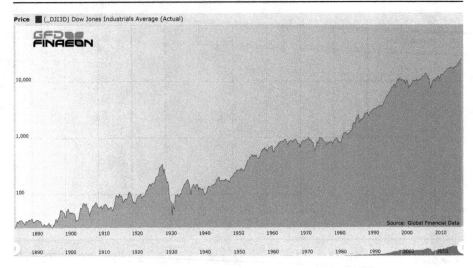

Figure 43.3 The Dow Jones Industrial Average 1885 to 2018.

chapter forty-four

August 1914: When Global Stock Markets Closed

On June 28, 1914, Austrian Archduke Franz Ferdinand was assassinated in Sarajevo. This event led to a month of failed diplomatic maneuvering between Austria-Hungary, Germany, France, Russia, and Britain, which ended with the onset of the Great War, as it was originally called.

Austria-Hungary declared war on Serbia on July 28, causing Germany and Russia to mobilize their armies on July 30. When Russia offered to negotiate rather than demobilize its army, Germany declared war on Russia on August 1. Germany declared war on France on August 3, and when Germany attacked Belgium on August 4, England declared war on Germany. Europe was at war, and millions died in the battles that followed.

The impact on global stock markets was immediate and fierce: the closure of every major European exchange and many of the exchanges outside of Europe. Although no one would have predicted this at the beginning of July 1914, by the end of the month, European stock exchanges were making preparations for the inevitable war and its impact.

Never before had all of Europe's major exchanges ceased trading simultaneously, but then never before had such a global cataclysm struck the world. There had been crises before when the stock market in the United States or other countries had shut their doors, such as the 1848 Revolution in France or the Panic of 1873 in New York, but never had all the world's major stock markets discontinued all trading simultaneously.

Open Financial Markets Led to Closed Exchanges

Ironically, it was because of the openness of global financial markets before the war that the global closure of stock markets occurred. At the beginning of 1914, capital was free to flow from one country to another. All the major countries of the world were on the gold standard, and differences in exchange rates were arbitraged through the buying and selling of government bonds listed on the world's stock exchanges. A country such as Russia would issue a bond that was simultaneously listed on the stock exchanges in London, New York, Paris, Berlin, Amsterdam, and St. Petersburg. Differences in exchange rates and the prices of bonds between countries could be arbitraged by buying and selling bonds in different markets. In effect, this made European stock exchanges a single, integrated market.

In 1914, currency flowed between countries with lightning speed. During the 1700s, money could only move as quickly as a ship could venture from one country to another. During the Napoleonic Wars, carrier pigeons were used to transmit information from the battlefronts to London, and in the United States, semaphores transferred information between New York and Philadelphia. By 1914, cables stretched across the oceans of the world, and money as well as stock orders could be wired telegraphically from one corner of the world to another in minutes.

Traders throughout the world could sell bonds and shares instantly, and it was the fear of massive selling, and the impact this would have on global markets, that led to the shutdown of European exchanges. There was a concern that investors would try to repatriate their money, leading to massive selling, a sharp fall in prices, and large amounts of capital flowing out of one country and into another.

The impact of selling on brokers and jobbers was exacerbated by the way shares were traded on the London Stock Exchange. Individual trades were made on a daily basis, then carried until Settlement Day when trades were matched and crossed. Brokers would make up the surplus or deficit on their accounts by settling outstanding trades with cash. As long as there were no significant swings in stock or bond prices, brokers had sufficient capital to settle their accounts. However, since traders relied on credit, large swings in prices could and would bankrupt many of the brokers, worsening the financial panic. A vicious cycle could be initiated that would lead to a collapse in stock prices. To avoid this problem, stock markets were closed until a solution could be found.

The War Drags Stock Prices Down

Of course, to investors, not being able to buy or sell shares is even worse than selling them at a loss. Although stocks could not be traded on the main exchanges, over-the-counter markets replaced exchanges for those who were desperate enough to sell.

Although the NYSE was closed between July 30 and December 12 of 1914, stocks were quoted by brokers and traded off the exchange. Global Financial Data has collected stock prices during the closure of the NYSE to recreate the Dow Jones Industrial Average while the NYSE was closed. We collected data for the twenty stocks in the new DJIA 20 Industrials and calculated the average of the bid and ask prices from August 24, 1914, to December 12, 1914. This enabled us to discover that the 1914 bottom for stocks actually occurred on November 2, 1914, when the DJIA hit 49.07, more than a month before the NYSE reopened. Few people realize

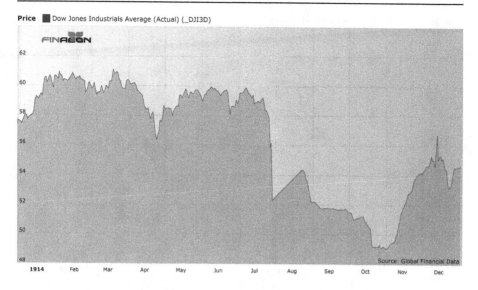

Figure 44.1 Dow Jones Industrial Average, 1914.

that stocks in the US had already bottomed out and was heading into a new bull market when the NYSE reopened on December 12, 1914. The DJIA did not revisit the lows of 1914 until the Great Depression in 1932.

Figure 44.1 shows how the Dow Jones Industrial Average behaved during 1914, including the period of the NYSE's closure. Although the market declined with the onset of war, investors eventually realized that war in Europe would bring opportunities to American companies to sell industrial goods and war materiel. Once this fact settled in, the stock market rose steadily for the next year.

The NYSE reopened trading for bonds under restrictions on November 28; the San Francisco Stock and Bond Exchange reopened on December 1; and the NYSE resumed trading at pegged prices on December 12, though the prospect of war profits soon made those restrictions irrelevant.

As Figure 44.2 shows, the Dow Jones Industrial Average almost doubled in price in the year following its bottom in November 1914. The market paused, then had another rally into 1916 before falling back once investors realized the strong profits they had anticipated from the war would not be realized.

The Closure of European Exchanges

In Europe, the problem of preventing catastrophic declines in stock prices was solved by putting a floor on share prices. Initially, stocks and bonds were not allowed to trade below the price they had been trading at on July 31, 1914. The government also placed restrictions on capital, limiting or preventing large flows of capital out of the country for the remainder of the war.

Price ■ Dow Jones Industrials Average (Actual) (_DJI3D)

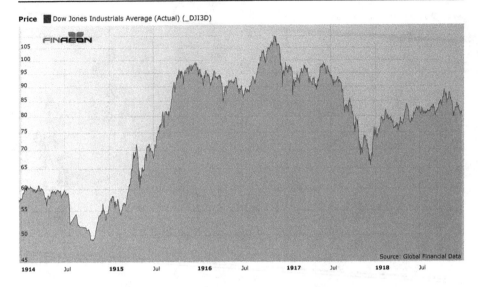

Figure 44.2 The Dow Jones Industrial Average, 1914 to 1918.

With these restrictions in place, markets reopened in Europe. The *London Times* began printing stock prices for London and Bordeaux on September 19, 1914, and for Paris on December 8, 1914. In January 1915, all shares were allowed to trade on the London Stock Exchange, though with price restrictions. The St. Petersburg exchange reopened in January 1917, only to close two months later because of the Russian Revolution. The Berlin Stock Exchange did not reopen until December 1917.

Unlike the United States, stocks on the London Stock Exchange declined in price during World War I. This was due not only to the decline in earnings that occurred and general selling of shares to raise capital, but just as importantly because of the lack of new buying and the shift of capital to government war debt. British companies were allowed to issue new shares only if the issue was in the national interest, and foreign governments and companies were not allowed to issue any new shares on the London Stock Exchange. The British government wanted to make sure that all available capital was used to fund the growing war debt.

Most of the new debt that listed on the London Stock Exchange was British government bonds, and their share of the London Stock Exchange's capitalization rose from 9 percent to 33 percent during the war. The performance of the London Stock Exchange between 1913 and 1919 is shown in Figure 44.3. As can be seen, stocks lost value continually during the war, hitting their bottom only in 1918. This occurred despite the general inflation that occurred in Britain during the war, which normally would have carried prices upward. Adjusted for inflation, the performance of British stocks during World War was even worse.

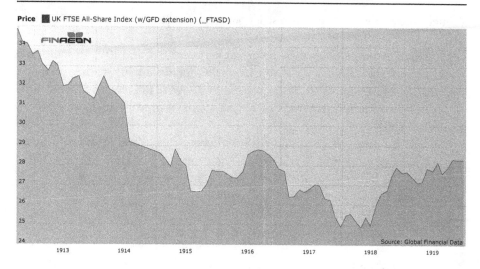

Price ■ UK FTSE All-Share Index (w/GFD extension) (_FTASD)

Figure 44.3 United Kingdom Stock Price Index, 1913 to 1919.

The Financial Costs of World War I

World War I destroyed the global integration of capital markets. The gold standard never returned, despite attempts after the war to revive it. The system of issuing bonds and shares internationally failed to recover after the war, and stock exchanges listed fewer international shares. The ownership of stocks and bonds from other countries shrank dramatically.

Exchanges were subjected to extensive regulation that did not exist prior to the war. Germans were not even allowed to trade on the London Stock Exchange for years after the war ended. London lost its place as the center of global finance, to be replaced by New York. Nevertheless, New York was not able to take on the pivotal role in capital markets that London held prior to World War I.

After the war was over, financial markets had to deal with the dislocations created by the war: inflation, increased government debt, reparation payments, the Russian Revolution, the emergence of new countries, England's failed attempt to return to the gold standard, the stock market crash of 1929, the Great Depression, debt defaults, competitive devaluations, the concentration of gold in France and the United States, and a hundred other financial repercussions that resulted directly or indirectly from World War I.

Governments and stock exchanges did learn how to manage financial markets during wartime. When World War II began, the London Stock Exchange closed for only a week, and the New York Stock Exchange never closed, save for August 15 to 16, 1945, when the NYSE closed to recognize V-J Day and celebrate the end of WWII. The Berlin Stock Exchange remained open during World War II,

231

though price floors and capital restrictions kept the prices of shares from falling until the devaluation of 1948.

Although global stock markets reopened between 1914 and 1917, in some cases it wasn't until the 1980s that the restrictions on financial markets that prevented the free flow of capital that had existed before 1914 were fully removed. Only after the fall of communism did stock markets become as globally integrated as they had been in 1914.

Though the focus of the hundredth anniversary of World War I will be on the massive destruction of World War I, the deaths of millions, and how World War I laid the foundations for World War II, the impact on stock markets and international finance should never be forgotten.

chapter forty-five

The World's First Bear Market

By our count, there have been twenty-five bear markets in the United States since 1792, and twenty-eight bear markets in the United Kingdom since 1692. Stock markets in the 17th century suffered from the effects of bear markets just as they do in the twenty-first century.

It is hard to tell exactly when the first bear market began because stock market data before 1692 is scarce. The price of East India Co. stock was at 500 in 1685 and declined to 158 in September 1691, but no consistent price data for stocks is available until March 1692. If we take the price of East India Company stock from March 1692 until November 1696, and the price of Bank of England stock from August 1694 until October 1696, the GFDatabase's London Stock Exchange Price index fell from 151 on April 1, 1692, to 42.57 on October 9, 1692, a decline of 72 percent (Figure 45.1). The first bear market was also one of the worst.

The Bear Beats the Bull during the Nine Years' War

What was the cause of the world's first bear market? We have no equivalent to the *Wall Street Journal* from the 1690s to tell us why the market declined, but the most likely source was the setbacks the British army and the Dutch suffered at the hands of French troops during the Nine Years' War (1688–1697), as well as the ongoing controversy over who was the true king of England. War and political crises have been the undoing of more than one bull market.

The groundwork for the Nine Year's War was laid a decade before in the 1670s. Louis XIV, the Sun King, emerged from the Franco-Dutch War in 1678 as the most powerful king in Europe. Louis XIV, of *"L'etat c'est moi"* fame, was not content with his gains from the Franco-Dutch War and wanted to extend his influence, increasing his territory, power, and control over Europe.

Louis XIV's (Figure 43.1) revocation of the Edict of Nantes in 1685 contributed to the deterioration in his military and political dominance outside of France.

Figure 45.1 Louis XIV.

Price ■ GFD Finaeon Equal Weight Daily London SE Price Index (1700s) (GFGBRBIG3EP)

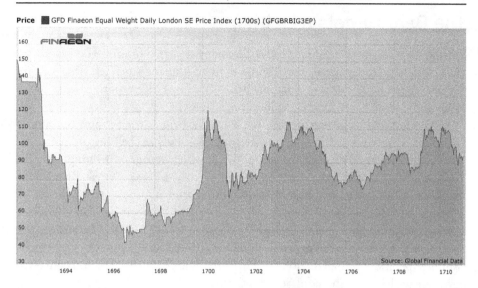

Figure 45.2 GFDatabase's London Stock Exchange Index, 1692 to 1710.

When Louis XIV's troops crossed the Rhine in September 1688, his opponents put together an alliance to stand up to the French king. Queen Mary of England, the Anglo-Dutch Stadtholder King William III, the Holy Roman Emperor Leopold I, King Charles II of Spain, Victor Amadeus II of Savoy, and major and minor princes of the Holy Roman Empire formed an alliance to stop Louis XIV.

Most of the fighting occurred near France's borders, mainly in the Spanish Netherlands and in the Rhineland. Although there was a fear of a French invasion of England at the beginning of the war, this never occurred, in part because of victories at the Battles of Barfleur and La Hogue between May 29 and June 4 in 1692. Nevertheless, Anglo-Dutch forces were defeated at the Battle of Steenkerqe on August 3, 1692, and the Dutch and English suffered defeats at the Battle of Lagos off Portugal on June 27, 1693, (N.S.) and at the Battle of Landen near Neerwinden on July 19, 1693 (N.S.). These defeats were soon reflected in the price of shares on the British and Dutch stock markets.

The expense of the war led to financial exhaustion of the participating countries. To help King William III fight these wars, the Bank of England was established on July 27, 1694, to provide funds to the English crown. In exchange for the establishment of the Bank of England, the king received a loan that never had to be repaid. After Queen Mary died on December 28, 1694, King William III became the sole ruler of England.

When Savoy defected from the Alliance, the Allies and France were eager to negotiate a settlement. The war came to an end with the Treaty of Ryswick, signed on September 20, 1697, in which Louis XIV retained Alsace, gave up Lorraine, and recognized William III as the sole ruler of England, Scotland, and Ireland.

The Bear Begets a Bubble

During the war, the price of East India Company stock fell from 158 on March 30, 1692, to 38 on November 6, 1696, while Bank of England stock fell from a par of 100 in August 1694 to 60 on October 16, 1696. From there, both stocks rose in value as the Nine Years' War drew to a conclusion.

Peace prevailed in Europe until 1701, when the War of the Spanish Succession was fought over who had the right to succeed Charles II as the king of Spain. The war ended with the Peace of Utrecht in 1713, which recognized Philip V as the king of Spain; however, the war further impoverished France, Great Britain, the Netherlands, and other participants with mounting debts.

Because of the burden of the war debts and a poorly performing economy, John Law was able to convince the French government to use his plan to convert war debts into stock in the *Compagnie des Indes* and to inflate the French economy by issuing paper money. England followed in France's footsteps in 1720 and converted government debt into shares of South Sea Stock.

Out of the ashes of the world's first bear market and the debts that were piled up from the British and French wars, the foundations were laid for the world's first stock market bubble in the *Compagnie des Index* in France in 1719 (see Chapter 9) and South Sea Stock in England in 1720 (see Chapter 6).

chapter forty-six

Donald Trump and the Brilliance of Bankruptcy

Global Financial Data includes information on thousands of businesses that entrepreneurs have created during the past two centuries, and two of these were run by Donald Trump. There are so many different aspects of Donald Trump's life that we could talk about, from real estate to television to politics, but the focus here is on Trump's two publicly traded companies, Trump Hotels & Casino Resorts Inc. and Trump Entertainment Resorts, Inc.

Making Atlantic City Great Again

After Atlantic City made gambling legal, Donald Trump got his casino license from the New Jersey Casino Control commission on March 15, 1982, and purchased hotels from Holiday Inn, Hilton, and Resorts International, which became the Trump Taj Mahal, Trump Plaza Hotel and Casino, and Trump's Castle Hotel Casino respectively. The Taj Mahal Casino opened in Atlantic City in 1990 at a cost of $1.1 billion. The hotel was financed with $675 million in Trump Taj Mahal Funding, Inc. 14 percent First Mortgage Bonds, Series A, due November 15, 1998.

Trump established Trump Hotels and Casino Resorts Inc. (Figure 46.3) in 1995, granting it ownership of Trump Plaza, sold the Trump Taj Mahal to the company for $890 million, and sold the Trump Castle for $485 million. The company also looked into opening casinos in Detroit, Kansas City, Coachella, California, and Gary, Indiana.

On June 7, 1995, the company went public, issuing 10 million shares at $14 per share using the symbol DJTC (Donald J. Trump Casinos) and with Trump maintaining a controlling 56 percent interest. As Figure 46.1 shows, at first the stock did well, reaching a high of 34 on June 5, 1996, giving the company a capitalization of $800 million, but there was just one problem. The company didn't make any money.

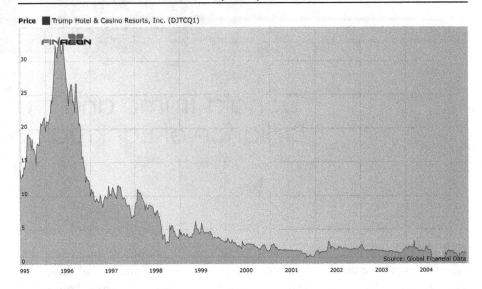

Figure 46.1 Trump Hotels & Casino Resorts, 1996 to 2005.

In fact, there wasn't a single year of the company's operation in which it made a profit. Talk about a one-armed bandit! By March 2005, shares were trading at 75 cents. Shareholders had lost over 95 percent of their investment and over $750 million in equity. Shareholders didn't have to go to the casinos to lose money. A chart of Trump Hotels & Casino Resorts, Inc. is provided in Figure 46.1, showing the nine-year decline in the price of its stock.

Now here is the brilliance of Donald Trump. If investors had put their money in the S&P 500 between June 1996 and March 2005, they would have doubled their money and had to pay taxes on these gains. By investing in Trump Hotels & Casino Resorts, Inc., they got large losses, which they could use to reduce their tax liability. Having discovered the secret of avoiding taxes through bankruptcy four times already, the Donald wanted to share his secret with investors. What a genius!

The 88 Cent Solution

Although the company earned a gross profit, it had about $1.8 billion in outstanding debt, generating around $220 million in interest expenses. After losing money for ten years in a row, the only solution was a restructuring of the company, which according to Trump was "really just a technical thing." Morgan Stanley took the lead to provide an additional $500 million in financing. In exchange for this, Trump reduced his interest in the company from 56 percent to 27 percent. Under the bankruptcy agreement, shareholders in Trump Hotels & Casino Resorts received 0.001 share in the new company, Trump Entertainment Resorts, Inc., 0.1106736 Class A Common Stock Purchase Warrant and 88 cents in cold cash.

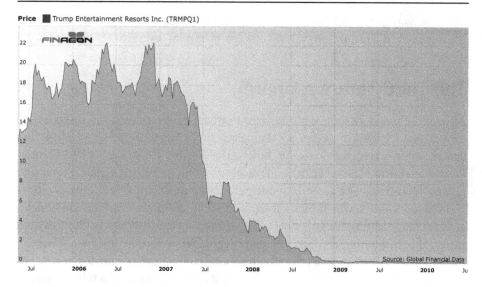

Price ■ Trump Entertainment Resorts Inc. (TRMPQ1)

Figure 46.2 Trump Entertainment Resorts, 2005 to 2010.

The Class A Warrants allowed its holders to buy shares in the new company at $123.74 per share. Given the fact that shares in Trump Entertainment Resorts started trading at $14 on May 23, 2005, it doesn't require a CFA degree to figure out the ultimate fate of these warrants.

Although the restructuring cut interest expenses in half to around $130 million, Trump still hadn't learned one of the basic tenets of running a public corporation. It is supposed to make a profit for its shareholders. Trump Entertainment Resorts lost money in every year of its existence. Between Trump's two companies, they managed to have a perfect record, losing money fifteen years in a row. How many other entrepreneurs can claim such a unique record?

As illustrated in Figure 46.2, Trump Entertainment Resorts shared the same experience as its predecessor. At first, the share price increased in value, peaking at $21 on August 1, 2005, but as it became clear that the company would continue its loss-making ways, the price of the stock began to decline until the shares were almost worthless. The company filed for bankruptcy in February 2009 with $1.2 billion in debt.

There were two groups competing for ownership of the company in bankruptcy court. One group of bidders was led by Andrew Beal and Carl Icahn, while the other was led by Avenue Capital Management. Trump announced that he would oppose the Beal/Icahn group if they tried to use his name on the casinos. The bankruptcy court eventually sided with Trump and Avenue Capital Management and gave them ownership and the right to reorganize the company.

On July 16, 2010, shares in Trump Entertainment Resorts, which were trading at 1 cent, were delisted and ceased to trade. Once again, Trump enabled shareholders to offset their profits from investing in the S&P 500 with losses in his company.

Between May 2006 and July 2010, the S&P 500 Return Index had broken even, but investors in Trump Entertainment Resorts had lost everything they had.

The Third Time's a Charm

Although Donald Trump never declared personal bankruptcy, his businesses filed for Chapter 11 bankruptcy protection seven times between 1991 and 2014. The bankruptcies included four of his hotels, the Trump Taj Mahal (1991), Trump Plaza Hotel and Casino (1992), Plaza Hotel (1992), Trump Castle Hotel and Casino (2004), as well as both of his publicly traded companies, Trump Hotels and Casino Resorts, which filed for bankruptcy in 2004 with $1.8 billion in debt, and Trump Entertainment Resorts, which filed for bankruptcy in 2009 with a mere $500 million in debt. The company again filed for bankruptcy in 2014.

During the thirteen years that Trump ran Trump Entertainment Resorts, the company lost over $1.1 billion and wrote down or restructured $1.8 billion in debt. Between 1994 and 2010, Trump's company lost over $1.8 billion. Over the same period of time, Trump was paid over $80 million by the company for his business acumen and expertise. Trump had the company base his bonus on EBITDA, earnings before interest, taxes, and depreciation allowance, but it was the interest on the highly leveraged company's debt, which was excluded from the calculation of his bonus, that undid the company. Trump Hotels & Casino Resorts paid out $1.96 billion in interest during its ten years in existence, and Trump Entertainment Resorts paid out $920 million in interest according to its financial filings.

Figure 46.3 Vignette on Trump Hotels & Casino Resorts, Inc. Stock Certificate.

Trump Entertainment Resorts sold off some of its assets to reduce its debt load, but this was insufficient to save the company. The company sold the Spotlight 29 Casino in Coachella, California, in 2005, the Majestic Star Casino in Gary, Indiana, for $253 million in 2005, and the Trump Marina in Atlantic City to Landry's Restaurants in 2011. The Trump's World Fair Casino was closed in 1999 and demolished in 2000. Harrah's at Trump Plaza was closed on September 16, 2014, and on October 10, 2016, the Taj Mahal closed down after losing money for its owners for twenty-five years.

Whether Trump goes public with any companies in the future remains to be seen, but if he does, only the short-sellers will be happy.

Sources for the Articles and Further Reading

Most articles used information from Wikipedia. Data for graphs are taken from the Global Financial Database. Sourcing for these graphs is included in the Global Financial Database.

Information on individual companies is taken from various sources. For the United States, the primary sources include *Poor's Manual of Railroads* from 1868/69 to 1940, *Poor's Public Utility Manual* (New York: Poor's Publishing Co.) from 1919 to 1940, and *Poor's Manual of Industrial Securities* (New York: Poor's Publishing Co.) from 1910 to 1940. Poor's Corp. was taken over by Standard Statistics Corp. to form Standard and Poor's in 1941 and these publications were discontinued. The *Manual of Statistics* (New York: Financial News Association), published between 1880 and 1923, proved to be a useful supplement to Poor's Manuals. Information on corporate actions were found in the annual issues of the Standard and Poor's *Dividend Record* (New York: Standard and Poor's Corp.) and Moody's Corp. *Dividend Record* (New York: Moody's Corp.). Both the *New York Times* (from 1851 on) and the *Commercial and Financial Chronicle* (New York: National News Service) from 1865 to 1972 were used to get contemporary views of some of the events discussed in the articles as well as price data and information on corporate actions.

Moody's/Mergent provided important information on individual companies both before and after the discontinuation of the Poor's Manuals in 1940. Sources include Moody's Corp., *Moody's Manual of Railroad Securities*, New York: Moody's Corp. published from 1909 through 1951, which changed its name to Moody's Corp., *Moody's Manual of Transportation Securities,* New York: Moody's Corp. in 1952. Moody's Corp., *Moody's Manual of Government and Municipal Securities,* New York: Moody's Corp. was used from 1919 to date, Moody's Corp., *Moody's Manual of Bank & Finance Securities,* New York: Moody's Corp. was used from 1929 to date, Moody's Corp., *Moody's Manual of Industrial Securities,* New York: Moody's Corp. from 1914 to date, Moody's Corp., *Moody's OTC Industrial Manual,* New York: Moody's Corp. from 1970 to date, and Moody's Corp., *Moody's OTC Unlisted Manual,* New York: Moody's Corp. from 1986 to date, and Moody's Corp., *Moody's Public Utility Manual,* New York: Moody's Corp. from 1914 until 2002. The Utility Manual merged with the Transportation Manual in 2003. Mergent Corp., *Mergent's International Manual,* New York: Moody's Corp. was published beginning in 1981 to date. All the Moody's Manuals changed their name to Mergent in 1999. These books were supplemented by Standard and Poor's Corp, *Standard and Poor's Stock Reports,* New York: Standard and Poor's Corp. for the NYSE, OTC/NASDAQ and ASE, which were published from the 1950s on.

Information on individual companies listed the London Stock Exchange was obtained primarily from London Stock Exchange, *The Stock Exchange Official Yearbook*, London: London Stock Exchange, published from 1875 until present and *The Stock Exchange Official Intelligence*, published from 1882 until 1933 when it merged with *The Stock Exchange Official Yearbook*, London: Spottiswoode, Ballantyne. Information on railway companies was obtained from *Bradshaw's Railway Manual, Shareholder's Guide and Directory*, London: W. J. Adams, which was published from 1869 through 1923 when British railways were consolidated into four companies. Information on government securities was taken from *Fenn's Compendium of the English and Foreign Funds, Debts and Revenues of all Nations*, London: Effingham Wilson. Both the *Statist* and the *Economist* also provided useful information at different points in time.

Stock Successes

For more information on Xerox, see "Xerox Xerox Xerox Xerox" in John Brooks, *Business Adventures* (New York: Open Road, 2014, pp. 166-200). A good corporate history is David Owen, *Copies in Seconds: How a Lone Inventor and an Unknown Company Created the Biggest Communication Breakthrough Since Gutenburg – Chester Carlson and the Birth of the Xerox Machine* (New York: Simon & Schuster, 2004) and Charles D. Ellis, *Joe Wilson and the Creation of Xerox* (Hoboken, N.J.: John Wiley & Sons, 2006) is also a good resource.

The story of Colonel Sanders is told in John Pearce's *The Colonel: The Captivating Biography of the Dynamic Founder of a Fast-Food Empire* (New York: Doubleday, 1982). For the Colonel's own version, see Col. Harland Sanders, *Life as I Have Known It Has Been Finger Lickin' Good* (Carol Stream, IL: Creation House, 1974). Information on the various incarnations of Dr. Pepper, Walt Disney Co., and Pepsi Co./Loft Inc. were taken from issues of the Moody's Manuals.

Two good books on the Bank of England are John Francis, *History of the Bank of England* (London: Willoughby & Co., 1847) and Richard Roberts and David Kynaston, eds. *The Bank of England, Money, Power & Influence* (Oxford: Oxford University Press, 1995). For information on other central banks, see Charles A. Conant, *A History of Modern Banks of Issue* (New York: G. P. Putnam & Sons, 1896, 6th Edition of 1926 republished by Augustus M. Kelley, Publishers, 1969). Malcolm Balen has written two books on the South Sea Bubble, *The Secret History of the South Sea Bubble: The World's First Great Financial Scandal* (New York: Fourth Estate, 2003) and *The King, The Crook, and the Gambler: The True Story of the South Sea Bubble and the Greatest Financial Scandal in History* (New York: Harper, 2004). To see how the South Sea Bubble affected Amsterdam and London stocks, see Larry Neal, *The Rise of Financial Capitalism* (Cambridge: Cambridge University Press, 1990). Another good overview of the 1720 bubble can be found in William N. Goetzmann, Catherine Labio, K. Geert Rouwenhorst, and Timothy

Young, eds., *The Great Mirror of Folly: Finance, Culture and the Crash of 1720* (New Haven: Yale University Press, 2013).

John Holdsworth's *The First and Second Banks of the United States* (Washington D.C.: Government Publication Office, 1910) provides a brief overview of both banks. For a general overview of banking in the United States in the early 1800s, see Bray Hammond's *Banks and Politics in America from the Revolution to the Civil War* (Princeton: Princeton University Press, 1991) and Murray N. Rothbard, *A History of Money and Banking in the United States* (Auburn, AL: Ludwig von Mises Institute, 2002). Two good books on the bank war are Robert Remini's *Andrew Jackson and the Bank War* (New York: W.W. Norton & Co, 1967) and Peter Temin's *The Jacksonian Economy* (New York: W.W. Norton & Co. 1969). For information on the Second Bank of the United States, see Ralph C.H. Catterall, *The Second Bank of the United States* (Chicago: University of Chicago, 1902), available from Google Books. There are many books about Alexander Hamilton with the best probably being Ron Chernow's *Alexander Hamilton* (New York: Penguin Books, 2005). Two good books on Andrew Jackson include H.W. Brands, *Andrew Jackson: His Life and Times* (New York: Doubleday, 2005), and Jon Meacham's *American Lion: Andrew Jackson in the White House* (New York: Random House, 2009).

For information on stock market bubbles, see the classic Charles P. Kindleberger, *Manias, Panics and Crashes* (New York: Basic Books, 1977) and Edward Chancellor, *Devil Take the Hindmost, A History of Financial Speculation* (New York: Plume Books, 2000).

Several books have been written on John Law and the Mississippi Bubble. See A. W. Wiston-Glynn and Gavin Adams, *John Law of Lauriston: Financier and Statesmen, Founder of the Bank of France, Originator of the Mississippi Scheme* (London: E. Saunders & Co., 1907) and Janet Gleeson, *Millionaire: The Philanderer, Gambler and Duelist Who Invented Modern Finance* (New York: Simon & Schuster, 2000).

For information on canals in Britain in the 1700s, see J. R. Ward, *The Finance of Canal Building in Eighteenth-Century England* (Oxford: Oxford University Press, 1974). On the railway mania, see Henry G. Lewin, *Railway Mania and Its Aftermath, 1845-1852* (London: David & Charles, 1968).

Two good sources on the history of the London Stock Exchange and its impact on foreign markets can be found in Ranald C. Michie, *The London Stock Exchange: A History* (Oxford: Oxford University Press, 1999) and Ranald C. Michie, *The Global Securities Market: A History* (Oxford: Oxford University Press, 2006). For changes in the center of the financial world over time, see Charles P. Kindleberger, *A Financial History of Western Europe* (London: George Allen & Unwin, 1984) and Charles P. Kindleberger, *World Economic Primacy, 1500-1990* (Oxford: Oxford University Press, 1996).

On the Dutch East India Company stock, see Larry Neal, "Venture Shares of the Dutch East India Company," in William N. Goetzmann and K. Geert

Rouwenhorst, editors, *The Origins of Value: The Financial Innovations that Created Modern Capital Markets* (Oxford: Oxford University Press, 2005, pp. 165-176). The best book on the VOC is Femme S. Gaastra, *The East India Company: Expansion and Decline* (Zulphen: Walburg Pers, 2003) as well as Charles R. Boxer, *The Dutch Seaborne, Empire* (Penguin Books, 1990). Stephen R. Bown, *Merchant Kings: When Companies Ruled the World 1600-1900* (New York: Thomas Dunne Books, 2010) covers the Dutch East India Company, the English East India Company, and several other sovereign multinationals.

For information on the English East India Company, see Nick Robbins, *The Corporation that Changed the World: How the East India Company Shaped the Modern Multinational* (London: Pluto Press, 2nd Edition, 2012); John Keay, *The Honourable Company: A History of the English East India Company* (New York: Scribner & Sons, 1994); and Antony Wild, *The East India Company: Trade and Conquest from 1600* (New York: The Lyons Press, 2000).

To read what Warren Buffett has written, get copies of the annual reports put out by Berkshire Hathaway. You can also read Warren E. Buffett, Lawrence A. Cunningham, *The Essays of Warren Buffett: Lessons for Corporate America*, 4th Ed., (Durham, NC: Carolina Academic Press, 2015). Alice Schroeder, *The Snowball: Warren Buffett and the Business of Life* (New York: Bantam Press, 2009) and Roger Lowenstein, *Buffett: The Making of an American Capitalist* (New York: Random House, 2008) provide good biographies. The foundation of Buffett's investment philosophy can be found in Benjamin Graham and Jason Zweig, *The Intelligent Investor* (New York: Harper Business, 2006).

Stock Scams

The story of Sir Gregor MacGregor is best told in David Sinclair's *The Land That Never Was* (Cambridge, MA: Da Capo Press, 2003). For a contemporary account, see "The Poyais Bubble," Quarterly Review (London) XXVIII (October 1822), pp. 157–161. The book written about Poyais, Thomas Strangeways, *Sketch of the Mosquito Shore Including the Territory of Poyais, etc.* (London: William Blackwood, 1822) can be found on Google Books.

The Florida Real Estate Bubble is briefly mentioned in Donald Rapp, *Bubbles, Booms and Busts: The Rise and Fall of Financial Assets* (New York: Copernicus, 2014).

The story of Anthony de Angelis is told in Norman C. Miller's *The Great Salad Oil Swindle* (New York: Penguin Books, 1965). See also Arthur Schroeder's "Salad-Oil King of the Universe: The Slippery Swindles of Tino De Angelis" in *Scams, Scandals and Skullduggery* (New York: McClelland & Stewart, Inc, 1996, pp. 44–59). For information on the settling of the accounts for the two brokerage firms that went bankrupt, see John Brooks's "Making the Customers Whole, The Death of a President" in *Business Adventures* (New York: Open Road, 2014, pp. 201–226).

The only book on John Keely is Theo Paijmans's *Free Energy Pioneer: John Worrell Keely* (Liburn, GA: Illuminet Press, 1998). There is also a chapter on Keely in Daniel W. Herring, *Foibles and Fallacies of Science, An Account of Celebrated Scientific Vagaries* (New York: D. Van Nostrand and Co., 1924).

Two good books on Ivar Kreuger are Allen Churchill's *The Incredible Ivar Kreuger* (New York: Rinehart & Co., 1957) and Frank Partnoy's *The Match King: Ivar Kreuger, The Financial Genius Behind a Century of Wall Street Scandals* (New York: Public Affairs, 2010). The movie about Ivar Kreuger, *The Match King*, filmed in 1932 right after his death is quite good, with Warren William playing the part of Kreuger.

Several books have been written on Barry Minkow, including two by Minkow himself. To get Minkow's version, you can read Barry Minkow, *Clean Sweep, The Inside Story of the ZZZZ Best Scam* (Nashville: Thomas Nelson Publishers, 1995). For more critical accounts, see Daniel Akst, *Wonder Boy, The Kid Who Swindled Wall Street* (New York: Charles Scribner's and Sons, 1990) and Joe Domanick, *Faking it in America Barry Minkow and the Great ZZZZ Best Scam* (Chicago: Contemporary Books, 1989).

The Story of Overend, Gurney & Co. is told in Geoffrey Elliott's *The Mystery of Overend & Gurney* (London: Methuen, 2006). The crisis of 1866 and Overend are discussed in both Walter Bagehot, *Lombard Street: A Description of the Money Market* (London, 1873) and Robert Baxter, *The Panic of 1866 with its Lessons on the Currency Act* (London: Longmans, Green, 1866), both of which are available online for free.

Stock Corners

For more information on the Panic of 1792, see the chapter in Robert Sobel's *Panic on Wall Street: A History of America's Financial Disasters* (New York: MacMillan, 1968). The panic is also covered in Ron Chernow's *Alexander Hamilton* (New York: The Penguin Press, 2004), David Jack Cowen, *The Origins and Economic Impact of the First Bank of the United States, 1791-1797* (New York: Garland Publishing, 2000); and David J. Cowen, Richard Sylla, and Robert E. Wright, "The US Panic of 1792: Financial Crisis Management and the Lender of Last Resort," mimeo (July 2006); and Federal Reserve Bank of Philadelphia, "The First Bank of the United States: A Chapter in the History of Central Banking," (June 2009).

Jacob Little is mentioned in Edwin Lefevre's *Reminiscences of a Stock Operator* (New York: John Wiley & Sons), as well as Matthew Hale Smith's *Sunshine and Shadow in New York* (J. B. Burr and Co.). Contemporary sources include the *New York Times* from December 7, 1856, May 13, 1859, and February 23, 1882, and the *Merchant's Magazine and Commercial Review*, vol. 52 (June 1865, pp. 407–415).

The story of the Northern Pacific Corner is best told in *Harriman vs. Hill: Wall Street's Great Railroad War* (Minneapolis: University of Minnesota Press, 2013). For contemporary accounts of the Northern Pacific corner and other speculative activities on Wall Street in the 19th century, see Edwin LeFèvre, *Reminiscences of a Stock Operator* (1923) (Burlington: Fraser Publishing Co, 1980) and James K. Medbery, *Men and Mysteries of Wall Street,* Fields, Osgood and Co. (1870) (Burlington: Fraser Publishing Co. 1968).

The principle source for the Stutz corner is provided in John Brooks's, "A Corner in Stutz," *The New Yorker*, August 23, 1959, pp. 74–88. The Piggly Crisis is covered in John Brooks, "The Last Great Corner," *Business Adventures* (New York: Open Road Integrated Media, 2014, pp. 255–282). For a thorough biography of Eddie Griffin, see Richard Whittingham's *Boy Wonder of Wall Street* (New York: Texere, 2003).

Stock Markets

The primary source for information on the Dow Jones Average, other than the S&P Dow Jones Indices website (www.djindexes.com), is Phyllis S. Pierce, editor, *The Dow Jones Averages, 1885-1995* (Chicago: Irwin Professional Publishing, 1996), which provides historical data on the Dow Jones Averages, but a more interesting overview is provided in John Prestbo, ed., *The Market's Measure* (New York: Dow Jones & Co., 1999).

Information on the Los Angeles stock averages is taken from the *Commercial and Financial Chronicle.* In 1790, when the first bull market occurred in the United States, Philadelphia was the dominant stock market in the country, as well as the capital of the United States until the government moved to Washington DC. Two interesting books on the Philadelphia stock exchange are Robert E. Wright, *The First Wall Street: Chestnut Street, Philadelphia and the Birth of American Finance* (Chicago: University of Chicago Press, 2005) and Domenic Vitiello with George E. Thomas, *The Philadelphia Stock Exchange and the City It Made* (Philadelphia: University of Pennsylvania Press, 2010). See also Edwin Perkins, *American Public Finance and Financial Services, 1700-1815* (Columbus: Ohio State University Press, 1997) and E. James Ferguson, *The Power of the Purse: A History of American Public Finance, 1776-1790* (Chapel Hill, NC: University of North Carolina Press, 1961) for information on the foundations of the transformation of the colonial economy and fiscal policy.

Henry Dent has written frequently on the impact of demographics on the stock market. See Harry S. Dent, *The Demographic Cliff: How to Survive and Prosper During the Great Deflation of 2014-2019* (New York: Atlantic Monthly, 1992). A good source on Japan's "lost decades" is Koichi Hamada, Anil K. Hashyap, and David E. Weinstein, eds., *Japan's Bubble, Deflation and Long-term Stagnation* (Cambridge, MA: MIT Press, 2010).

Wikipedia includes an article on the 2012–13 Cypriot Financial Crisis, which contributed substantially to its bear market, though I know of no formal review of the Cyprus Stock Market Bubble of 1999–2001.

A good discussion of the impact of World War I on the New York Stock Exchange can be found in Charles R. Geisst, *Wall Street: A History* (Oxford: Oxford University Press, 2012). The impact of World War I on the London Stock Exchange is covered in Ranald Michie, *The London Stock Exchange: A History* (Oxford: Oxford University Press, 1999).

John Childs has written two books on the Nine Years' War, including *The Army, James II and the Glorious Revolution* (New York, St. Martin's Press, 1980), as well as *The British Army of William III 1698–1702* (Manchester: Manchester University Press, 1987). The result in England was the Glorious Revolution, which changed England both politically and economically. See Peter Temin and Hans-Joachim Voth, *Prometheus Shackled: Goldsmith Banks and England's Financial Revolution after 1700* (Oxford: Oxford University Press, 2013); Carl Wennerlind, *Casualties of Credit: The English Financial Revolution, 1620-1720* (Cambridge, MA: Harvard University Press, 2011). To learn about the problems of lending to kings, see Mauricio Drelichman and Hans-Joachim Voth, *Lending to the Borrower from Hell: Debt, Taxes and Default in the Age of Philip II* (Princeton: Princeton University Press, 2014).

The quintessential book by Donald Trump is *Trump: The Art of the Deal* (New York: Random House, 1988). He has written several other books along the same theme: *Trump: How to Get Rich* (New York, Random House, 2004), *Trump 101: The Way to Success* (Hoboken, NJ: John Wiley & Sons, 2007), *Trump, Never Give Up: How I Turned My Biggest Challenges into Success* (Hoboken, NJ: John Wiley & Sons, 2008), and *Trump: Think Like a Billionaire: Everything You Need to Know about Success, Real Estate and Life* (New York, Random House, 2004) among others. These books were co-authored with Meredith McIver. Several books have been written about Donald Trump, including *Trump Revealed: An American Journey of Ambition, Ego, Money and Power* (New York: Scribner, 2016) and David Cay Johnston, *The Making of Donald Trump* (Brooklyn: Melville House, 2016). More are sure to follow.

Index

Dr. Bryan Taylor is President and Chief Economist for Global Financial Data. He received his Ph.D. from Claremont Graduate University in Economics writing about the economics of the arts. He has taught both economics and finance at numerous universities in southern California and in Switzerland. He began putting together the Global Financial Database in 1990, collecting and transcribing financial and economic data from historical archives around the world. Dr. Taylor has published numerous articles and blogs based upon the Global Financial Database, the US Stocks Database, the UK Stocks Database and the GFD Indices, all collected by Global Financial Data over the past 25 years. Dr. Taylor's research has uncovered previously unknown aspects of financial history. He has written two books on financial history, a novel and several short stories. He resides in a Southern California Beach community with his dogs, Trouble and Shadow.